Parties, Politics, and Public Policy in America

Third Edition

William J. Keefe
University of Pittsburgh

HOLT, RINEHART AND WINSTON
New York Chicago San Francisco Dallas
Montreal Toronto London Sydney

For my family

Library of Congress Cataloging in Publication Data
Keefe, William J
  Parties, politics, and public policy in America.

  Includes bibliographical references and index.
  1. Political parties—United States. I. Title.
JK2265.K44   1980   329'.02   79-20031
ISBN 0-03-054116-6

Preface

The American party system is in serious trouble. Its loss of vitality appears both in government and in the electorate. Voters ignore parties, politicians dismiss them, and activists bypass them. Almost everyone, it seems, distrusts them. Across the nation, party organizations frequently have been reduced to bystanders in the campaign struggles between candidates. Political "outsiders"—the political action committees of interest groups, the media, campaign management firms, political consultants —are often more visible in campaigns than the parties. In the midst of party devitalization, interest-group politics flourishes.

The weakness of the parties has been especially noticeable in presidential elections. Ironically, perhaps, party and governmental "reforms" have contributed to this. Presidential primaries have all but displaced the national convention. Party caucuses have become candidate gatherings; the local caucus now belongs to whoever attends. Party spending in presidential campaigns has been supplanted by public financing. The preferences of party leaders in presidential politics count for less and less, those of amateur activists for more and more. For candidates and public officials alike, it is the party label that matters, not the party mission. All in all, no decade in the last century took a larger toll on the parties than that of the 1970s. And further tests of the party system are promised for the 1980s.

The parties have suffered from prolonged neglect by the public and from overattention by the reformers. Scholars, meanwhile, continue to be intrigued by them. Numerous books, monographs, and articles have been published on American parties in recent years. I have drawn extensively on this literature.

This brief volume attempts to depict what we now know about this basic political institution; it is brief because, for the nonspecialist reader in particular, some things are more important to know than others. Moreover, it is worth recalling the observation of the late E. E. Schattschneider, a scholar whose work touches all who write about American politics: "The compulsion to know everything is the road to insanity." On that unassailable ground, this book leaves some lesser aspects of party unexplored, some things unsaid.

The purpose of this third edition, like that of the previous two, is one of exegesis: to bring into focus the salient features of the parties, to account for their form and functions, and to examine and interpret their present condition. It pays special attention to the changes that have come to the

parties, to the difficulties that confront them as agencies for managing
conflict and managing government, and to the forces that play upon and
shape them.

   With this, as with the other editions, I have benefited from the sugges-
tions of friends, students, and colleagues, mainly at the University of Pittsburgh: Paul A. Beck, Keith Burris, Holbert N. Carroll, Edward F. Cooke,
Robert L. Donaldson, Charles O. Jones, Paul Lopatto, Roger McGill, Michael Margolis, Morris S. Ogul, Bert A. Rockman, Robert S. Walters, and
Sidney Wise. Such errors of fact and interpretation that remain in this
book, as I see it, are properly theirs! Larry Boyle of the Federal Election
Commission gave me valuable counsel concerning the campaign finance
act. Robin Gross of Holt, Rinehart and Winston provided excellent edito-
rial assistance. Finally, I want to thank my wife, Martha, for helping to
prepare this edition, as well as the earlier ones. In particular, I want to
acknowledge her inspired typing, consummate pasting, and above-aver-
age proofreading.

Oakmont, Pennsylvania   W.J.K.
June 1979

Contents

Figures

Tables

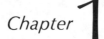

POLITICAL PARTIES AND THE POLITICAL SYSTEM

$\mathbf{A}$ny attempt to unravel the mysteries of American political parties might well begin with the recognition of this fact: The parties are less what they make of themselves than what their environment makes of them.[1] To a remarkable extent, the party owes its form and substance to the impact of four external elements: the design of the legal–political system, the election system, the political culture, and the heterogeneous quality of American life. Singly and in combination, these elements contribute in significant and indelible ways to the shape of the parties, to the manner in which they carry on their business, to the behavior of both their elite and rank-and-file members, and to their capacity to control the political system and to perform as central policy-making agencies.

THE PARTIES AND THEIR ENVIRONMENT

The Legal–Political System

No careful student of American history can escape the conclusion that the Constitution was designed by men who were suspicious of popular majorities and who had little sympathy for the functions of party. Line after line of the Constitution discloses their basic intent: to establish a government that could not easily be brought under the control of any one element, however large, that might exist within the country. The underlying philosophy of the Founding Fathers was both simple and pervasive:

power was to check power, and the ambitions of some men were to check the ambitions of other men. The two main features in this design were federalism and the separation of powers—the first intended to distribute power between different levels of government; the second, to distribute power among the legislative, executive, and judicial branches. Division of the legislature into two houses, with their memberships elected for different terms and by different methods, was thought to reduce further the risk that a single faction (or party) might gain ascendancy. E. E. Schattschneider developed the argument in this fashion:

> The theory of the Constitution, inherited from the time of the Glorious Revolution in England, was legalistic and preparty in its assumptions. Great reliance was placed in a system of separation of powers, a legalistic concept of government incompatible with a satisfactory system of party government. No place was made for the parties in the system, party government was not clearly foreseen or well understood, government by parties was thought to be impossible or impracticable and was feared and regarded as something to be avoided. . . . The Convention at Philadelphia produced a constitution with a dual attitude: it was proparty in one sense and antiparty in another. The authors of the Constitution refused to suppress the parties by destroying the fundamental liberties in which parties originate. They or their immediate successors accepted amendments that guaranteed civil rights and thus established a system of party tolerance, *i.e.,* the right to agitate and to organize. This is the proparty aspect of the system. On the other hand, the authors of the Constitution set up an elaborate division and balance of powers within an intricate governmental structure designed to make parties ineffective. It was hoped that the parties would lose and exhaust themselves in futile attempts to fight their way through the labyrinthine framework of the government, much as an attacking army is expected to spend itself against the defensive works of a fortress. This is the antiparty part of the constitutional scheme. To quote Madison, the "great object" of the Constitution was "to preserve the public good and private rights against the danger of such a faction [party] and at the same time to preserve the spirit and form of popular government."[2]

Federalism also works against the development of centralized parties. The federal scheme of organization guarantees that not only will there be 50 separate state governmental systems, but also 50 separate state party systems. No two are exactly alike. The prevailing ideology in one state party may be vastly different from that of another state party; for example, it takes no great imagination to picture the extraordinary differences that separate the state Democratic party of Mississippi from that of New York. And within each state all manner of local party organizations exist, sometimes functioning in harmony with state and national party bodies and sometimes not. Not only do the parties differ from state to state and from community to community, but the election laws that govern their activities differ. There are state laws of great variety, for example, that govern the organizational features of parties, nominating procedures, ballots, campaign finance, and elections. The thrust of federalism is thus dispersive and parochial.[3]

The Election System

Another element in the environment of political parties is the election system. So closely linked are parties and elections that it is impossible to understand much about one without understanding a great deal about the other. Parties stay in business by winning elections. Election systems influence how the parties compete for power and the success with which they do it. Consider several examples.

Although a state's election calendar may appear neutral, even innocuous, it has a substantial bearing on party fortunes. Many state constitutions provide election calendars that separate state from national elections—for example, gubernatorial from presidential elections. The singular effect of this arrangement is to insulate state politics from national politics.[4] The national tides that sweep one party into the presidency may be no more than ripples by the time a state election is held two years later. Although the Democratic party won presidential election after presidential election during the 1930s and 1940s, a great many governorships and state legislatures remained safely Republican, in part because of their off-year election calendars. In similar fashion, the use of staggered terms of office for legislative and executive offices diminishes the likelihood that one party can take control of both branches of government at any one time. When the governor is elected for four years and the lower house is elected for two years, prospects increase that the governor's party will lose legislative seats, and perhaps its majority, in the off-year election. The same is true in the case of the president and Congress. Whatever their virtues, staggered terms and off-year elections heighten the probability of divided control of government.

The use of single-member districts with plurality elections for the selection of legislative bodies also carries ramifications for the parties. When an election is held within a single-member district, only one party can win; the winning candidate need receive only one more vote than any other candidate, and all votes for candidates other than the victor are lost. Although the single-member district system discriminates against the second party in any district, its principal impact is virtually to rule out the possibility that a minor party can win legislative representation. Indeed, only a handful of minor party candidates have ever held seats either in Congress or in the state legislatures. The device of single-member districts with plurality elections has long been seen as one of the principal bulwarks of the *two*-party system.[5]

Few, if any, electoral arrangements apparently have had a greater impact on political parties than the direct primary, a product of the reformist movement in the early twentieth century. The primary was introduced as a means of combating the power of those party oligarchs who, shielded from popular influences, dominated the process of selecting nominees in state and local party conventions. By contrast, the primary was designed to democratize the nominating process by empowering the voters to choose the party's nominees. Today, all states employ some form of primary system, though the convention method survives for the nomination of presidential and vice-presidential candidates. The proliferation of presidential primaries in recent years has, of course, diminished the significance of the national convention.

Although the precise impact of the primary on the parties is difficult to evaluate, it seems plain that its influence has been substantial. The usual arguments look like this: First, by transferring the choice of nominees from party councils to the voters, the primary has increased the probability that candidates with significantly different perspectives on public policy will be brought together in the same party. Whatever their views or policy orientations, the victors in primary elections become the party's nominees, and there is not much the party can do about it. Second, as a result, party responsibility has declined—candidates who win office largely on their own, who have their own distinctive followings within local electorates, have less reason to defer to party leaders or to follow party imperatives. Their party membership is what they choose to make it. Third, the presence of the primary has contributed to numerous intraparty clashes; particularly bitter primary fights sometimes render the party incapable of generating a united campaign in the general election.[6] Finally, the argument has often been advanced that the primary has contributed to the spread and maintenance of one-party politics. Where one party ordinarily dominates the politics of an area, its primaries tend to become the arena where political battles are fought out. The growth of the second party is inhibited not only by the lack of voter interest in its primaries but also by its inability to attract strong candidates to its colors. One-party domination reveals little about the party's organizational strength—indeed, the prospects are high that one-party political systems will be characterized more by factionalism and internecine warfare than by unity, harmony, or ideological agreement.

Such are the arguments that have been developed against the primary. There are, of course, a number of arguments that can be made on its behalf.[7] Moreover, in some jurisdictions the dominant party organization is sufficiently strong that "independent" candidates are seldom able to upset the "organization slate." Potential challengers may abandon their campaigns once the party organization has made known its choices. Other candidacies may never materialize because the prospects for getting the "nod" from party leaders appear so unpromising. Nevertheless, taking the country as a whole, the evidence is persuasive that the use of the primary has led to a general weakening of party organization. Unable to control its nominations, a party forfeits some portion of its claim to be known as a party, some portion of its *raison d'être*. The loose, freewheeling character of American parties owes much to the advent, consolidation, and extension of the direct primary.

To call down a further example of the relationship between the election system and the party system, one may consider the use and impact of nonpartisan elections. In their search for a formula to improve city government early in the twentieth century, reformers hit upon the idea of the nonpartisan ballot—one in which party labels would not be present. The purpose of the plan was to free local government from the issues and divisiveness of national and state party politics and from the grip of local party bosses, which in turn, it was thought, would contribute to the effectiveness of local units. The nonpartisan ballot immediately gained favor and, once established, has been hard to dislodge; indeed, the plan has grown in popularity over the years. Today, well over half of the American cities with populations over 5000 have nonpartisan elections.

A variety of political patterns hide behind the nonpartisan system. In some cities with nonpartisan ballots, such as Chicago, the party presence continues to be highly visible, and there is no doubt as to which candidates are affiliated with which parties. These elections are partisan in everything but label. In other cities, local party organizations compete against slates of candidates sponsored by various nonparty groups. In still other cities, the local parties are virtually without power, having lost it to interest groups that recruit, sponsor, and finance candidates for office. Finally, there are nonpartisan elections in which neither party nor nonparty groups slate candidates—thus leaving individual candidates to their own devices. The latter type is particularly prevalent among small cities.

It is difficult to say how much nonpartisan elections have diminished the vitality of local party organizations. Here and there the answer is plainly, "very little if at all"; elsewhere, the impact appears to have been substantial. Whatever the case, it is clear that where parties are shut out of the local election process, other kinds of politics enter—possibly centered around interest groups (including the press), "celebrity" or "name" politics (the latter favoring incumbents), or the idiosyncratic appeals of individual office-seekers. Where party labels are absent, power is up for grabs. Whether the voters in any real sense can hold their representatives accountable, lacking the guidance that party labels furnish, is problematical at best.[8]

Myths to the contrary, elections systems are never wholly neutral. There are election laws and constitutional arrangements that bolster the two-party system (such as the single-member district system or the rigorous requirements that minor parties must meet to gain a place on the ballot), and those which make party government difficult and sometimes impossible (such as staggered terms of office, off-year elections, direct primaries, and nonpartisan ballots). The major parties, of course, are not always passive witnesses to existing electoral arrangements. At times they simply endure them because it is easier to live with customs and conventional arrangements than to try to change them, or because they recognize the benefits which they confer. At other times they seek new electoral dispositions because the prospects for party advantage are sufficiently promising to warrant the effort and the risk. It is a good bet that no one understands or appreciates American election systems better than those party leaders responsible for defending party interests and winning elections.

The Political Culture and the Parties

A third important element in the environment of American political parties is the political culture—"the system of empirical beliefs, expressive symbols, and values which defines the situation in which political action takes place."[9] As commonly represented, the political culture of a nation is the amalgam of public attitudes toward the political system, its subunits, and the role of the individual within the system. It includes the knowledge and beliefs people have about the political system, their feelings toward it and their identification with it, and the evaluations that they make of it.

Although there is little systematic information on the public's political orientations toward the party system, there is scattered evidence that large sections of the public do not evaluate parties or party functions in a favorable light. An instructive study of a cross section of the Wisconsin electorate in the mid-sixties by Jack Dennis bears on these points. Table 1 shows the range of public attitudes on a series of propositions about American parties, including those which reveal diffuse or generalized support for the party system as a whole and the norm of partisanship and those which reveal acceptance of ideas or practices congruent with a system of responsible parties.[10]

The principal conclusion to be drawn from the table is that the public is highly skeptical of the parties and their activities. Better than eight out of ten respondents believe that "the best rule in voting is to pick the man regardless of his party label." A clear majority of the public believes that the parties do more to confuse issues than to clarify them, that government would perform better without conflict between the parties, and that the parties create unnecessary conflicts.[11]

Two items in this survey evoke a mild proparty response: 67 percent of the sample reject the proposal to remove party labels from the ballot in *all* elections—the effect of which would be to institutionalize nonpartisan government—and 68 percent believe that those people who engage in campaign work for the parties perform a valuable function. Even this general level of support, however, no longer obtains. A 1974 study finds that only 38 percent of the Wisconsin electorate reject the proposition that party labels should be removed from the ballot—a decline in support of nearly 30 percent in a decade.[12]

Of equal interest, the Wisconsin data reveal that support for cohesive and disciplined parties is relatively thin. Less than a quarter of the respondents agree on the key proposition that "a senator or representative should follow his party leaders, even if he doesn't want to." A slightly larger number agree to a variant of the first item—that "we would be better off if all Democrats in government stood together and all Republicans did the same." Overall, there is little in this profile of popular attitudes that portends public understanding or acceptance of the tenets of a responsible party system.

Generalizing about national attitude patterns from the data gathered in one state is risky. Nevertheless, it appears likely that the orientations of the Wisconsin voters to the parties are fairly representative of the nation as a whole. Although most people vote within the framework of their party affiliations, their interest in parties often stops at that point. Nationwide surveys of voter attitudes toward control of the presidency and Congress by the same party, shown in Table 2, help to make the case. Only about one-third of the voters believe that the country is better off when the same party controls both the executive and legislative branches of government. Figure 1 shows the principal advantages that the public believes result from divided party control. Chief among these is the belief that it increases the likelihood that corruption will be detected and that power will not be abused. It seems clear from these data that most Americans are dubious of government by party.

Further evidence of popular dissatisfaction with the two-party system can be found in trends concerning party identification and straight party voting. The number of people who identify themselves as either Democrats or Republicans has dropped from 80 percent in 1940 to 72 percent in 1978; indeed, on several occasions during the 1960s and 1970s, the proportion of party identifiers fell below 70 percent. Correspondingly, the number of people who classify themselves as independents has grown, to the point that almost one-third of the electorate is now regarded as independent of party.

An analysis of trends in straight-ticket voting shows a similar erosion of citizen linkage to the parties. Figure 2 depicts the proportion of voters who reported that they voted a straight ticket (supporting all the candidates of one party) in each presidential election between 1952 and 1976. The decline in straight-ticket voting has been sharp—from 66 percent of the electorate in 1952 to 41 percent in 1976. Straight-ticket voting in off-year elections (not shown in the figure) has also declined markedly in recent years. For a great many voters, it is apparent, partisan consistency no longer is a matter of much importance.

The evidence of these pages is that American political parties rest on a relatively narrow and uncertain base of popular support. Scarcely anyone

TABLE 1. The Distribution of Sentiment on Items Pertaining to Support for the Party System

Items Diffuse Support	1 Strongly Agree	2 Agree	3 Agree- Disagree	4 Disagree	5 Strongly Disagree	6 Don't Know	7 Not Ascertained	Total Percent
The parties do more to confuse the issues than to provide a clear choice on them.	4%	50	19	20	1	5	1	100%
The party leaders make no real effort to keep their promises once they get into office.	6%	30	28	31	2	3	1	101%†
Our system of government would work a lot more efficiently if we could get rid of conflicts between the parties altogether.	9%	44	8	28	6	4	1	100%
The political parties more often than not create conflicts where none really exist.	5%	59	13	15	*	7	1	100%
It would be better if, in all elections, we put no party labels on the ballot.	3%	19	7	54	13	3	1	100%

People who work for parties during political campaigns do our nation a great service.	7%	61	19	10	*	4	*	101%†
The best rule in voting is to pick the man regardless of his party label.	23%	59	6	9	1	2	*	100%

Support for Responsible Party Government

A senator or representative should follow his party leaders, even if he doesn't want to.	1%	22	9	56	7	4	1	100%
We would be better off if all the Democrats in government stood together and all the Republicans did the same.	2%	28	12	49	5	4	1	101%†
It is good to stick with your party through thick and thin.	3%	33	14	41	6	3	1	101%†

Source: Jack Dennis, "Support for the Party System by the Mass Public," *American Political Science Review*, LX (September 1966), p. 605 (as adapted).
* Less than 1%.
† Totals do not add to 100% due to rounding.

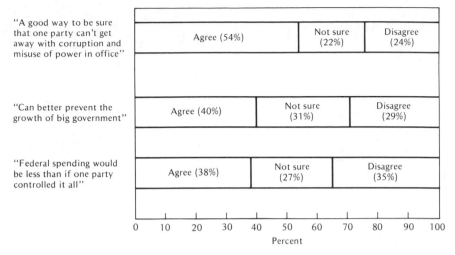

Figure 1.
THE PUBLIC'S PERCEPTIONS OF THE ADVANTAGES OF DIVIDED GOVERNMENT
Source: Adapted from Louis Harris, "Survey Report," *Pittsburgh Post Gazette,* September 27, 1976.

can fail to notice the widespread skepticism of politics and politicians that pervades popular thought. Few vocations stir so little interest as that of the politician. The language of American politics is itself laced with suspicion and hostility. In the argot of popular appraisal, political organizations turn into "machines," party workers emerge as "hacks," political leaders become "bosses," and campaign appeals degenerate into "empty promises" or "sheer demagoguery." The fact that some politicians have contributed to this state of affairs, by debasing the language of political discourse or by their behavior, as in the Watergate affair, is perhaps beside the point. The critical fact is that the American political culture contains a strong suspicion of the political process and the agencies that try to dominate it, the political parties. Though it is difficult to evaluate in any

TABLE 2.   Voter Attitudes Toward Party Control of Government

Do you think it is better or worse for the country to have a president of one party and a Congress controlled by the other party, or doesn't it make much difference?

	1973 Total Voters	1976 Total Voters
Better	50%	40%
Worse	29	38
Makes no difference or not sure	21	22
	100%	100%

Source: Louis Harris Survey Report, January 1973, *Pittsburgh Post Gazette*, September 27, 1976 (as adapted).

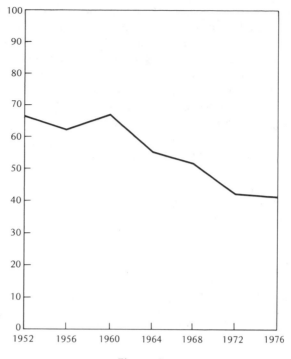

Figure 2.

STRAIGHT-TICKET VOTING IN PRESIDENTIAL ELECTIONS, 1952–1976, IN PERCENTAGES
Source: Jack Dennis, "Trends in Public Support for the American Party System," a paper delivered
at the Annual Meeting of the American Political Science Association, Chicago, Illinois, August
29–September 2, 1974, p. 5 (as updated). The data for 1952–1972 were drawn from surveys by
the Center for Political Studies and the Survey Research Center of the University of Michigan. The
1976 data were taken from the Gallup Poll.

precise way, there is little doubt that the skepticism that pervades popular
thought about the parties contributes to their devitalization as organizations.

A Heterogeneous Nation

To complete the analysis of the environment of American parties, it is
necessary to say something about the characteristics of the nation as a
whole. No array of statistics is required to make the point that in the
magnitude of its diversity, no nation can lay greater claim than the United
States. The American community is composed of an endless variety of
economic and social interests, class configurations, ethnic and religious
groups, occupations, regional and subregional interests and loyalties, values, and beliefs. There are citizens who are deeply attached to inherited
patterns and those who are impatient advocates of change, those who care
intensely about politics and those who can take it or leave it, and those who

elude labeling—those who are active on one occasion and passive on another. There are citizens who think mainly in terms of farm policy, some who seek advantage for urban elements, others whose lives and political interests revolve around businesses or professions. Diversity abounds. Sometimes deep, sometimes shallow, the differences that separate one group from another and one region from another make the formation of public policy that suits everyone all but impossible.

The essential requirement for any major party is that it be able to accommodate itself to the vast diversity that lies within the nation. The result has been the emergence of major parties that, by and large, are remarkably hospitable to all points of view and to all manner of interests and people. From one point of view they are loose and untidy systems characterized more by their coalition quality than by unity. Herbert Agar makes the case succinctly:

Most politics will be parochial, most politicians will have small horizons, seeking the good of the state or the district rather than of the Union; yet by diplomacy and compromise, never by force, the government must water down the selfish demands of regions, races, classes, business associations, into a national policy which will alienate no major groups and which will contain at least a plum for everybody. This is the price of unity in a continentwide federation.[13]

PARTY ORGANIZATION

Regardless of variations in emphasis, there are two features that are common to party organizations throughout the United States. First, parties are organized in a series of committees, extending from the precinct level to the national committee. And second, party committee organization has been developed to parallel the arrangement of electoral districts. With the exception of heavily one-party areas, party committees of some type will be found in almost all jurisdictions within which government officials of importance are elected. The presence of party committees, of course, reveals nothing at all about their activities or their effectiveness in campaigns.

A familiar description of American parties begins by likening their organizational structure to that of a pyramid. At the top of the pyramid rests the national committee, at the bottom the precinct organizations, with various ward, city, county, and state committees lodged in between. Although it is convenient to view party organization within this pattern, it is misleading if it suggests that power flows steadily from top to bottom, from major national leaders to local leaders and local rank-and-file. The truth is that subnational committees have substantial autonomy, particularly in the crucial matters of selecting and slating candidates for public office (including federal), raising and spending money, and conducting campaigns.

The National Committee

The most prestigious and visible of all party committees is the national committee.[14] The committeemen and committeewomen who serve on the national committee of each party are prominent state politicians, chosen in a variety of ways and under a number of constraints. Their official tenure begins when they are accepted by the national convention of each party.

The selection of national committee members is not a simple matter. The Democratic party, operating under its 1974 charter, has especially elaborate provisions governing the composition of its national committee. Among its membership are the chairperson and the highest ranking official of the opposite sex of each recognized state party, 200 additional members allotted to the states on the same basis as delegates are apportioned to the national convention, and a number of delegates representing the Democratic Governors' Conference, the Congress, the National Finance Council, the Conference of Democratic Mayors, and the Young Democrats of America. As in the case of delegates to the party's national convention, members of the national committee must be selected "through processes which assure full, timely, and equal opportunity to participate" and with due attention to "affirmative action" standards.

To know what the national committee is, it is necessary to look at what it does. By and large, its activities are not impressive. One of its principal responsibilities is to make arrangements for the national convention every four years. In this capacity it chooses the convention site, prepares a temporary roster of convention delegates, and selects convention speakers and temporary officers who will manage the assembly in its opening phase. The committee is especially active during presidential campaigns in coordinating campaign efforts, publicizing the party and its candidates, and raising money. Following the election, the committee often faces the task of raising the necessary funds to pay off campaign debts.

The influence of the president on his party's national committee is substantial. "I don't think the Republican National Committee can ever really be independent," a long-time Committee staff member has said. "[The Committee has] a responsibility to the leader. Policy is always made at the White House, not here. We accept it and support it."[15] The same is true in the case of the Democratic National Committee. "The president [Jimmy Carter] likes a party that serves as a supportive tool for the president," observes a state party chairman. "An independent organization is looked upon as a nuisance. That is inevitable." Or, as a White House aide remarked, the president "is turned on to the DNC as a service institution."[16]

The national committees come to life during presidential election years, for their major efforts are directed toward the election of their party's presidential candidate. During nonpresidential years most of the national committee's work is carried on by committees or the national chairman. Study groups occasionally are created by the committee (perhaps under instructions from the national convention) to examine certain problems such as party organization, party policy, or convention management. In 1969, for example, the Democratic National Committee created the Commission on Party Structure and Delegate Selection, known as the McGovern–Fraser Commission, to hold hearings and to suggest proposals for changes in party procedures. Included in its wide-ranging report were recommendations urging state parties (and, in certain cases, state legislatures) to eliminate discrimination of all kinds in party rules, to open party meetings and processes to participation by all members of the party, to remove or moderate restrictive voter registration laws or practices, and to provide for the fair representation of blacks, women, and young persons in state delegations to the national convention. Two subsequent reform commissions, the Mikulski Commission (1972–1973) and the Winograd Commission (1975–1978), further refined party rules to increase intraparty democracy. The broad thrust of the 1969–1978 reforms was to increase popular participation in the presidential nominating process while at the same time diluting the power of party professionals.

The National Chairman

The head of the national party is the national chairman.[17] Although the chairman is officially selected by the members of the national committee, in practice he is chosen by the party's presidential candidate shortly after the national convention has adjourned. Very few chairmen in either party have held the position for an extended period of time—the chairman of the party winning the presidency usually receives a major appointment in the new administration, and the chairman of the losing party is replaced by a new face. When a vacancy in the chairmanship of the "out" party occurs, selection of the new chairman is made by the national committee. Factional conflicts may come to the surface when the committee is faced with the responsibility of finding a replacement, since the leading candidates will invariably be identified with certain wings of the party.

The central problem with which the national chairman must come to terms in presidential election years is the direction and coordination of the national campaign. The chairman has few powers but important responsibilities. In raising presidential campaign funds, he competes with other campaign managers and party units for scarce resources; in seeking to focus attention on the presidential campaign, he competes with other politicos concerned with other campaigns; in seeking to unify the party, he is often thwarted by party elements whose interests run counter to his and those of the presidential candidate; in attempting to influence and publicize national party policies, he collides with the nagging realities of parochialism, sectionalism, and indifference. Apart from the prestige that attaches to the office, there are few rewards that flow regularly to the national chairman. He holds a job without much security, heads a committee that has no independent base of power, stands for unity in a party that often appears to be flying apart, and speaks for a party for whom in fact no one person can speak. This is not a job for tidy-minded or doctrinaire politicians.

Nor is it a job for politicians who weary of the frustrations that come from leading a party agency that has no authentic powers and many debts. When Kenneth M. Curtis resigned as chairman of the Democratic National Committee in 1978, after only one year in office, he commented:

> Have you ever tried to meet the payroll every two weeks of a bankrupt organization and deal with 363 bosses [national committee members] and 50 state chairs? . . . I tried it for a year and simply decided I'd like to do something else with my life. It's not the sort of job that you lay down in the street and bleed to keep. . . .[18]

Congressional and Senatorial Campaign Committees

The other principal units of the national party organization are the congressional and senatorial campaign committees, one for each party in each house. These committees, composed of members of Congress, are independent of the national committees. The campaign committees are an outgrowth of the need of members of Congress to have organizations concerned exclusively with their political welfare. As such, they raise campaign funds for members, help to develop campaign strategies, conduct research, and otherwise provide assistance to members running for reelection. In addition, the committees make available limited funds for party candidates in states or districts where the party has no incumbent. A certain degree of informal cooperation takes place between the party committees of Congress and the national committees, but for the most part they go their separate ways, one preoccupied with the presidential race, the others bent on securing reelection of incumbent legislators and on improving the party's prospects for winning or retaining control of Congress.

State Committees

Midway between the national party apparatus and local party organizations are the state party committees, often called state central committees. So great are the differences between these committees from state to state —in membership selection, size, and function—that it is difficult to generalize about them. In some states the membership is made up of county chairmen; more commonly, state committeemen and women are chosen in primaries or by local party conventions. Their size ranges from less than a hundred members to several hundred. There are states in which the state central committee is a genuinely powerful party unit and is charged by custom with drafting the party platform, slating statewide candidates, and waging an intensive fund-raising campaign. In other states the committee's impact on state politics is scarcely perceptible. In a fashion similar to that found at the national level, the state chairman is ordinarily selected by the party's gubernatorial candidate. And like the national chairman, the state chairman is usually a key adviser to the governor on party affairs, particularly on matters involving the distribution of patronage.

Local Party Organization

Below the state committee of the party is the county committee, ordinarily a very large organization composed of all the precinct officials within the county. At the head of this committee is the county chairman, who is usually elected by the members of the county committee. Often a key figure in local party organization, the county chairman is active in the campaign planning, in the recruitment and slating of party candidates, in the supervision of campaign financing, and in the allocation of patronage to the party faithful. In many counties, the county chairman's power is enhanced by the fact that he actively recruits candidates for precinct committeemen and committeewomen—the very people who in turn elect him to office. In some states there are congressional district party organizations, developed around the office of congressman. Where these committees exist, they function essentially as the congressman's personal organization, set off from the rest of the party and preoccupied with "errand running" for constituents and the election of the congressman. Although local party officials, such as the county chairman, may be instrumental in controlling the original congressional nomination, their influence on the congressman's policy orientations is virtually nil. Indeed, one of the dominant characteristics of congressional district organization is its autonomy.[19] Further down the line are the city and ward committees, which vary in size and importance throughout the country. Their activities, like those of other committees, are centered around campaigns and elections.

The cornerstone of American party organization is the precinct committee, organized within the tens of thousands of election or voting districts of the nation. In metropolitan areas a precinct is likely to number 1000 or 2000 voters, while in open-country areas, perhaps only a dozen. The complexity of party organization at the precinct level is mainly a function of precinct size. The precinct committeeman and/or committeewoman is chosen in one of two ways: by the voters in a primary election or by the vote of party members attending a precinct caucus.

In the lore of American politics, elections are won or lost at the precinct level. A strong precinct organization, the argument runs, is essential to party victory, and the key to a strong organization is a precinct leader bent on carrying his precinct. In attempting to advance his party's fortunes, the committeeman engages in four main activities: those associated with the campaign itself, party organizational work (for example, recruitment and organization of workers), promulgation of political information, and identification and recruitment of candidates for local office.[20] For most jurisdictions, it appears, his most important activities are those related to the campaign, such as inducing and helping people to register, contacting voters, raising money, campaigning for votes, and transporting voters to the polls. Undoubtedly there are differences in the role perceptions of party officials. A study of precinct leaders in Massachusetts and North Carolina, for example, found that about 60 percent saw their principal task as that of mobilizing voters.[21] In the Detroit metropolitan area, by contrast, less than half (45 percent) evaluated their primary task as the production of votes; surprisingly large numbers in this sample (24 percent) defined their role as that of "ideological mentor"—that is, charged with the responsibility of educating voters concerning government and public issues; and others (18 percent) defined their role as that of promoting social and economic welfare efforts.[22] Whether variations in the role perceptions of precinct officials have an important bearing on party efforts to win elections is difficult to say. There is very little systematic evidence concerning the components present in winning elections or, for that matter, in losing them.

Extraparty Groups

In a few states and localities, the most important party agencies are not the formal party organizations but rather extralegal associations formed by party members to accomplish various purposes. These unofficial organizations come in all sizes and shapes. Some were formed in order to wrest political power away from the regular party organizations, while others were established as a means of fostering greater concern with issues in state and local politics. Among the most prominent examples of these associations are the California Republican Assembly, the California Democratic Council, the voluntary associations in both parties in Wisconsin, and the Democratic reform clubs of New York City. Composed of dues-paying, well-educated, mainly middle-class members, these organizations have at times been more effective than the regular organizations in California and Wisconsin; indeed, the party national committees have sometimes dealt with these associations rather than with the official organizations.[23] The political clubs differ sharply from "old-style" political organizations in their lack of interest in patronage, their preoccupation with public policy and ideological problems, and the professional–business–university back grounds of their members.

In addition to the extralegal party groups noted above, which both complement and compete with the regular organizations, there are a host of auxiliary organizations that spring up during campaigns. Presidential campaigns are replete with groups such as Independents for Nixon, Lawyers for Humphrey, Citizens for Eisenhower, Volunteers for Stevenson, Businessmen for Kennedy, and Independents for Carter. In some cases closely linked to the formal party apparatus and in other cases largely independent, these groups raise and spend money, develop campaign plans, and solicit votes. One appeal of these groups is that they permit citizens who are reluctant to be identified with the formal party organizations to play a role in campaigns. From the party's perspective, these organizations provide additional sources of campaign money and political workers, not to mention an added measure of legitimacy for its candidates.

There are, finally, the youth groups in the party organizations—in particular, the Young Democrats, with a membership of about 250,000, and the Young Republicans, with a membership of about 450,000. Neither group has been especially active in youth voter registration drives, even though the turnout of young persons has regularly been much lower than that of any other age group.[24] The activity of youth groups is variable. In some communities they are active in the recruitment and training of young candidates and in raising funds for their campaigns, while in other communities they are little more than social organizations.

The Changing Parties: "Old-Style" and "New-Style" Politics

In the late nineteenth and early twentieth centuries the best examples of strong party organization could be found in the large cities of the Northeast and Midwest—New York City, Boston, Philadelphia, Jersey City, Kansas City, and Chicago. Well-organized and strongly disciplined, the urban "machine" during this era was well-nigh invincible. Precinct and ward officials maintained steady contacts with their party constituencies, finding jobs for people out of work, helping those who were in trouble with the law, aiding others to secure government benefits such as welfare payments, assisting neighborhoods to secure government services, helping immigrants to cope with a new society, and facilitating merchants and tradespeople in their efforts to obtain contracts, licenses, and the like. The party organization was at the center of community life, an effective mediary between the people and their government. Party officials were "brokers," exchanging information, access, and influence for loyalty and support at the polls.

Today the picture is much different. Although the party organizations continue to provide social services in certain large cities, the volume of such exchanges has declined sharply. Numerous factors have contributed to this loss of function, including: 1) the growth of civil service systems and the corresponding decline in patronage; 2) the relative decline in the value of patronage jobs; 3) the arrival of the "welfare state" with its various benefits for low-income groups; 4) the steady assimilation of immigrants; 5) the growing disillusionment among better educated voters over many features of "machine" politics; and 6) the coming of age of the mass media with its potential for contacts between candidates and their publics. There remain, of course, many disadvantaged citizens, particularly in large cities, who continue to rely on local party leaders for assistance in solving the problems in their lives. But most Americans scarcely give a thought to using party officials in this way. Where the parties have suffered a loss of functions, it is reasonable to assume that they have also suffered a loss of vitality. The result, undoubtedly, has been a decline in their ability to "deliver the vote" on election day.

The most interesting and significant struggle within both national parties over the past decade has been that occurring between "purists" and "professionals"—the distinction first drawn by Nelson Polsby and Aaron Wildavsky.[25] As seen by the purists:

> The party itself has no value and merits no loyalty. Its only legitimate reason for being is to advance true ideals and good policies. The essence of politics is not the mere competition for office among parties and interest groups; it is standing up and being counted for what is right regardless of whether it is popular. Any compromise or soft-pedaling of principle is immoral, hypocritical, and a sure sign of a candidate's unfitness for the nomination. Hence the candidacy of a Goldwater or a McCarthy or a McGovern or a Wallace is not to be judged by whether he won or lost, but by whether he stuck to his principles.[26]

By contrast, the professionals set great store by the party itself:

> They have served it before the nomination contest and expect to serve it after the election. They regard threats to bolt the party as dirty pool; their morality requires the candidates and factions to compete in good faith and the losers to unite behind the winners—though a particularly unsuitable candidate may incline even the professionals to "go fishing" on election day. Winning the election is the party's prime goal, for it is an indispensable prerequisite for everything else it wants to do. Therefore the professionals seek a candidate whose style they think will appeal to the voters they need to win, not necessarily to party leaders. They judge a candidate by how well or badly he runs in the election and by how much he has helped or hurt the rest of the ticket. And they see negotiation, compromise, and accommodation not as hypocrisy or immorality but as the very essence of what keeps parties—and nations— from disintegrating.[27]

The "new politics" of recent years has changed familiar political terrain. Today there are far more activist newcomers engaged in party activities and political campaigns, particularly in the Democratic party, than in the past. Younger, leery of party "machines," repelled by patronage and "deals," committed to an "open" political process, often suspicious of the Washington "establishment," stimulated by "high principle" and "rectitude" appeals, and greatly concerned with issues, the new class of reformers has had a dramatic impact on American politics. Enthusiastically committed to Eugene McCarthy, they influenced Lyndon Johnson's decision to withdraw from the presidential contest in 1968. In 1972, still held together by opposition to the Vietnam war, they worked ceaselessly to win the nomination for George McGovern, using party rules on delegate selection that gave unprecedented representation to women, blacks, and youth in the national convention. In 1976, as members of the "peanut brigade," amateur activists helped an "outsider," a relatively unknown former Georgia governor, Jimmy Carter, to win the Democratic nomination and ultimately the election. Throughout the 1970s, the new activists supported efforts to "democratize" the Democratic party, to make it an "open party with open rules."

THE ACTIVITIES OF PARTIES

Among the principal thrusts of scholarship on political parties is the thesis that political parties are indispensable instruments in the functioning of democratic political systems. Scholars have differed sharply in their approaches to the study of parties and in their appraisals of the functions or activities of parties, but they are in striking agreement as to the linkage between parties and democracy. Representative of a wide band of analysis, the following statements by V. O. Key, Jr., and E. E. Schattschneider sketch the broad outlines of the argument:

> Governments operated, of course, long before political parties in the modern sense came into existence.... The proclamation of the right of men to have a hand in their own governing did not create institutions by which they might exercise that right. Nor did the machinery of popular government come into existence overnight. By a tortuous process party systems came into being to implement democratic ideas. As democratic ideas corroded the old foundations of authority, members of the old governing elite reached out to legitimize their positions under the new notions by appealing for popular support. That appeal compelled deference to popular views, but it also required the development of organization to communicate with and to manage the electorate.... In a sense, government, left suspended in mid-air by the erosion of the old justifications for its authority, had to build new foundations in the new environment of a democratic ideology. In short, it had to have machinery to win votes.[28]

The rise of political parties is indubitably one of the principal distinguishing marks of modern government. The parties, in fact, have played a major role as *makers* of governments, more especially they have been the makers of democratic government.... [Political] parties created democracy and ... modern democracy is unthinkable save in terms of the parties. ... The parties are not ... merely appendages of modern government; they are in the center of it and play a determinative and creative role in it.[29]

The contributions of political parties to the maintenance of democratic politics can be judged in a rough way by examining the principal activities in which they engage. Of particular importance are those activities associated with the recruitment and selection of leadership, the representation and integration of interests, and the control and direction of government.

Recruitment and Selection of Leaders

The processes by which political leaders are recruited, elected, and appointed to office form the central core of party acitivity.[30] Except where authentic nonpartisan elections exist, political parties are the dominant agencies for identifying potential officeholders, sorting them out, channeling them into candidacies, and mobilizing the voters necessary to their election. The party interest, moreover, extends to the appointment of administrative and judicial officers—for example, cabinet members, justices of the Supreme Court—once the party has captured the executive branch of government.[31] As noted earlier, the party organizations do not necessarily dominate the process by which candidates are recruited or nominated. Increasingly, in fact, candidates are "self-starters," choosing to enter primaries without waiting for approval from party chieftains. With their own personal followings and sources of campaign money, they often pay scant heed to party leaders or party policies. Some candidates are recruited, groomed, and financed by political interest groups. The looseness of the American party system creates conditions under which party control over many of the candidates who run under its banner is thin or nonexistent.

Still and all, the political parties play an important role in finding candidates and in electing them to office. It is difficult to see how hundreds of thousands of elective offices could be filled in the absence of parties without turning each election into a free-for-all, conspicuous by the presence of numerous candidates holding all varieties of set, shifting, and undisclosed views. Composing a government out of an odd mélange of officials, especially at the national level, would be very difficult. Any form of collective accountability to the voters would vanish. Hence, whatever their shortcomings, by proposing alternative lists of candidates and campaigning on their behalf, the parties bring certain measures of order, routine, and predictability to the electoral process.

The constant factors in party politics are the pursuit of power, office, and advantage. Yet, in serving their own interest in winning office, parties make other contributions to the public at large and to the political system. Among other things, they help to educate the voters concerning issues and mobilize them for political action, provide a linkage between the people and the government, and simplify the choices to be made in elections. The parties do what voters cannot do by themselves: from the totality of interests and issues in politics, they choose those that will become "the agenda of formal public discourse."[32] In the process of shaping the agenda, they provide a mechanism by which voters can not only make sense out of what government does, but also relate to the government itself. The role of the parties in educating voters and in structuring opinion has been described by Robert MacIver in this way:

> Public opinion is too variant and dispersive to be effective unless it is organized. It must be canalized on the broad lines of some major division of opinion. Party focuses the issues, sharpens the differences between contending sides, eliminates confusing cross-currents of opinion. . . . The party educates the public while seeking merely to influence it, for it must appeal on grounds of policy. For the same reason it helps to remove the inertia of the public and thus to broaden the range of public opinion. In short the party, in its endeavors to win the public to its side, however unscrupulous it may be in its modes of appeal, is making the democratic system workable. It is the agency by which public opinion is translated into public policy.[33]

Representation and Integration of Group Interests

The American nation is extraordinarily complex and heterogeneous. All kinds of political interest groups exist within its borders. Given the diversity in the objectives of different groups, conflict inevitably arises between one group and another and between various groups and the government. The parties help to keep conflict of this sort within tolerable limits. Relations between the parties and private organizations take on the character of a marriage of convenience—groups need the parties as much as the parties need them. No group can expect to move far toward the attainment of its objectives without coming to terms with the realities of party power; the parties, through their public officeholders, are in a strategic position to advance or obstruct the policy objectives of any group. Similarly, no party can expect to achieve broad electoral successes without a firm base of group support.

In one sense, the parties, particularly their public officials, serve as "brokers" among the organized interests of American society, weighing the claims of one group against those of another, accepting some programs, and modifying or rejecting others. The steady bargaining that occurs between interest groups and key party leaders (in the executive and legislative branches) tends to produce settlements to which the participants can accommodate for a time, even though they may not be wholly satisfactory to any one. The processes of bargaining and compromise are essential elements in the strategy of American parties. The legitimacy of government, moreover, may depend on the capacity of the parties to represent diverse interests and to integrate the claims of competing groups in a broad program of public policy.

The thesis that the major parties are steadily sensitive to the representation of group interests cannot be advanced without a caveat or two. The stubborn fact is that the parties are far more solicitous toward the claims of organized interests than toward those of unorganized interests. The groups that regularly engage the attention of the parties and their representatives in government are those whose support (or opposition) can make a difference at the polls. Organized labor, organized business, organized agriculture, organized medicine—all have multiple channels for gaining access to decision-makers. Indeed, party politicians are about as likely to search out the views of these interests as to wait to hear from them. In recent years, special "cause" groups—those passionate and uncompromising lobbies concerned with single issues such as gun control, abortion, tax rollbacks, equal rights, nuclear power, and the environment —have kept legislators' feet to the fire, exerting extraordinary influence as they judge each member on the "correctness" of his or her position. By contrast, many millions of Americans are all but shut out of the political system. The political power of such groups as agricultural workers, sharecroppers, migrants, and unorganized labor has never been commensurate with their numbers or, for that matter, with their contribution to society. With low participation in elections, weak organizations, low status, and poor access to political communications, their voices are often drowned out in the din produced by organized interests.[34]

No problem of representation in America is more important than that of finding ways by which to move the claims of the unorganized public onto the agenda of politics. But the task is formidable: "All power is organization and all organization is power. . . . A man who has no share in any form of organized power is not independent of organized power. He is at the mercy of it. . . ."[35]

Control and Direction of Government

A third major activity of the parties involves the control and direction of government. Parties recruit candidates and organize campaigns in order to win political power, gain public office, and take control of government. Given the character of the political system and the parties themselves, it is unrealistic to suppose that party management of government will be altogether successful. In the first place, the separate branches of government may not be captured by the same party. Only one-half of the elections from 1950 to 1980, for example, resulted in control of both houses of Congress and the presidency by the same party. Division of party control complicates the process of governing, forcing the president not only to work with his own party in Congress but also with elements of the other party. Party achievements in majority-building tend to be blurred in the mix of coalition votes, and party accountability to the voters suffers. In the second place, even though one party may dominate both the legislative and the executive branches, there is a good possibility that its margin of seats in the legislature will be too thin to permit it to govern effectively. Moreover, internal disagreement within the majority party may be so great on certain kinds of issues that it is virtually impossible for it to pull its ranks together and to develop coherent positions. When majority party lines are shattered, opportunities come into view for the minority party to assert itself forcefully in the policy-making process. Overall, what has been said about the problem of the majority party in managing the government at the national level applies in about the same fashion to most state governments.

The upshot of this is that although the parties organize governments, they do not completely control decision-making activities. In some measure they compete with political interest groups bent on securing public policies advantageous to their clienteles, and there are times when certain groups have fully as much influence on the behavior of legislators and bureaucrats as legislative party leaders, national and subnational party leaders, or the president. Yet, to point out the difficulties that confront the parties in seeking to manage the government is not to suggest that the parties' impact on public policy is insubstantial. Not even a casual examination of party platforms, candidates' and officeholders' speeches, or legislative voting can fail to detect the contributions of the parties to shaping the direction of government or, in fact, ignore the differences that separate the parties on public policy matters.[36]

One begins to understand American parties by recognizing that party politicians are more likely to set great store in the notion of winning elections than in using election outcomes to achieve a broad range of policy goals. To be sure, they have interests and commitments in policy questions but rarely to the point that rules out bargaining and compromise in the interest of achieving half a "party loaf." Politicians tend to be intensely pragmatic and adaptable men. For the most part, they are attracted to a particular party more because of its promise as a mechanism for moving into government than as a mechanism for governing itself. Party is a way of organizing activists and supporters in order to make a bid for office. This is the elemental truth of party politics. That the election of one aggregation of politicians as against another has policy significance, as indeed it does, comes closer to representing an unanticipated dividend than a triumph for the idea of responsible party government.

NOTES

1. This proposition is arguable. For the counter position—one that stresses the capacity of parties to shape themselves—see Austin Ranney, *Curing the Mischiefs of Faction: Party Reform in America* (Berkeley, Calif.: University of California Press, 1975), especially Chapter 1; Jeane Jordan Kirkpatrick, *Dismantling the Parties: Reflections on Party Reform and Party Decomposition* (Washington, D.C.: American Enterprise Institute for Public Policy Research, 1978); and, of a different order, Kenneth Janda, "Environmental Constraints on the Degree of Party Organization," a paper delivered at the Conference on Political Parties in Modern Societies, Northwestern University, September 21–22, 1978.

2. From *Party Government* by E. E. Schattschneider. Copyright 1942 by E. E. Schattschneider. Reprinted by permission of Holt, Rinehart and Winston, Inc., pp. 6–7.

3. The Democratic party's adoption of new rules (particularly regarding the selection of national convention delegates) and a party charter (in 1974) has diminished the variability among states in their practices concerning presidential nominating politics, participation in party activities, and the conduct of party affairs. See the discussion in Chapter 3, pp. 66–70.

4. The behavior of voters also serves to separate state politics from national politics. Even in those states in which governors are elected at the same time as the president, the chances are nearly one out of two that the party that carries the state in the presidential contest will lose at the gubernatorial level. Party "splits" in presidential and gubernatorial outcomes occurred in 11 out of 25 cases in 1964, 8 out of 20 in 1968, 11 out of 18 in 1972, and 5 out of 14 in 1976.

5. For a careful exposition of this argument, see Schattschneider, *Party Government,* pp. 67–84.

6. For evidence on the disruptive impact of primaries on campaign workers, see the instructive article by Donald B. Johnson and James R. Gibson, "The Divisive Primary Revisited: Party Activists in Iowa," *American Political Science Review,* LXVIII (March 1974), pp. 67–77. The authors find that campaign workers for candidates who are defeated in contested primaries are typically less active in the *general election campaign* and, not infrequently, decide not to vote for either candidate or decide to work and vote for the opposition party. For an earlier study that finds that contested primaries, in and of themselves, have relatively little impact on *general election outcomes,* see Andrew Hacker, "Does a Divisive Primary Harm a Candidate's Election Chances?" *American Political Science Review,* LIX (March 1965), pp. 105–110. But also see Robert A. Bernstein, "Divisive Primaries Do Hurt: U.S. Senate Races, 1956–1972," *American Political Science Review,* LXXI (June 1977), pp. 540–545.

7. For a more extensive analysis of the primary, see Chapter 3, pp. 61–63.

8. This analysis is based principally on the research of Charles R. Adrian. See his article, "Some General Characteristics of Nonpartisan Elections," *American Political Science Review,* LXVI (September 1952), pp. 766–776, and his book, *Governing Urban America* (New York: McGraw-Hill, 1961), pp. 98–102.

9. Lucian W. Pye and Sidney Verba (eds.), *Political Culture and Political Development* (Princeton, N.J.: Princeton University Press, 1965), p. 513.

10. A system of "responsible parties" would be characterized by centralized, unified, and disciplined parties committed to the execution of programs and promises offered at elections and held accountable by the voters for their performance.

11. The data and general line of argument developed in these paragraphs are derived from Jack Dennis, "Support for the Party System by the Mass Public," *American Political Science Review,* LX (September 1966), pp. 600–615.

12. Jack Dennis, "Trends in Public Support for the American Political Party System," a paper delivered at the Annual Meeting of the American Political Science Association, Chicago, Illinois, August 29–September 2, 1974, p. 9.

13. Herbert Agar, *The Price of Union* (Boston: Houghton Mifflin, 1950), p. xiv.

14. For an instructive study of the national committee and the national chairman, see Cornelius P. Cotter and Bernard C. Hennessy, *Politics Without Power: The National Party Committees* (New York: Atherton Press, 1964).

15. *Congressional Quarterly Weekly Report,* February 16, 1974, p. 352.

16. *Congressional Quarterly Weekly Report,* January 14, 1978, p. 61.

17. See Cotter and Hennessy, *Politics Without Power,* pp. 67–80. They see the roles of the national chairman as "image-maker, hell-raiser, fund-raiser, campaign manager, and administrator."

18. *Congressional Quarterly Weekly Report,* January 14, 1978, p. 58.

19. See Avery Leiserson, "National Party Organization and Congressional Districts," *Western Political Quarterly,* XVI (September 1963), pp. 633–649.

20. The capacity of local party organizations to perform these activities may be dependent in part on the political and demographic environments in which they are lodged. Recent research has sought to identify whether interparty competitiveness (political environment) or income–educational–racial configurations (demographic environment) have a bearing on the parties' performance of traditional activities, such as providing services to voters or persuading them how to vote. The findings are far from conclusive. It is by no means clear, for example, that the more competitive the constituency, the better will each party perform its organizational and campaign activities. For an examination of this and other hypotheses, see Paul Allen Beck, "Environment and Party: The Impact of Political and Demographic County Characteristics on Party Behavior," *American Political Science Review,* LXVIII (September 1974), pp. 1229–1244.

21. Lewis Bowman and G. R. Boynton, "Activities and Role Definitions of Grassroots Party Officials," *Journal of Politics,* XXVIII (February 1966), pp. 121–143. Also see Lee S. Weinberg, "Stability and Change Among Pittsburgh Precinct Politicians," *Social Science* (Winter 1975), pp. 10–16.

22. Samuel J. Eldersveld, *Political Parties: A Behavioral Analysis,* © 1964 by Rand McNally & Company, Chicago, pp. 253–254.

23. See Hugh A. Bone, *American Politics and the Party System* (New York: McGraw-Hill, 1971), pp. 139–141.

24. *Congressional Quarterly Weekly Report,* July 15, 1978, pp. 1792–1795.

25. Nelson W. Polsby and Aaron B. Wildavsky, *Presidential Elections* (New York: Scribner 1971), pp. 35–39.

26. Ranney, *Curing the Mischiefs of Faction,* pp. 139–140.

27. Ranney, *Curing the Mischiefs of Faction,* p. 141. Like Polsby and Wildavsky, Ranney recognizes that there are few politicians who are completely "unsullied purists or unprincipled professionals."

28. V. O. Key, Jr., *Politics, Parties, & Pressure Groups* (New York: Crowell, 1964), pp. 200–201.

29. From *Party Government* by E. E. Schattschneider. Copyright 1942 by E. E. Schattschneider. Reprinted by permission of Holt, Rinehart and Winston, Inc., p. 1.

30. Agreement among students of political parties as to the nature of party functions, their relative significance, and the consequences of functional performance for the political system is far from complete. Frank J. Sorauf points out that among the functions that have been attributed to American parties have been those of simplifying political issues and alternatives, producing automatic majorities, recruiting political leadership and personnel, organizing minorities and opposition, moderating and compromising political conflict, organizing the machinery of government, promoting political consensus and legitimacy, and bridging the separation of powers. The principal difficulty with listings of this sort, according to Sorauf, is that "it involves making functional statements about party activity without necessarily relating them to functional requisites or needs of the system." He suggests that at this stage of research on parties emphasis should be given to the activities performed by parties, thus avoiding the confusion arising from the lack of clarity about the meaning of

function, the absence of consensus on functional categories, and the problem of measuring the performance of functions. See his instructive essay, "Political Parties and Political Analysis," in William Nisbet Chambers and Walter Dean Burnham (eds.), *The American Party Systems: Stages of Political Development* (New York: Oxford, 1967), pp. 33–53.

31. In about four-fifths of the states, judges are chosen in some form of partisan or nonpartisan election. In the remaining states they come to office through appointment. A few states employ the so-called Missouri Plan of judge selection, under which the governor makes judicial appointments from a list of names supplied by a nonpartisan judicial commission composed of judges, lawyers, and laymen. Under this plan, designed to take judges "out of politics," each judge, after a trial period, runs for reelection without opposition; voters may vote either to retain or to remove him from office. If a majority of the voters cast affirmative ballots, the judge is continued in office for a full term; if the vote is negative, the judge loses office and the governor makes another appointment in the same manner. Even under this plan, of course, the governor may give preference to aspirants of his own party. The truth of the matter is that irrespective of the system used to choose judges, party leaders and party interest will nearly always be involved.

32. Theodore J. Lowi, "Party, Policy, and Constitution in America," in William Nisbet Chambers and Walter Dean Burnham (eds.), *The American Party Systems,* p. 263.

33. Robert MacIver, *The Web of Government* (New York: Macmillan, 1947), p. 213.

34. There are few facts about the political participation of Americans of greater significance than those that reveal its social class bias. A disproportionate number of the people who are highly active in politics are drawn from the upper reaches of the social order, from among those who hold higher-status occupations, are more affluent, and are better educated. Citizens from lower socioeconomic levels constitute only about 10 percent of the participants who are highly active in politics. See Sidney Verba and Norman H. Nie, *Participation in America: Political Democracy and Social Equality* (New York: Harper & Row, 1972), especially Chapter 20.

35. Harvey Fergusson, *People and Power* (New York: Morrow, 1947), pp. 101–102.

36. For an analysis of the differences between the platforms of the parties, see Gerald M. Pomper, *Elections in America* (New York: Dodd, Mead, 1970), pp. 149–170.

Chapter 2

THE CHARACTERISTICS OF AMERICAN PARTIES

The major parties are firm landmarks on the American political scene. In existence for over a century, the major parties have made important contributions to the development and maintenance of a democratic political culture and to democratic institutions and practices. In essence, the parties form the principal institution for popular control of government, and this achievement is all the more remarkable for the limitations under which they function. This chapter examines the principal characteristics of the American party system.

THE PRIMARY CHARACTERISTIC: DISPERSED POWER

Viewed at some distance, the party organizations may appear to be neatly ordered and hierarchical—committees are piled, one atop another, from the precinct to the national level, conveying the impression that power flows from the top to the bottom. In point of fact, however, the American party is not nearly so hierarchical. State and local organizations have substantial independence on most party matters. The practices that state and local parties follow, the candidates they recruit or help to recruit, the campaign money they raise, the auxiliary groups they form and re-form, the innovations they introduce, the organized interests to which they respond, the campaign strategies and issues they create and, most important, the policy orientations of the candidates who run under their label—all bear the distinctive imprints of local and state political cultures, leaders, traditions, and interests.[1]

28

Although there is no mistaking the overall decentralization of American parties, it is also apparent that the power of the national party has grown immensely in terms of control over the presidential nominating process —particularly in the case of the Democratic party. The Democratic reform movement, begun in the late 1960s, drastically altered the rules and practices of state parties in matters related to the selection of national convention delegates. In 1974, the Democratic party held a mid-term convention for the purpose of drafting a charter—the first in the history of either major party—to provide for the governance of the party. The charter formally establishes the Democratic national convention as the highest authority of the party and requires state parties to observe numerous standards in the selection of convention delegates. As a result of a Supreme Court decision in 1975, moreover, it is now clear that if there is a conflict between national and state party rules concerning the selection of delegates, national party rules must govern. "The convention serves the pervasive national interest in the selection of candidates for national office," the Supreme Court ruled, "and this national interest is greater than any interest of an individual state."[2]

The centralizing reforms of the Democratic party, however, need to be kept in perspective. Indeed, they have done more to devitalize national party organizations than to strengthen them. The spread of presidential primaries and the "opening up" of party caucuses, for example, have transformed the national convention, diminishing its independent role in choosing the presidential nominee. In the 1976 Democratic convention, the delegates did little more than ratify the choice made earlier in the party primaries and caucuses of the states. Four years earlier the choice of the nominee had been only slightly less predictable at the opening of the convention. In effect, the "average party voter" and the "candidate enthusiast," not the Democratic convention, nominated George McGovern and Jimmy Carter. Moreover, neither the 1972 nor the 1976 convention was in any real sense a party gathering. Rather, each was an assemblage dominated by the front-running candidate, his organization, and the amateur activists drawn to his preconvention campaign. Party leaders and public officeholders were conspicuous either by their absence or by their powerlessness.

The influence of national party agencies on state and local organizations is largely confined to the presidential nominating process. Should national party leaders seek to influence the nomination of candidates for Congress, for example, the prospects are that they would be rebuffed. Custom dictates that the national party follow a "hands-off" policy in the choice of congressional candidates.[3] These nominations are seen as local matters. Moreover, it is rare for party leaders in Congress to attempt to discipline fellow party members who stray off the reservation, voting with the other party on key legislative issues or otherwise failing to come to the aid of their party.[4] Congressmen who neglect or demean their party not only escape sanctions but also, by dramatizing their capacity to resist party pressures, may improve their fortunes with the voters back home—such is the case in a party system in which power is concentrated nowhere.

The weakness of the national party apparatus is also revealed in the character and activities of the national committee. For the party in power, it is essentially an arm of the president. Neither national committee has more than minimal leverage on fellow party members in Congress, on the party's governors, or on the party's public officials further down the line. The public financing of presidential elections, in effect since 1976, has sharply constricted the national committee's role in campaign finance.

Much of the energy of national party leaders is devoted to efforts to keep the party united. And as one would expect in a party composed of divergent interests, the price of unity is usually accommodation. The shaping of party positions on major questions of public policy is thus well beyond the capacity of the committee.

Factors Contributing to the Dispersal of Party Power

It is no happenstance that the national parties lead a furtive existence, under ordinary circumstances visible only during presidential election campaigns. The situation could hardly be otherwise, given the legal and constitutional characteristics of the American political system. American parties must find their place within a federal system where powers and responsibilities lie with 50 states as well as with the national government. The basic responsibility for the design of the electoral system in which the parties compete is given to the states, not to the nation. Not surprisingly, party organizations have been molded by the electoral laws under which they contest for power. Local and state power centers have naturally developed around the thousands of governmental units and elective offices found in the states and localities. With his distinctive constituency (frequently a "safe" district), his own coterie of supporters, and his own channels to campaign money, the typical officeholder has a remarkable amount of freedom in defining his relationship to his party. The organization's well-being and his well-being are not identical. To press this point, it is not too much to say that officeholders are steadily engaged in the process of evaluating party claims and objectives in the light of their own career aspirations. When the party's claims and the officeholder's aspirations diverge, the party ordinarily loses out. The broad point is that a federal system, with numerous elective offices, opens up an extraordinary range of political choices to subnational parties and especially to individual candidates.

For all of its significance for the party system and the distinctiveness of American politics, however, federalism is but one of several explanations for the fragmentation of party power. Another constitutional provision, separation of powers, also contributes to this condition. One of the frequent by-products of this system is the emergence of a truncated party majority—that is, a condition under which one party controls one or both houses of the legislature and the other party controls the executive. At worst, this leads to a dreary succession of narrow partisan clashes between the branches; at best, it may contribute occasionally to the clarification of certain differences between the parties; at no time does it contribute a particle to the development and maintenance of party responsibility for a program of public policy. A glance at Table 3 will reveal the dimensions of this "party problem" in the American states. Currently, about one-half of all gubernatorial–legislative elections lead to divided party control of the branches. The pattern at the national level is not much different.

TABLE 3.   Incidence of Party Division (Governor versus Legislature) Following Elections of 1976 and 1978

Relation between Governor and Legislature	Following Election of 1976		Following Election of 1978	
	Number	Percent	Number	Percent
Governor opposed	20	41	24*	49
Governor unopposed	29	59	25	51

Source of data: *Congressional Quarterly Weekly Report*, November 18, 1978, p. 3302. Nebraska is excluded because it has a nonpartisan legislature.

*Following the election of 1978, the governor faced opposition party majorities in *both* houses in 17 of these 24 states.

A third factor is the method used to make nominations. It was noted earlier that nominations for national office are sorted out and settled at the local level, ordinarily without interference of any sort by national party functionaries. One of the principal supports of local control over this activity is the direct primary. Its use virtually guarantees that candidates for national office will be tailored to the measure of local specifications. Consider this analysis by Austin Ranney and Willmoore Kendall:

A party's *national* leaders can affect the kind of representatives and senators who come to Washington bearing the party's label only by enlisting the support of the state and local party organizations concerned; and they cannot be sure of doing so even then. Assume, for example, that the local leaders have decided to support the national leaders in an attempt to block the renomination of a maverick congressman, and are doing all they can. There is still nothing to prevent the rank and file, who may admire the incumbent's "independence," from ignoring the leaders' wishes and renominating him. The direct primary, in other words, is *par excellence* a system for maintaining *local* control of nominations; and as long as American localities continue to be so different from one another in economic interests, culture, and political attitudes, the national parties are likely to retain their present ideological heterogeneity and their tendency to show differing degrees of cohesion from issue to issue.[5]

Fourth, the distribution of power within the parties is affected by patterns of campaign finance. Few, if any, campaign resources are more important than money. A large proportion of the political money donated in any year is given directly to the campaign organizations of individual candidates rather than to the party organizations. Candidates with access to campaign money, moreover, are automatically in a strong position vis-à-vis the party organization. Not having to rely on the party for campaign funds, the candidate can stake out his independence from it.

Fifth, there is a pervasive spirit of localism that dominates American politics and contributes to the decentralization of political power. There are literally countless ways in which local interests find expression in national politics. Even the presidential nominating process may become critical for the settlement of local and state political struggles. A prominent political leader who aligns with the candidate who wins the presidential nomination, particularly if he does so early in the race, can put new life into his own career. He gains access to the nominee and increased visibility. If his party wins the presidency, an appointment in the new administration may be offered to him. Or if he chooses to run for a major public office, he is likely to secure the support of the president. National conventions, in a word, settle more than national matters.

Congress has always shown a remarkable hospitality to the idea that governmental power should be decentralized. A great deal of the major legislation that has been passed in recent decades, for example, has been designed in such a way as to make state and local governments participants in the development and implementation of public policies. Locally based political organizations profit from these arrangements. A basic explanation for Congress's defense of state and local governments lies in the backgrounds of the congressmen themselves. Many of them will have been elected to state or local office prior to their election to Congress. They are steeped in local lore, think in local terms, meet frequently with local representatives, and work for local advantage. Their steady attention to the local dimensions of national policy helps not only to safeguard their own careers but also helps to promote the interests of those local politicians who look to Washington for assistance in solving community problems.

Finally, the fragmentation of party power owes much to the growing importance of "outsiders" in the political process. Chief among them are the media, campaign management firms, and political interest groups. Increasingly, candidates hire expert consultants to organize their campaigns, to shape their strategies, and to mold their images. And they use the media to present themselves to the voters—what counts, the modern candidate knows, is how he or she is perceived by the voters. As for political interest groups, their role in campaigns, particularly in their financing, probably has never been more important than it is right now. In the congressional elections of 1978, political action committees of various business, labor, and professional groups funneled over $30 million to the campaigns of House and Senate candidates—nearly three times as much as they contributed in 1974.[6] In modern campaigns, the role of the party organization has become less and less conspicuous, their impact on election outcomes less and less important.

The Power of Officeholders

The structure, tone, and mood of American parties bear the heavy imprint of decentralization. This concept, more than any other, brings into focus the essential weakness of national party leaders and institutions. But to stress this characteristic is perhaps to create an illusion of great organizational strength among state and local party units. In point of fact, however, only a few state and local party organizations, *qua* organizations, have any real strength. James M. Burns makes the point this way:

> At no level, except in a handful of industrial states, do state parties have the attributes of organization. They lack extensive dues-paying memberships; hence they number many captains and sergeants but few foot soldiers. They do a poor job of raising money for themselves as organizations, or even for their candidates. They lack strong and imaginative leadership of their own. They cannot control their most vital function—the nomination of their candidates. Except in a few states, such as Ohio, Connecticut, and Michigan, our parties are essentially collections of small cliques and they are often shunted aside by the politicians who understand political power. Most of the state parties are at best mere jousting grounds for embattled politicians; at worst they simply do not exist, as in the case of Republicans in the rural South or Democrats in the rural Midwest.[7]

The malaise that tends to characterize party organizations at all levels of government results in a concentration of power in the hands of public officeholders and candidates for public office. Sometimes in their own names and sometimes in the name of their party, they assume the critical functions associated with campaigns and elections. In most jurisdictions it is the officeholders (or aspirants) who develop issues and strategies, who recruit the corps of campaign workers, who raise the necessary political money, who mobilize the voters, and who carry the party banner. Their power comes not as the result of wresting leadership from party officials but rather from taking over campaign responsibilities that otherwise would be met inadequately, or perhaps not at all, by the formal party organization.

VARIATIONS IN PARTY COMPETITION FROM STATE TO STATE AND FROM OFFICE TO OFFICE

Familiar and conventional interpretations in American politics are never easy to abandon. Old labels persist even though their descriptive power has been sharply eroded; such is the case in the designation of the

American two-party system. Vigorous two-party competition in all jurisdictions is, of course, clearly unattainable. No one should expect it. It is
surprising, however, how little two-party competition is to be found in
certain electoral districts of the nation. The American party system is in
places and at times strongly two-party, and in other places and at other
times, dominantly one-party. In addition, there are states and localities in
which factional politics within one or both of the major parties is so pervasive and persistent as to suggest the presence of a multiple-party system.
Competition between the parties is a condition not to be taken for
granted, despite the popular tendency to bestow the two-party label upon
American politics.

Competitiveness in Presidential and Congressional Elections

Although in many states and localities there is little more than a veneer
of competitiveness between the parties, this is not the case in presidential
elections. Contests for this office provide the best single example of authentic two-party competition, particularly in recent decades.[8] With but
two exceptions in all two-party presidential contests since 1940, the losing
presidential candidate has received at least 45 percent of the popular vote;
the exceptions occurred in 1964 when Barry Goldwater received slightly
under 39 percent of the vote and in 1972 when George McGovern gar-
nered only 38 percent. Several recent elections have been extraordinarily
close: in 1960 John Kennedy received 49.7 percent of the popular vote to
Richard Nixon's 49.5 percent; in a turnabout in 1968 Nixon obtained 43.4
percent to Hubert Humphrey's 42.7 percent (with George Wallace receiving 13.5 percent). In another extremely close race in 1976, Jimmy Carter
received 50.1 percent of the vote, while Gerald R. Ford received 48.0
percent. The plain fact is that the two major parties are now so evenly
matched in presidential contests that the losing party has excellent reason
to expect that it can win the office within an election or two.

A view of presidential elections from the states is worth examining. In
the last two decades there has been a sharp decline in the number of
one-party states and regions in presidential elections. The point is readily
verified in Figure 3, which shows the tempo of Republican growth in the
once-solid Democratic South. The watershed in southern political history
appears to have been 1952. Dwight D. Eisenhower carried four southern
states (Florida, Tennessee, Texas, and Virginia), narrowly missing victories
in several other states, while receiving over 48 percent of the popular vote
throughout the South. Richard Nixon's victory in 1968 was similarly impressive. In the District of Columbia and 39 states outside the South,
Hubert Humphrey led Nixon by about 30,000 votes; in the 11 southern
states Nixon led Humphrey by over 500,000 votes. The high point of
Republican appeal was reached in 1972, when Nixon received 70 percent
of the southern vote, a much larger proportion than he received in 1968.

One result of the 1976 nomination by the Democrats of Jimmy Carter, a native of Georgia, was that the Republican surge in the South was arrested; although Gerald Ford ran well in nearly all states of the Confederacy, he carried only Virginia.

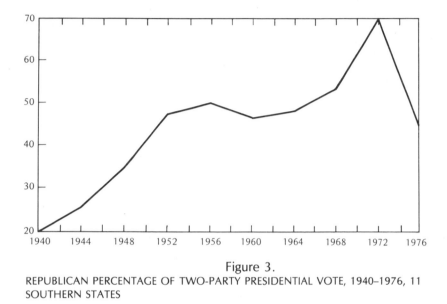

Figure 3.
REPUBLICAN PERCENTAGE OF TWO-PARTY PRESIDENTIAL VOTE, 1940–1976, 11 SOUTHERN STATES

At the other end of the scale, certain traditionally Republican strongholds have become more competitive. At one time immoderately Republican, such states as Maine, New Hampshire, and Vermont are no longer "in the bag." Each election puts a further strain on old party loyalties. Landslide elections occur from time to time, as in 1964 and 1972, but they are often followed by "cliffhangers," as in 1968 and 1976. It is a good guess that most future presidential elections will be closely competitive, decided by thin margins in a handful of states.

Congressional elections are another story. Indeed, the attribute that most congressional districts have in common is a history of one-party domination. Table 4 shows the extent to which House and Senate elections have been diverted from the main stream of competitive politics at the national level. In most recent elections, about 15 to 20 percent of the House elections have been in the "marginal" (or competitive) category—that is, elections in which the winning candidate receives less than 55 percent of the vote. In only about 65 to 100 districts out of 435 is there ordinarily any chance that the incumbent party will lose—so safe are the vast majority of congressional districts. Though more competitive than those of the House, Senate elections usually result in control by the same party. Not surprisingly, party control is most likely to shift when a seat is "open"—that is, when no incumbent is running.

TABLE 4. Marginal, Safer, and Uncontested Seats in Elections to U.S. House of Representatives and Senate, 1970–1978, by Percentage of Total Seats

Election Margin	House					Senate				
	1970	1972	1974	1976	1978	1970	1972	1974	1976	1978
	Percent					Percent				
Marginal ⎰ Seats won by Democrats, by less than 55 percent of the vote	6.0	6.2	10.1	11.9	9.2	21.2	20.6	17.1	22.6	5.9
Seats won by Republicans, by less than 55 percent of the vote	6.5	8.7	12.2	5.6	5.8	21.2	26.5	22.8	12.9	23.5
Safer ⎰ Seats won by Democrats, by 55 percent or more of the vote	42.1	41.4	46.7	49.2	43.0	45.5	29.4	48.5	38.7	35.3
Seats won by Republicans, by 55 percent or more of the vote	34.2	33.8	20.7	26.2	26.4	12.0	23.5	8.6	19.3	32.4
Uncontested seats	11.2	9.9	10.3	7.1	15.6	0.0	0.0	3.0	6.5	2.9
Total	100.0	100.0	100.0	100.0	100.0	100.0	100.0	100.0	100.0	100.0

Source: Data drawn from various issues of Congressional Quarterly Weekly Report.

TABLE 5.   Electoral Margins by Region,* House and Senate, 1978

Chamber and Region	Seats Won by Less Than 55 Percent of the Vote	Seats Won by 55 Percent or More of the Vote	Uncontested**
House			
South	14.9%	51.2%	33.9%
East	18.0	69.2	12.8
Midwest	11.6	82.6	5.8
West	15.8	77.6	6.6
Senate			
South	30.8	61.5	7.7
East	28.6	71.4	0.0
Midwest	37.5	62.5	0.0
West	16.7	83.3	0.0

South: Ala., Ark., Fla., Ga., Ky., La., Miss., N.C., Okla., S.C., Tenn., Tex., and Va.
   East: Conn., Del., Maine, Md., Mass., N.H., N.J., N.Y., Pa., R.I., Vt., and W. Va.
   Midwest: Ill., Ind., Iowa, Kan., Mich., Minn., Mo., Neb., N.D., Ohio, S.D., and Wis.
   West: Alaska, Ariz., Calif., Colo., Haw., Ida., Mont., Nev., N.M., Ore., Utah, Wash., and Wyo.
   **Includes some elections in which the only opposition was that presented by a minor party candidate.

Decisive party victories are not confined to any region of the country. Table 5 shows the electoral margins by region in the off-year election of 1978. Over 80 percent of the House elections in all parts of the country were won by 55 percent or more of the vote. Indeed, many were uncontested. In the Midwest, the proportion of one-sided elections was almost 90 percent. This analysis is, of course, "after the fact." Many members of Congress view each election with trepidation, never feeling that their constituencies are as secure as postelection analyses usually stamp them.[9]

Table 6 helps to fill out this account of noncompetitiveness at the congressional level. It is not uncommon to find that 90 percent or more of the incumbents in the House and Senate are reelected. Ordinarily, not many incumbents fall by the wayside in the primaries. All this comes down to the fact that Congress is an arena for two-party politics not because its members are produced by competitive environments but because *both* parties have managed to develop and to maintain large blocs of "noncompetitive" seats.[10] American politics, it seems, has been fashioned out of such anomalies.

Competitiveness at the State Level

A glance at Table 7, borrowed from a study by Austin Ranney, reveals the wide range of competitiveness in the 50 states. The degree of interparty competition was calculated for each state by blending four separate

TABLE 6. The Advantage of Incumbency in House and Senate Elections, 1956–1978

Year	Defeated in Primary	Total Number of Incumbents Running in General Election	Elected in General Election	Defeated in General Election	Percentage of Incumbents Running in General Election Elected
1956					
House	6	404	389	51	96.29
Senate	0	28	25	3	89.29
1958					
House	3	393	355	38	90.33
Senate	0	31	20	11	64.52
1960					
House	6	400	374	26	93.50
Senate	0	29	28	1	96.55
1962					
House	12	396	381	22	94.34
Senate	1	34	29	5	85.29
1964					
House	5	389	344	45	88.43
Senate	1	32	28	4	87.50
1966					
House	11	402	362	40	90.05
Senate	3	29	28	1	96.55
1968					
House	3	401	396	5	98.75
Senate	4	24	20	4	83.33
1970					
House	7	391	379	12	96.93
Senate	1	29	23	6	79.31
1972					
House	13	380	367	13	96.58
Senate	2	25	20	5	80.00
1974					
House	8	383	343	40	89.56
Senate	2	25	23	2	92.00
1976					
House	3	381	368	13	96.59
Senate	0	25	16	9	64.00
1978					
House	5	377	358	19	94.96
Senate	3	22	15	7	69.18

Source: *Congressional Quarterly Weekly Report*, March 25, 1978, p. 755 (as updated by Congressional Quarterly research department).

state "scores": the average percentage of the popular vote received by Democratic gubernatorial candidates, the average percentage of Democratic seats in the state senate, the average percentage of Democratic seats in the state house of representatives, and the percentage of all terms for governor, senate, and house in which the Democrats were in control. Taken together, these percentages produced an "index of competitiveness," ranging (theoretically) from .0000 (total Republican domination) to 1.0000 (total Democratic domination). At midpoint, .5000, perfect competition would exist between the parties.[11]

In over one-half of the American states, party competition for *state* offices lacks an authentic ring. Over the period of this study, 1962–1973,

TABLE 7. The Fifty States Classified According to Degree of Interparty Competition, 1962–1973

One-party Democratic	Modified One-party Democratic	Two-party		Modified One-party Republican
Louisiana (.9930)	North Carolina (.7750)	Nevada (.6057)	Delaware (.4947)	North Dakota (.3463)
Alabama (.9520)	Maryland (.7647)	California (.6020)	Michigan (.4903)	Idaho (.3445)
Mississippi (.9145)	Virginia (.7543)	Alaska (.5760)	Pennsylvania (.4705)	Colorado (.3390)
South Carolina (.8935)	Tennessee (.7443)	Connecticut (.5670)	Utah (.4647)	Kansas (.3380)
Texas (.8780)	Florida (.7410)	Montana (.5553)	Arizona (.4377)	South Dakota (.3373)
Georgia (.8710)	Hawaii (.7313)	New Jersey (.5437)	Illinois (.4245)	Vermont (.3307)
Arkansas (.8645)	Oklahoma (.7297)	Washington (.5420)	Wisconsin (.4245)	Wyoming (.3205)
	New Mexico (.7107)	Nebraska (.5127)	Indiana (.4160)	
	Missouri (.7085)	Oregon (.5075)	Iowa (.4113)	
	Kentucky (.7037)	Minnesota (.5037)	New York (.4053)	
	West Virginia (.6945)		Maine (.4045)	
	Rhode Island (.6860)		Ohio (.3693)	
	Massachusetts (.6730)		New Hampshire (.3600)	

Source: From Austin Ranney, "Parties in State Politics," in Herbert Jacob and Kenneth N. Vines, eds., *Politics in the American States: A Comparative Analysis*, 3rd Ed., copyright © 1976, Little, Brown and Company (Inc.). Reprinted by permission.

seven states (all southern) were classified as one-party Democratic; another 20 states were designated as either modified one-party Democratic or modified one-party Republican. Twenty-three states met the test of two-party competition.

Two particularly interesting correlations with competitiveness appear. One concerns the relationship between one-party domination and membership in the Confederacy—all seven one-party Democratic states withdrew from the Union, as did Florida, North Carolina, Tennessee, and Virginia (all modified one-party Democratic states). It is plain that for many of the states that today have a low level of party competition (in particular for state offices), the Civil War was the great divide. The second correlation to be noted centers on urbanization: not surprisingly, the two-party states are significantly more urbanized than the other states. In similar fashion, these states are also distinguished by having high per capita incomes, a significant proportion of "foreign stock," a high proportion of labor devoted to manufacturing, and a low proportion of labor devoted to agriculture.[12]

The degree of interparty competitiveness cannot, of course, be measured only in terms of the struggle for state offices, as this study notes. Some of the states in the one-party or modified one-party categories during this period had vigorous two-party competition in certain presidential, congressional, and senatorial elections. Virginia, for example, classified as a modified one-party Democratic state, has long had a large number of "presidential Republican" voters. Indeed, this nominally Democratic state voted Republican in six of the eight presidential elections between 1948 and 1976. Competitiveness must therefore be explored along several dimensions.

Competitiveness at the Office Level

Party competition varies sharply not only between states but between *offices* in the same state.[13] Figure 4, the work of Joseph Schlesinger, reveals the complexity inherent in the concept of competitiveness. To unravel the figure, examine the location of each state office on the horizontal and vertical axes. The horizontal axis shows the extent to which the parties have controlled each office over the period of the study; the vertical axis shows the rate of turnover in control of the office between the parties. It is readily apparent that some offices are steadfastly held by one party and that other offices are genuinely competitive. Wide variations exist within each state. Taking the northern states as a group, there is less competition for seats in the House than for any other office. By contrast, the offices of governor and senator are the most competitive—even these offices, however, are not significantly competitive.

Overall, the pattern of competition depicted in Figure 4 testifies to the inability of state parties to compete for and to control a range of offices. To emphasize a point made earlier, the figure suggests, albeit subtly, that

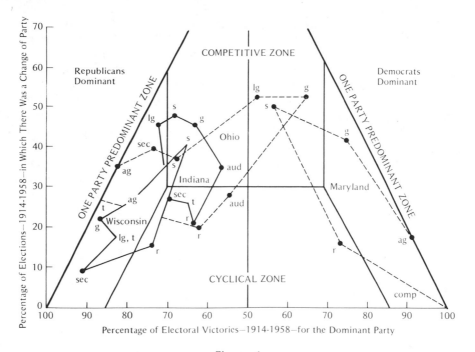

Figure 4.

PARTY COMPETITION FOR INDIVIDUAL OFFICES (SELECTED STATES)

Office Key

g: governor
s: senator
r: congressman
lg: lieutenant governor
sec: secretary of state
ag: attorney general
aud: auditor
t: treasurer
comp: comptroller

". . . the more centrally located on the horizontal axis the more competitive an office was in overall terms; the higher on the diagram the more rapid the rate of turnover; and correspondingly, the lower on the diagram an office falls, the longer the cycles of one-party control, regardless of the degree of overall competition."

Source: Joseph A. Schlesinger, "The Structure of Competition for Office in the American States," *Behavioral Science,* V (July 1960), p. 203.

the successful officeholder is one who develops and maintains his own campaign resources, knowing that the party organization is about as likely to be a spectator to his career as a guardian of it.

Competitiveness in a One-Party Environment

No discussion of American one-party systems can proceed far without encountering the peculiar and inevitable dynamic of such systems: factional politics. Not by any means are all one-party systems alike in their

factional characteristics. Some one-party states are characterized by multifactionalism, and others, by bifactionalism. Although it is true, of course,
that factional struggles sometimes occur within parties in a two-party
system, their significance is ordinarily much less pronounced than in heavily one-party jurisdictions, especially those of the South.[14]

Factionalism in the South grew up around the Democratic primary.
Because of the weakness of the Republican party, the "real" election in
most southern states usually has taken place in the Democratic primary.
Candidates winning at this stage ordinarily have run little risk of defeat
in the general election, perhaps not even having a Republican opponent
with whom to contend. The absence of strong interparty competition
(especially for state and local offices) has inflated the importance of the
dominant party's primary, and this in turn has led to freewheeling, indi-
vidualistic politics in which candidates of all kinds struggle for the Democratic nomination in a virtual "no-party" environment.[15] This pattern is
changing, of course, as a result of growing Republican strength in the
South.

Some southern states have been characterized by a persistent bifactionalism, with two relatively well-organized groups contesting election after
election. For several decades following the arrival of Huey Long on the
scene, the principal political division in Louisiana (Democratic) politics
was between the Long and the anti-Long factions, the first identified with
the low-income groups (both in rural areas and in New Orleans), and the
second, with the conservative elements of business and agriculture.[16] The
Louisiana experience shows that in limited measure bifactional struggles
resemble two-party competition: there were recognized sets of leaders,
identifiable policy orientations, well-developed campaign organizations,
and more or less stable popular followings. More typical is multifactionalism, which is characterized by numerous candidates for the same office,
each with his own personal organization (ordinarily strong in his own and
neighboring counties and weak statewide), each concerned with his own
survival. Candidacies are rarely linked together by any form of "ticket,"
as has been used in Louisiana. Where multifactionalism prevails, it is
virtually impossible for the voter to sort through the candidates, identifying those with something of a common ideology, in order to elect a group
of men who are disposed to cooperate with one another. Rather, multifactionalism produces a free-for-all; candidates of all stripes vie with one
another in a barrage of charges and countercharges, leaving the electorate
confused as to the direction the government will take once the winners
have come to power.

Factional politics lack structure and coherence, even in a bifactional
state. Despite the superficial resemblance of bifactional politics to two-
party politics, the issues that separate the factions are never as clear-cut
as they are in a two-party system. Uncertainty plagues political careers.
Aspiring politicians link their candidacies to one or the other of the two

factions, but their affiliations may shift from one election to the next. The paths of advancement are never clearly marked, either for potential candidates or for officeholders. Improbable alliances develop, only to disappear as frustrations mount and as new opportunities come into view. By and large, the faction that wins is unprepared to assume generalized control over the government. Overall, the label of the party in power conceals more than it illuminates. And there is slim prospect that the voter will be able to make sharp distinctions among the candidates or, following the election, to hold any group even roughly accountable for its performance in office.

The Persistent Two-Party System in America

Despite the existence of one-party systems here and there, political competition in the United States usually comes down to competition between the two major parties, Democratic and Republican. It is not easy to depict clearly why American politics has been hospitable to a two-party rather than a multiple-party system, as in many European democracies. Without attempting a detailed analysis of this complex question, we can summarize the principal hypotheses that have been offered. Less than "laws" and more than hunches, they include the following explanations.

A familiar explanation is that election of members of the U.S. House of Representatives from single-member districts by plurality vote helps to support the two-party pattern. Under this arrangement a single candidate is elected in each district, and he needs to receive only a plurality of the vote. There is slight inducement for third-party candidates to run, since the prospects are poor that they could defeat the candidates of the two major parties. On the other hand, if congressmen were elected under a proportional representation scheme, with several members chosen in each district, third-party candidates would undoubtedly have a better chance of winning some seats. Third parties are up against the same obstacle in presidential elections: only one party can capture the presidency. For this office, the nation as a whole takes on the cast of a single-member district. Each state's electoral votes are awarded as a unit to the candidate receiving a plurality of the popular vote; all other popular votes are in effect wasted. In 1968, for example, George Wallace, candidate of the American Independent party, received about five million popular votes in states *outside* the South but won electoral votes only in the five southern states he carried. If electoral votes were divided in proportion to popular votes in each state, third-party candidates would likely make a bigger dent in the electoral vote totals of the major parties. Electoral practices in the United States, it is plain, are hard on third parties.

The diversity and flexibility that characterize the two major parties also contribute to the preservation of the two-party system. The policy orientations of the parties are rarely so firmly fixed as to preclude a shift in emphasis or direction in order to attract emerging interests within the electorate. Moreover, each party is made up of officeholders with different views; almost any political group, as a result, can discover some officials who share its values and predilections and who are willing to represent its point of view. The adaptability of the parties and officeholders not only permits them to siphon off support that otherwise might contribute to the development of third parties but also creates a great deal of slack in the political system. Groups pressing for change know that there is always some chance that they can win acceptance for their positions within the existing party framework.

Another central explanation for the durability of the two-party system in America is found in a tradition of dualism.[17] Early political struggles took place between those who favored adoption of the Constitution and those who opposed it. Subsequently, dualism was reflected in struggles between Federalists and Anti-Federalists and, later still, between Democrats and Whigs. Since the Civil War, the main party battle has been fought out between Democrats and Republicans. In sum, the main elements of conflict within the American political system have ordinarily found expression in competition between two dominant groups of politicians and their followings. This, in a nutshell, is the essence of American party history. Third parties have cropped up from time to time to challenge the major parties, but their lives ordinarily have been short and uneventful—so deep-seated is the attachment of a majority of Americans to inherited institutions and practices.

A profusion of other themes might be explored in seeking to account for the two-party character of American politics. Election law, for example, makes it difficult for all but the most well-organized and well-financed third parties to gain a place on the ballot; in presidential elections, they must struggle in state after state to recruit campaign workers and funds and to collect signatures for their nominating petitions. Even audiences may be hard to come by. Moreover, because the risk of failure looms so large, new political organizations must strain to find acceptable candidates to run under their banner; aspiring politicians are not notable for their willingness to take quixotic risks for the sake of ideology or principle, particularly if there is some chance that a career in one of the major parties is available. The extraordinary costs of organizing and conducting major campaigns, the difficulties that attend the search for men and women to man party outposts, and the frustrations that plague efforts to cut the cords that bind American voters to the traditional parties all serve to inhibit the formation and maintenance of third parties. Finally, it appears that the restless impulse for new alternatives that often dominates other nations, leading to the formation of new parties, is found less commonly in the United States.

Despite the obstacles that confront the creation of a new national party, the possibility cannot be ruled out. Plainly, not all American citizens are highly satisfied with the political, economic, and social systems of the country. A national survey taken in the mid-seventies, for example, revealed that 25 percent of all voters would be likely to support a new party more conservative than the Republican party. Interestingly, support for a conservative party was as great among Democrats as among Republicans, as great among young as among older voters.[18] A later poll found that 41 percent of a national sample were in favor of the creation of a new "center" party, one that would be flanked on the left by the Democratic party and on the right by the Republican party. Independents and young voters led all other groups in favoring a new middle-of-the-road party.[19] Whether this mood for change can be translated into both organization and durable electoral support is, of course, problematical. The impediments to launching and sustaining a new party are persistent and formidable in a system shaped, either deliberately or fortuitously, to benefit the existing major parties.

PARTIES AS COALITIONS

Viewed from afar, the American major party is likely to appear as a miscellaneous collection of individual activists and voters, banded together in some fashion in order to attempt to gain control of government. But there is more shadow than substance in that view, for when the party is brought into sharp focus, its basic coalitional character is revealed. The point is simple but important: the party is much less a collection of individuals that it is a collection of social interests and groups. In the words of Maurice Duverger, "A party is not a community but a collection of communities, a union of small groups dispersed throughout the country. . . ."[20]

Functioning within a vastly heterogeneous society, the major parties have naturally assumed a coalitional form. Groups of all kinds—social, economic, religious, and ethnic—are organized to press demands on the political order. In the course of defending or advancing their interests, they contribute substantial energy to the political process—through generating innovations, posing alternative policies, recruiting and endorsing candidates, conducting campaigns, and so on. It is safe to say that no party seriously contesting for office could ignore the constellation of groups in American political life.

Party leaders are accustomed to thinking in coalition terms. The candidates to be slated, the issues to be developed, the decisions on the allocation of resources, and the jobs to be filled—all such choices are made with one eye on the coalitions that compose the party and the other eye on the overall objectives of the party. The test of party leadership, perhaps especially at the local level, is its capacity to "harmonize" group interests, bringing them into accord with each other and with the broad goals of the party. The picture portrayed in these interviews with Detroit party leaders, taken from a study by Samuel Eldersveld, suggests the central tasks posed for party management:

> The district chairman has to be a Sherlock Holmes in the Republican party. We have, as you know, many splits in our party, and there is a constant battle of wits as to who is for whom. You have to be flexible—to meet these people on their own level, talk shop, pat them on the back, and get the work out of them.

> In our district we have a Polish section, a Negro section, a Jewish section, and any number of smaller groups. I have to be a jack of all trades. My job is to get as many people in these groups happy as I can and see that they get the votes out.[21]

Although the coalitions that make up the parties may look illogical and untidy to the outsider, they are fundamental to party organization and strategy. The capacity of a party to win an election depends on the skill of its leaders in putting together or maintaining a majority coalition of groups, some of which will hold sharply conflicting views. The presence of incompatible groups within the same party coalition is not uncommon. Since the early days of the New Deal, for example, the Democratic coalition has been the principal home of southern Democrats, blacks, and a variety of ethnic groups (Polish, Italian, and so on) located mainly in large northern cities; conflicts between these groups have been inevitable as civil rights questions have gained in significance and visibility. The urban working classes, Catholics, and Jews have also been important elements in the Democratic coalition. In counterpoise, the Republican coalition in recent decades has drawn a disproportionate number of supporters from such groups as big business, industry, farmers, small-town and rural dwellers, small businessmen, Protestants, suburbanites, and "old stock" Americans. It, too, is an uneasy alliance.

The generalization that describes the American major parties as coalitions cannot be advanced without a caveat or two. No group, it should be emphasized, is exclusively identified with one party; a significant number of union members, for example, will always be found voting Republican even though their unions endorse and support candidates of the Democratic party. Moreover, coalitions are always in flux as members grow restive over developments within their party and attentive to the attractions of the other party. In recent years, for example, southern Democrats have found it painful to remain within the coalition that makes up the national Democratic party. Disillusioned over the liberal thrust of the party, many life-long southern Democrats bolted in 1964 to support Barry Goldwater. In even greater number they moved into the ranks of the American Independent party in 1968, voting for George Wallace in preference to Hubert Humphrey or Richard Nixon. Four years later they voted overwhelmingly for Nixon. With a Georgian at the head of the Democratic ticket in 1976, southern voters abandoned their newly-found Republicanism and returned to the Democratic fold. American parties are fragile because they are coalitions, held together by generality, personality, and promise. What is surprising is that they hold together in campaigns as well as they do.

The American major party is anything but clannish. It will devote a friendly ear to almost any request. All groups are invited to support it, and in some measure, all do. Ordinarily, everything about the major party, functioning at the election stage, represents a triumph for those who press for accommodation in American politics. Platforms and candidate speeches, offering something to almost everyone, provide the hard evidence that the parties attempt to be inclusive rather than exclusive in their appeals and to draw in a wide rather than a narrow band of voters. "No matter how devoted a party leadership may be to its bedrock elements," V. O. Key observed, "it attempts to picture itself as a gifted synthesizer of concord among the elements of society. A party must act as if it were all the people rather than some of them; it must fiercely deny that it speaks for a single interest."[22]

But problems develop once the election is over and the party has been placed in office. It is at this point that the coalition put together so carefully in the campaign runs the risk of flying apart. The behavior of the Democratic party in Congress offers a good example of the coalition dilemma. Table 8 reports on the extent to which southern Democrats have split off from northern Democrats at the roll-call stage in a number of recent sessions. The table is a study in divergence: on roughly one-fourth to one-third of all roll calls, a majority of southern Democrats opposed a majority of "northern" (all other) Democrats.

The evidence of Table 8 is that a great deal of disagreement hides behind the party label, especially in the case of the congressional Democrats. When party coalitions come apart in Congress, biparty coalitions are often brought to life. The most persistent and successful biparty coalition in the history of Congress has been the "conservative coalition," formed by a majority of southern Democrats and a majority of Republicans. In existence in one form or another since the late 1930s, this coalition comes together on essentially the same policy issues that divide northern from southern Democrats. It is no exaggeration to say that the most effective majority in some recent sessions of Congress has been the southern Democrat–Republican coalition. Indeed, about the only recent Congress in which a lid was put on the coalition's power was the Eighty-ninth Congress (1965–1966)—a brief interval in which the Democratic majority, under President Lyndon Johnson, was so overpowering that even the defection of many southerners ordinarily could not bring the party down.

TABLE 8.   Northern versus Southern Democrats in Congress

Year	Total Roll Call Votes Both Chambers	North–South Democratic Splits*	Percentage of Splits
1957	207	64	31
1958	293	84	29
1959	302	83	27
1960	300	119	40
1961	320	107	33
1962	348	74	21
1963	348	84	24
1964	308	75	24
1965	459	160	35
1966	428	124	29
1967	560	148	26
1968	514	173	34
1969	422	153	36
1970	684	233	34
1971	743	279	38
1972	861	330	38
1973	1,135	318	28
1974	1,081	326	30
1975	1,214	409	34
1976	1,349	378	28
1977	1,341	375	28
1978	1,350	323	24

Source: This table is used with the permission of the Congressional Quarterly Service. See the *Congressional Quarterly Weekly Report*, January 14, 1978, p. 76, and December 23, 1978, p. 3480.

*A majority of voting southern Democrats opposed to a majority of voting northern Democrats.

PARTIES OF IDEOLOGICAL HETEROGENEITY

To win elections and gain power is the unabashedly practical aim of the major party. As suggested previously, this calls for a strategy of coalition-building in which the policy goals of the groups and candidates brought under the party umbrella are subordinated to their capacity to contribute to party victory. The key to party success is its adaptability, its willingness "to do business" with groups and individuals holding all manner of views on public policy questions. The natural outcome of a campaign strategy designed to attract all groups (and to repel none) is that the party's ideology is not easily placed in sharp focus. It is, in a sense, up for grabs, to be interpreted as individual party members and officeholders see fit.

Figure 5 gives a clue to the ideological distance that separates members of the same party in the U.S. Senate on a series of proposals of key interest

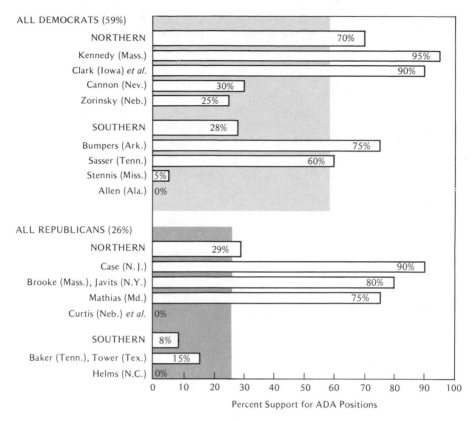

ALL DEMOCRATS (59%)
NORTHERN — 70%
Kennedy (Mass.) — 95%
Clark (Iowa) et al. — 90%
Cannon (Nev.) — 30%
Zorinsky (Neb.) — 25%

SOUTHERN — 28%
Bumpers (Ark.) — 75%
Sasser (Tenn.) — 60%
Stennis (Miss.) — 5%
Allen (Ala.) — 0%

ALL REPUBLICANS (26%)
NORTHERN — 29%
Case (N. J.) — 90%
Brooke (Mass.), Javits (N.Y.) — 80%
Mathias (Md.) — 75%
Curtis (Neb.) et al. — 0%

SOUTHERN — 8%
Baker (Tenn.), Tower (Tex.) — 15%
Helms (N.C.) — 0%

0   10   20   30   40   50   60   70   80   90   100
Percent Support for ADA Positions

Figure 5.
DEMOCRATIC AND REPUBLICAN SUPPORT OF ADA POSITIONS, BY SECTION AND
INDIVIDUAL MEMBERS, NINETY-FIFTH CONGRESS, FIRST SESSION, U.S. SENATE
This graph was prepared from data presented by the *Congressional Quarterly Weekly Report,* April
15, 1978, p. 916. The eleven states of the Confederacy are classified as "southern," while all others
are classified as "northern." Other northern Democrats with 90 percent pro-ADA scores were
Muskie (Me.), Sarbanes (Md.), Metzenbaum (Ohio), and Nelson (Wis.). Other northern Republicans
with "O" ratings on the ADA scale were Goldwater (Ariz.), Bartlett (Okla.), Hatch (Utah), and
Wallop (Wyo.).

to the Americans for Democratic Action—a group long known for its
identification with liberal policies. Those senators voting in harmony with
ADA objectives in the Ninety-fifth Congress favored such measures as
federally assisted housing for low- and moderate-income persons, stricter
standards for automobile emissions, use of federal funds for busing students, use of federal funds for abortions, limitations on spending for the
Clinch River breeder reactor project, prohibition of the production of the
neutron bomb and the B-1 bomber, reduced utility rates for elderly persons, limitations on the importation of Rhodesian chrome, and liberal

provisions for the distribution of food stamps. Viewed in ideological terms, Figure 5 shows clearly, each party is a mass of tensions and contradictions, with party members marching to a variety of drums.

The internal divisions within each major party can be easily identified. Southern Democrats do not view the world in the same light as northern Democrats, nor do they respond to the same cues and constituency clienteles as their northern colleagues. Many eastern Republicans have more in common with northern Democrats than they do with fellow party members from the South or the Midwest.[23] But tempting as it is to fasten on intraparty differences as a way of explaining the performance of the parties in policy-making arenas, the argument can easily get out of hand. In truth, the parties are far from identical, and each has more unity than is commonly supposed.

Although the structure of voting in Congress does not exhibit a high degree of ideological coherence within each party, it nevertheless does show important and continuing policy differences between the parties— at least, between majorities of each party. Taken as a whole, Democratic members of Congress[24] and Democratic congressional candidates[25] are much more likely to support social welfare legislation and an expanded role for the federal government, for example, than are Republican office-holders and Republican candidates. Programs to advance minority rights, to assist public education, to improve the lot of the poverty stricken, to provide medical care for the elderly, or to promote the interests of organized labor typically produce substantial disagreement between the parties, with most Democrats aligned on the "liberal" side and most Republicans aligned on the "conservative" side. Hence, to return to the metaphor of an earlier paragraph, while party members may be marching to different drums, most of them are playing the same tune.

THE PARTY AS AN INTEREST GROUP

Although American parties are sometimes criticized for their cool detachment from important social issues, the same cannot be said for their attitude toward a band of issues having high relevance for the party, *qua* party. Certain kinds of issues, or policy questions, which come before legislatures present the party with an opportunity to advance its interests as an organization—in much the same fashion as political interest groups attempt to secure or block legislation that would improve or impair their fortunes. There is, E. E. Schattschneider wrote some years ago, both a "private" and a "public" personality within each party.[26] The public dimension of the party is on display when larger questions of public policy are brought before the legislature; as often happens on these questions, party lines fail to hold, factions ease away from the party, and biparty coalitions come to life, empowered for the moment as the majority. The party's public appearance, in the judgment of many critics, leaves much to be desired; the fundamental flaw is that the party nominally in control of government, but rent by factionalism and fragmentation, cannot be held responsible by the public for its decisions. The problem is not that party unity collapses on all issues but that it collapses with sufficient frequency to make it less than a dependable agent for carrying out commitments presumably made to the electorate.

In sharp contrast is the private personality of the party. Though it is an exaggeration to argue that the party is engaged in steady introspection, it is surely true, as Schattschneider has observed, that "the party knows its private mind better than it knows its public mind."[27] It has a sharp sense of where the best opportunities lie for partisan advantage, and an equally keen sense of the perils and pitfalls that can threaten or damage party interests. Numerous opportunities are available for transmitting benefits to the party organization and its members. Patronage can be extracted from government at all levels; in some jurisdictions there are literally hundreds and thousands of jobs available for distribution to party stalwarts. At the national level, the custom of "senatorial courtesy" guarantees that senators will have the dominant voice in the selection of candidates to fill various positions, such as those of district court judges and U.S. marshals. This custom provides that before nominating a person for a position in a state, the president will consult with the senators of that state (if they belong to the same party as he does) to learn their preference for the position. If he should nominate someone objectionable to the senators of that state, the prospects are strong that the Senate as a whole will reject the nominee, irrespective of his qualifications for the position. On questions of this sort—those which touch the careers and political fortunes of members—party unity is both high and predictable.

Legislators have never won reputations for queuing up behind proposals that might limit maneuvering in the interest of their careers or their party's welfare. With only a few exceptions, for example, they have been opponents of plans to extend the merit system, to take judges "out of politics," and to empower independent boards or commissions to assume responsibility for reapportionment and redistricting. There is a private side to such public questions as these—to extend the merit system is to cut back party patronage, to remove judges from the election process is to cut off a career avenue for legislators with their sights on the court, and to give a nonlegislative commission control over redistricting is to run the risk of a major rearrangement of legislative districts and a resultant loss of offices. What is plain is that legislators and the parties they represent take seriously their role as guardians of the welfare of the organization and the personal interests of its members. As a collectivity, the American party is never more resourceful or more cohesive than when it is monitoring party business. And party business, it is worth noting, is about as likely to intrude on the great public questions as it is on those of narrow or parochial concern. Opportunities to advance the party cause—through debate, legislation, or investigations—are limited only by a failure of imagination.

THE AMBIGUITY OF PARTY MEMBERSHIP

For those people who set great store by neat and orderly arrangements, the American major party is vastly disappointing. There are, of course, numerous examples of the party in disarray. A particularly good one, in the judgment of some students of American politics, involves the concept of party "membership."

Who is a party member in the United States? The answer is far from clear, though a stab at the question can be made by considering the legal aspects of party membership. In closed-primary states there are minimum tests of membership. In these states, roughly four-fifths of the total, the person who registers as a Democrat or as a Republican must in some fashion establish the authenticity of his affiliation. Ordinarily this is no more than a pro forma affirmation by the voter that he regards himself as a Democrat or Republican or that he customarily votes for the candidates of one of the parties. In any case, legal party membership in these states is determined by self-classification at the stage of registration; the significance of establishing membership is that each party's primary is open only to members of that party.[28] By contrast, in open-primary states there is no test of party affiliation; the "act" of gaining membership consists merely of the voter's request for the ballot of the party in whose primary he wishes to participate. In certain open-primary states, the voter is automatically given the ballots of all the parties, with instructions to mark one and discard the rest.

The simple fact is that, apart from primary voting in closed-primary states, membership in an American major party is of slight moment. In effect, anyone who considers himself a Democrat is a Democrat; anyone who considers himself a Republican is a Republican. A citizen may register one way and vote another or not vote at all. No obligations intrude on the party member. He can be a member without applying for admission, a beneficiary without paying dues or contributing to campaigns, a critic without attending meetings, an interpreter without knowing party vocabulary, an apostate without fearing discipline. To the citizen who takes politics casually, it may be the best of all worlds. The typical American is insensitive to the claims, problems, and doctrine of his party. His principal participation in party life is through the act of voting—sometimes for his party and, of course, sometimes not.

THE INDOMITABLE PARTY?

The party in America is at the center of the political process. Nonetheless, its grip on political power is far from secure. To be sure, the men and women who are recruited for party and public offices, the issues that they bring before the electorate, the campaigns in which they participate, and the government that they help to organize and direct—all are influenced by party. The basic problem remains, however, that the party is unable to control all the routes to political power. In some jurisdictions, nonpartisan election systems have been developed to try to remove parties from politics, and to a degree they have succeeded. Moreover, so thoroughly are some states and localities dominated by one party that party itself has come to have little relevance for the kinds of men and women recruited for office or for the voters in need of cues for casting their votes. Devices such as the direct primary have also cut into the power of the party organization, serving in particular to discourage national party agencies from attempting to influence nominations, including those for national office, and to open up the nominating process to all kinds of candidates. Perhaps most important, the growing influence of the mass media, public relations experts, and campaign management firms has diminished the role of party organizations in political campaigns.[29]

The wonder of American politics is that the party system functions as well as it does. From the perspective of party leaders, the American Constitution is a vast wasteland, scarcely capable of supporting vigorous parties; federalism, separation of powers, checks and balances, and staggered elections all have proved inimical to the organization of strong parties. The burden of the evidence is that national and state constitutions were drafted by men suspicious of the concentration of power in any hands; their designs have served to fracture or immobilize party power. The party itself is an uneasy coalition of individuals and groups brought together for limited purposes. Within government, power is about as likely to be lodged in nooks and crannies as it is in central party agencies. Conflict within the parties is sometimes as intense as it is between the parties. As for the individual party member, he has a great many rights but virtually no responsibilities for the well-being of the party.

Public disillusionment over the parties places a further strain on their capacities. Many voters believe that the parties have not posed imaginative solutions for such nagging issues as racial injustice, urban decay, inflation, unemployment, and poverty. Similarly, citizens are concerned over the "old" politics that seems to dominate the parties, manifested in a preoccupation with patronage,[30] perquisites, and the welfare of the organization rather than with public policy. The parties are also subject to harsh criticism for their apparent willingness to yield to the blandishments of pressure groups and local interests, while too frequently ignoring broad national interests and problems. For many citizens, it is all too clear, the parties appear as starkly conservative institutions, fearful of innovation and unable to shape intelligent responses to contemporary dilemmas. At no time in the last century have the American major parties occupied such troubled ground as they do today.

The reforms of the 1970s did more to weaken the parties than to strengthen them. The spread of presidential primaries, the opening of caucuses, the ideology of popular participation, and the federal campaign finance law sharply diminished the role of parties and party leaders in presidential elections. They have become spectators to the campaign clashes of candidate organizations. As for the members of Congress, if anything, they have become even more independent of party. In the free-floating politics of today, interest groups, especially those organized around narrow issues, have gained increasing influence over election outcomes and public policies. The politics of the 1980s looks vastly different from that of the 1960s.

For those citizens who believe that democratic politics depends on the presence of viable parties, the current conditions must surely appear grim. Even so, it is by no means clear that the major parties are in the process of withering away, to be replaced by government without parties or government by multiple-party coalitions. Survival in this weakened condition seems much more likely. And finally, it is useful to remember that, whatever else may be said of American parties, they have never been particularly strong.

NOTES

1. American political parties not only are more decentralized than their counterparts in European nations, they are clearly among the most decentralized parties in the world. For evidence on this point, see Kenneth Janda, "American and European Parties Compared on Organization, Centralization, Coherence, and Involvement," a paper delivered at the Annual Meeting of the American Political Science Association, Chicago, Illinois, August 29–September 2, 1974, especially pp. 23–24.

2. *Cousins* v. *Wigoda*, 419 U.S. 477, 490 (1975). This case involved the seating of the Illinois delegation to the 1972 Democratic national convention. The Court upheld the right of the Democratic convention to refuse to seat the Illinois delegation which, according to the findings of the credentials committee, had violated national party rules concerning the selection process for delegates and whose make-up inadequately represented youth, women, and minorities.

3. History dictates the same course. Disturbed by congressional opposition to certain New Deal legislation, President Franklin D. Roosevelt attempted in 1938 to "purge" several southern Democrats by openly endorsing their primary opponents. His action ended in embarrassment for him and disaster for his plan, for the voters' response was to elect the very men he had marked for defeat. The lesson is evident that national party leaders must tread warily on local party grounds.

4. Exceptions can be noted. During the Eighty-ninth Congress (1965-1966), the House Democratic caucus, in an unusual exercise of disciplinary powers, took away the seniority rights of two southern Democrats who had publicly endorsed the Republican presidential candidate, Barry Goldwater, in the 1964 election.

5. Austin Ranney and Willmoore Kendall, *Democracy and the American Party System* (New York: Harcourt, 1956), p. 497.

6. See the discussion of political action committees in Chapter 3, pp. 86–87 and 89–92.

7. James M. Burns, *The Deadlock of Democracy: Four Party Politics in America* (Englewood Cliffs, N.J.: Prentice-Hall, 1963), pp. 236–237. For an instructive study of state party organizations and leaders, see Robert J. Huckshorn, *Party Leadership in the States* (Amherst, Mass.: University of Massachusetts Press, 1976).

8. The competitiveness of presidential elections also can be examined from the perspective of the electoral college. Of the 46 presidential elections held between 1876 and 1968, 21 can be classified as "hairbreadth elections"—those in which a slight shift in popular votes in a few states would have changed the outcome in the electoral college. See Lawrence D. Longley and Alan G. Braun, *The Politics of Electoral College Reform* (New Haven, Conn.: Yale University Press, 1972), especially pp. 37–41.

9. On this point, see especially Richard F. Fenno, Jr., *Home Style: House Members in Their Districts* (Boston: Little, Brown, 1978), pp. 10–18; and Thomas E. Mann, *Unsafe at any Margin: Interpreting Congressional Elections* (Washington, D.C.: American Enterprise Institute for Public Policy Research, 1978).

10. The presence of numerous noncompetitive seats in both national and state legislative elections may be due as much, if not more, to the incumbency factor as to the influence of party on voting behavior. Incumbent members of Congress have enormous advantages over their challengers, including greater voter recognition (in the vast majority of cases), superior access to the media, sizable allowances for staff, office space, travel expenses, the franking privilege and, typically, a personal campaign organization and ready access to a variety of campaign resources. Small wonder so few incumbents lose! See a study by Warren L. Kostroski that finds that in the last quarter-century incumbency has become increasingly important, while the influence of party has declined, in determining elections to the U.S. Senate. "Party and Incumbency in Postwar Senate Elections," *American Political Science Review*, LXVII (December 1973), pp. 1213–1234.

11. Austin Ranney, "Parties in State Politics," in Herbert Jacob and Kenneth Vines (eds.), *Politics in the American States*, p. 60. Copyright © 1976, Little, Brown and Company, Inc.

12. Ranney, "Parties in State Politics," pp. 63–65.

13. It is worth noting here that the elements that influence voting decisions also vary by office. A recent study suggests that the importance of parties (as cue-givers), experience and incumbency, personal qualifications, and issues in shaping voter decisions varies according to the nature and level of the office—for example, presidential–subpresidential, executive–legislative, incumbent–nonincumbent. Taken as a whole, the personal qualifications of candidates appear to have the greatest impact on the vote. Issues usually loom more important in presidential and gubernatorial voting, parties more important in gubernatorial and senatorial voting, and candidate experience most important in senatorial voting. Typically, voters have much less political information about senatorial candidates than they do about presidential and gubernatorial candidates. See Barbara Hinckley, Richard Hofstetter, and John Kessel, "Information and the Vote: A Comparative Election Study," *American Politics Quarterly*, II (April 1974), pp. 131–158.

14. The leading studies of southern factionalism are V. O. Key, Jr., *Southern Politics in State and Nation* (New York: Knopf, 1949) and Allan P. Sindler, *Huey Long's Louisiana* (Baltimore: Johns Hopkins Press, 1956).

15. The presence of numerous candidates in southern Democratic primaries often has meant that the vote is highly fragmented, with no candidate receiving a majority. To inject the majority idea into the election system, southern states employ a "runoff" primary. If no candidate garners a majority of the vote in the first primary, a second or runoff primary is held several weeks later between the two candidates who received the most votes. With the field thus narrowed to two, one of the candidates is assured of a majority.

16. Currently, Louisiana would be classified as a multifactional state. See Donald R. Matthews and James W. Prothro, *Negroes and the New Southern Politics* (New York: Harcourt, 1966), pp. 159–160.

17. For analysis of the dualism theme, see V. O. Key, Jr., *Politics, Parties, & Pressure Groups* (New York: Crowell, 1964), pp. 207–208.

18. "The Gallup Poll," *Pittsburgh Press*, April 20, 1975.

19. "The Gallup Poll," *The Washington Post*, November 13, 1978.

20. Maurice Duverger, *Political Parties* (New York: Wiley, 1965), p. 17.

21. Samuel J. Eldersveld, *Political Parties: A Behavioral Analysis*, © 1964 by Rand McNally & Company, Chicago, pp. 75–76.

22. Key, *Politics, Parties, & Pressure Groups*, p. 221.

23. For a study of the decline of party unity in *both* parties in the lower house of Congress, see Barbara Deckard and John Stanley, "Party Decomposition and Region: The House of Representatives, 1945–1970," *Western Political Quarterly*, XXVII (June 1974), pp. 249–264. A major explanation for the decline has been the growth of regional and ideological cleavages within the parties. Most notable for their declining party unity scores over this period were eastern Republicans (more liberal than their party colleagues) and southern Democrats (more conservative than their party colleagues). For the most part, regional cleavages within the parties are due to ideological differences.

24. The differences between Democratic and Republican members of Congress are examined at greater length in Chapter 5.

25. See an analysis by Jeff Fishel of the ideological differences between Democratic and Republican candidates who challenge incumbent congressmen. A majority of Democratic challengers in his study see themselves as "liberal," while a majority of the Republican challengers see themselves as "conservative." About one-third of the candidates in each party see themselves as "middle of the road." Only a handful of candidates label themselves as conservative Democrats or liberal Republicans. *Party and Opposition: Congressional Challengers in American Politics* (New York: McKay, 1973), pp. 64–94.

26. From *Party Government*, by E. E. Schattschneider. Copyright 1942 by E. E. Schattschneider. Reprinted by permission of Holt, Rinehart and Winston, pp. 133–137.

27. From Schattschneider, *Party Government*, p. 134.

28. In 1973, the U.S. Supreme Court upheld, in a 5–4 decision, a state law in New York that requires a voter to register his or her party affiliation 30 days in advance of a general election in order to be eligible to vote in that party's next primary election. Had the Court not upheld this "closed" provision, there would be nothing to prevent voters from switching parties as often as they like, permitting Democrats to vote in Republican primaries and Republicans to vote in Democratic primaries. *Rosario* v. *Rockefeller*, 410 U.S. 752 (1973).

29. The impact of the mass media and professional campaign management firms on the electorate and the party system is considered in Chapter 6.

30. As a result of a Supreme Court decision in 1976, it seems probable that patronage dismissals will be limited in the future. In *Elrod* v. *Burns*, the Supreme Court ruled that the newly-elected Democratic sheriff of Cook County, Illinois, could not fire noncivil service, nonpolicymaking employees simply because they were Republicans and had obtained their jobs under the previous administration. Undoubtedly, new litigation will test the extent to which the First Amendment protects the rights of lower- and middle-level patronage employees to retain their jobs when their offices come under the control of a different party. *Elrod* v. *Burns*, 427 U.S. 347 (1976).

Chapter 3

POLITICAL PARTIES AND THE ELECTORAL PROCESS

It is probable that no nation has ever experimented as fully or as fitfully with mechanisms for making nominations as has the United States. The principal sponsor of this experimentation is the federal system itself. Under it, responsibility for the development of election law lies with the states. Their ingenuity, given free rein, has often been remarkable. A wide variety of caucuses, conventions, and primaries—the three principal methods of making nominations—have been tried out in the states. Those devices that have lasted owe their survival not so much to a widespread agreement on their merits as to the inability of opponents to settle upon alternative arrangements and to the general indifference of the public at large to major institutional change.

NOMINATING METHODS

Caucus

The oldest device for making nominations in the United States is the caucus. In use prior to the adoption of the Constitution, the caucus is an informal meeting of political leaders held to decide questions concerning candidates, strategies, and policies. The essence of the caucus idea, when applied to nominations, is that by sifting, sorting, and weeding out candidates prior to the election, leaders can assemble substantial support behind a single candidate, thus decreasing the prospect that the votes of like-minded citizens will be split among several candidates. Historically, the most important form of caucus was the *legislative caucus,* which was used successfully for the nomination of candidates for state and national offices, including the presidency, until 1824. The major drawback to the legislative caucus was that membership was limited to the party members in the legislature, thereby exposing the caucus to the charge that it was unrepresentative and undemocratic. A modest reform in the legislative caucus took place when provisions were made for seating delegates from districts held by the opposition party. Nevertheless, when the (Jeffersonian) Republican caucus failed to nominate Andrew Jackson for the presidency in 1824, it came under severe criticism from many quarters and shortly after was abandoned for the selection of presidential nominees.

Party Conventions

Advocates of reform in the nominating process turned to the party convention, already in use in some localities, as a substitute for the legislative caucus. The great merit of the convention system, it was argued, was that it could provide for representation, on a geographical basis, of all elements within the party. The secrecy of the caucus was displaced in favor of a more public arena, with nominations made by conventions composed of delegates drawn from various levels of the party organizations. As the convention method gained in prominence, so did the party organizations; state and local party leaders came to play a dominant role in the selection of candidates.

The convention system, however, failed to consolidate its early promise. Although it has been used for the nomination of presidential candidates from the 1830s to the present, it has given way to the direct primary for most other offices. Critics found that it suffered from essentially the same disabling properties as the caucus. In their view, it was sheer pretense to contend that the conventions were representative of the parties as a whole; rather, they were run by party bosses without regard either for the views of the delegates or for the rules of fair play. An endless array of charges involving corruption in voting practices and procedures were made, and doubtless there was much truth in them. Growing regulation of conventions by the legislatures failed to assuage the doubts of the public. The direct primary came into favor as reformers came to understand its potential as a device for dismantling the structure of boss and "machine" influence and for introducing popular control over nominations.

The Direct Primary

Popular control of the political process has always been an important issue in the dogma of reformers. With its emphasis on voters rather than party organization, the direct primary was hard to resist; once Wisconsin adopted it for nomination of candidates for state elective offices in 1903, its use spread steadily throughout the country. Connecticut became the last state to adopt it, in 1955, but only after much tampering with the idea.[1] The Connecticut model (the "challenge" primary) combines convention and primary under an arrangement in which the party convention continues to make nominations, but with this proviso: if the party nominee at the convention is challenged by another candidate who receives as much as 20 percent of the convention votes, a primary must be held later. Otherwise, no primary is required, and the name of the convention nominee is automatically certified for the general election.

Part of the attractiveness of the primary is its apparent simplicity. From one perspective, it is a device for transferring control over nominations from the party leadership to the rank-and-file voters; from another, it shifts this control from the party organization to the state. The primary rests on state law: it is an official election held at public expense, on a date set by the legislature, and supervised by public officials. It has often been interpreted as an attempt to institutionalize intraparty democracy.

It is not surprising that the direct primary has always had a better reception in reformist circles than anywhere else. For the party organization, it poses problems rather than opportunities. Should the organization become involved in a contested primary for a major office, it is certain to have to raise large sums of money for the campaign of its candidate. If it remains neutral, it may wind up with a candidate who either is hostile to the organization or is unsympathetic toward its programs and policies. Even if it abandons neutrality, there is no guarantee that its candidate will win; indeed, a good many political careers have been launched in primaries in which the nonendorsed candidate has convinced the voters that a vote for him is a vote to crush the "machine." Finally, the primary often works at cross purposes with the basic party objective of harmonizing its diverse elements by creating a "balanced" ticket for the general election. The voters are much less likely to nominate a "representative" slate of candidates, one that recognizes all major groups within the party, than is the party leadership. Moreover, if the primary battle turns out to be bitter, the winner may enter the general election campaign with a sharply divided party behind him. It is no wonder that some political leaders have viewed the primary as a systematically conceived effort to bring down the party itself.

TYPES OF PRIMARIES

There are three basic types of primaries in use in the American states: *closed, open,* and *blanket.* Also in use among the states are three special forms of primaries: *nonpartisan, runoff,* and *presidential* (discussed in the next section).

Closed Primary

The most common form of primary, in use in about four-fifths of the states, is the closed primary. The key feature of this primary is that the voter may participate in the nomination of candidates only in the party to which he belongs. Ordinarily, in closed primary states, the voter is required to indicate his party affiliation at the time he registers to vote. This determines the party ballot he will be given at the primary election. Some states have a less rigorous requirement under which the voter merely reports his party affiliation at the time of the primary election and is given the ballot of that party. Where the tests of party membership are handled casually, there is some likelihood that voters cross over to participate in the selection of candidates of the other party.

Open Primary

From the point of view of the party organization, the open primary is less desirable than the closed primary. Used in about one-fifth of the states, the open primary poses no party membership requirements for the eligible voter. The voter may vote in the primary of any party. In the most common form of open primary, the voter is given the ballots of all parties, with instructions to vote for the candidates of one party and to discard the other ballots. There is nothing to prevent Democrats from voting to nominate Republican candidates or Republicans from voting to nominate Democratic candidates. Party leaders suffer from a special anxiety in open primary states: the possibility that voters of the competing party will "raid" their primary, hoping to nominate a weak candidate who would be easy to defeat in the general election. Whether "raiding" occurs with any frequency is difficult to say, but there is no doubt that in some states large numbers of voters cross over to vote in the other party's primary when an exciting contest is present. Probably the strongest appeal for the open primary is that it preserves the secrecy of the voter's party affiliation.

Blanket Primary

The states of Alaska and Washington complete the circle of open primary states with what is known as a blanket primary. No primary is quite so open. Under its provisions the voter is given a ballot on which all candidates of all parties are listed under the separate offices. A voter may vote for a Democrat for one office and, responding to other impulses, vote for a Republican for another office. He cannot, of course, vote for more than one candidate for one office. The blanket primary is an invitation to "ticket splitting."

Nonpartisan Primary

In a number of states, judges, school board members, and other local government officials are selected in nonpartisan primaries. State legislators in Nebraska are also selected on this basis. The scheme itself is simple: the two candidates obtaining the greatest number of votes are nominated; in turn, they oppose each other in the general election. No party labels appear on the ballot in either election. The nonpartisan primary is defended on the grounds that partisanship should not be permitted to intrude upon the selection of certain officials, such as judges. By eliminating the party label, runs the assumption, the issues and divisiveness that dominate national and state party politics can be kept out of local elections and local offices. In point of fact, however, although nonpartisan primaries muffle the sounds of party, they do not eliminate them. It is not at all uncommon for the party organizations to slip quietly into the political process and to recruit and support candidates in these primaries; in such cases, about all that is missing is the party label on the ballot.

Runoff Primary

Another form of primary, the runoff or second primary, is a by-product of a one-party political environment. As used in southern states, this arrangement provides that if no candidate obtains a majority of the votes cast for that office, a runoff is held between the two leading candidates. The runoff primary is an attempt to come to terms with a chronic problem of a one-party system—essentially all competition is jammed into the primary of the dominant party. With numerous candidates seeking nomination for the same office, the vote is likely to be sharply split, with no candidate receiving a majority. A runoff between the top two candidates in the first primary provides a guarantee, if only statistical, that one candidate will emerge as the choice of a majority of voters. This is no small consideration in those southern states where the Democratic primary has long been the "real" election and where factionalism within the party has been so intense that no candidate would stand much of a chance of consolidating his party position without two primaries—the first to weed out the losers, and the second to endow the winner with the legitimacy a majority can offer.

AN OVERVIEW OF THE PRIMARY

In the perspectives of its early Progressive sponsors, the great virtue of the direct primary was its democratic component, its promise for changing the accent and scope of popular participation in the political system. Its immediate effect, it was hoped, would be to diminish the influence of political organization on political life. What is the evidence that the primary has accomplished its mission? What impact has it had on political party organization?

An important outcome of the primary is that it has served to sensitize party elites to the interests and feelings of the most highly motivated rank-and-file members. Under the primary fewer nominations are "cut and dried." Even though candidates "slated" by the organization win more often than they lose, there is usually some uncertainty over their prospects.[2] The possibility of a revolt against the organization, carried out in the primary, forces party leaders to take careful account of the elements that make up the party and to pay attention to the claims of potential candidates. As a result, intraparty relationships cannot as easily be taken for granted: there is always a chance—in some jurisdictions, a strong possibility—that the aspirant who is overlooked by the party chieftains will decide to challenge their choice in the primary. The primary thus induces caution among party leaders. A "hands-off" policy—one in which the party makes no endorsement—is sometimes the party's only response. If it has no candidate, it cannot very well lose—some party leaders have been able to stay in business by avoiding the embarrassment that comes from primary defeats. In some jurisdictions, the possibility of party intervention in the primary is never even seriously considered, so accustomed is the electorate to party-free contests. From the perspective of the public at large, it seems apparent that the main contribution of the primary is that it opens up the political process.

The primary has not immobilized party organizations, but it has caused a number of problems for them. It is not hard to understand party leaders' lack of enthusiasm for primaries when it is recognized that, among other things, the primary: 1) greatly increases party campaign costs (if the party backs a candidate in a contested primary); 2) diminishes the capacity of the organization to reward its supporters through nominations; 3) makes it difficult for the party to influence nominees who establish their own power bases in the primary electorate; 4) creates the possibility that a person hostile to party leadership and party policies can capture a nomination; 5) permits anyone to wear the party label and opens the possibility that the party will have to repudiate a candidate who has been thrust upon it; and 6) increases intraparty strife and factionalism.[3] The imagination boggles at the thought of an institution better designed than the primary to stultify party organization and party processes.

Despite the pernicious effects that sometimes accompany the primary, the party has learned to live with it. This results, in part, from the failure of the primary to fulfill the expectations of its sponsors. Two things have gone awry. First, there has often been a lack of competitiveness in primaries. The surprising number of nominations that go by default may be due to any of several explanations. On the one hand, the lack of contested primaries may be evidence of party strength—that is, potential candidates stop short of entering the primary because their prospects appear slim for defeating the organization choice. On the other hand, the "deserted" primary simply may testify to the pragmatism of politicians: they do not struggle to win nominations that are unlikely to lead anywhere. As V. O. Key, Jr., and others have shown, primaries are most likely to be contested when the chances are strong that the winner will be elected to office in the general election and least likely to be contested when the nomination appears to have little value.[4] (See Figure 6.) The tendency is thus for competition to occur in competitive districts or in the primary of the dominant party. Whatever the explanation, in this respect the primary often bears little resemblance to its original design.

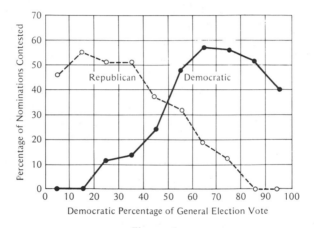

Figure 6.
PRIMARY COMPETITION AND THE PROSPECTS FOR GENERAL ELECTION VICTORY: RELATION BETWEEN PROPORTION OF NOMINATIONS CONTESTED AND PERCENTAGE OF GENERAL ELECTION VOTE POLLED BY REPUBLICAN AND DEMOCRATIC NOMINEES FOR MISSOURI HOUSE OF REPRESENTATIVES, 1942–1950
Source: V. O. Key, Jr., *American State Politics: An Introduction* (New York: Knopf, 1956), p. 173.

Second, experience with the primary has also shown that it is one thing to shape an institution so as to induce popular participation and quite another to realize it. No fact about primaries is more familiar than that large numbers of voters assiduously ignore them. It is not at all uncommon for a majority of voters to stay away from the polls on primary day, even when there are major statewide races to be settled. What this means concretely is that the impact of the wider public on the choice of candidates is minimized. The rule is starkly simple: when the turnout in primary elections is low, the probability is high that the "organization slate" will prevail. Although much of the public may pay little heed to primaries, a vigorous party will have little trouble turning out its workers and loyalists to support the party's choices. In a limited primary electorate the party organization wins far more often than it loses.

THE NATIONAL CONVENTION

The American national convention is surely one of the most remarkable institutions in the world for making nominations. In use since the Jacksonian Era, it is the official agency for the selection of each party's candidates for president and vice-president and for the ratification of each party's platform. At the same time, it is the party's supreme policy-making authority, empowered to make the rules that govern party affairs.

The national convention historically has served another function of prime importance to the parties. It has been a meeting ground for the party itself, one where leaders could tap rank-and-file sentiments and where the divergent interests that make up each party could, at least in some fashion, be accommodated. In its classic role, the great virtue of the national convention has been that it presents an opportunity for the national party—the 50 state parties assembled—to come to terms with itself, permitting leading politicians to strike the necessary balances and to settle temporarily the continuing questions of leadership and policy. Under the press of other changes in the presidential nominating process, however, the party role in conventions has recently been diminished.

Until the 1970s, national convention decisions could best be explained by examining the central role of national, state, and local party leaders and the behavior of state delegations. These were the "power points" in the classic model of convention politics, aptly described by the authors of *Explorations in Convention Decision Making:*

> Historically, state delegations have been thought to be the key units for bargaining in conventions; operating under the unit rule, they bargain with each other and with candidate organizations. The rank-and-file delegates are manipulated by hierarchical leaders holding important positions in national, state, or local party organizations. In order to enhance their bargaining position, these leaders often try to stay uncommitted to any candidate until the moment that their endorsement is crucial to victory for the ultimate nominee. After the presidential balloting is over, the vice presidential nomination is awarded to a person whose selection will mollify those elements of the party who did not support the presidential choice. At the end of the convention, all groups rally around the ticket and the party receives a boost in starting the fall campaign.[5]

The classic model of convention decision making bears only modest resemblance to the influence patterns in the most recent party conventions. State delegations have given way to candidate blocs in importance, while party leaders have been displaced by the leaders of candidate organizations. Party leaders have few resources with which to bargain in state delegations split among candidate followings. The governor who heads a state delegation may be nothing more than a figurehead; meetings of many state delegations are concerned more with announcements (for example, bus departures for the convention site) and ceremonies than with strategy. In contrast, the "action" is to be found in the candidate caucuses, where the strategy sessions occur on candidates, rules, and platform planks. Uncommitted delegates decline in number. In sum, the outstanding fact concerning today's party conventions is that they are dominated by candidates and their organizations. Accordingly, the influence that party and elected officials wield in conventions is largely a product of their affiliation with one of the candidate organizations.

The decline of the party presence in national conventions results from a confluence of forces: the new delegate selection rules that both opened up the parties to amateur activists and contributed to the spread of presidential primaries, to the capacity of candidates to dominate campaign fund-raising (using government subsidies under a matching system since 1976), and to the general weakness of state and local party organizations.[6] The reliance of candidates on party leaders in the preconvention period has never been less—in most states, party leaders cannot do much either to help or to hurt a candidate's chances to win delegates. What matters to the candidate is winning the immediate primary or placing well (as judged by the mass media) in order to attract new funds and to build momentum for the next contest. In the modern scheme of campaigning, expert consultants, an active personal organization spread out around the state, and the mass media loom much more important to the candidates than party structures and party leaders.

Selection of Delegates

Convention delegates historically have been chosen by caucus/convention systems, by party state central committees, and by presidential primaries. Until the early 1970s, nearly two-thirds of the states chose their delegates through the caucus/convention system, commonly selecting some delegates at local levels (for example, congressional district) and others at the party's state convention. A few states empowered party state central committees to choose delegates. Thus, in states that did not employ some version of the primary, the selection process took place within the party structure. The result was that most of the delegates selected were established party leaders and public officials.

Presidential primaries came on the scene in the early twentieth century. Like the direct primary used to nominate national, state, and local officials, the presidential primary was designed to wrest control over nominations from the "bosses" (the party professionals) and to place it in the hands of the people by permitting them to choose the delegates to the nominating conventions in a public election. The first state to adopt a presidential primary law was Florida, in 1904. In scarcely more than a decade, over one-half of the states had adopted some version of it. Other states, however, found it difficult to break away from their familiar arrangements, and the zeal supporting this reform soon subsided. Several states that had eagerly adopted presidential primary laws discarded them, returning to the older system of party caucuses and conventions. In 1968, only 16 states and the District of Columbia held presidential primaries.

The picture has changed radically since then. In 1972, 23 states held presidential primaries; by 1976, the number had increased to 30. What is more, nearly three-fourths of the 1976 convention delegates in both parties were chosen directly by the voters in primaries. Thus, by 1976 this method was fully as dominant as the caucus/convention system had been in 1968. Table 9, the work of Austin Ranney, shows the details of the expanding participation of the public in the presidential nominating process.

The adoption of primary laws is the work of state legislatures. Their astonishing hospitality to presidential primaries stems from several factors. The most important was the party reform movement launched by the Democrats following their turbulent national convention in 1968. The reforms centered on the delegate selection process and were designed to facilitate the participation of all Democratic voters in presidential nominations. Prompted by the party's new ideology of "openness" and "participation," many state legislatures turned to presidential primaries, adopting a

TABLE 9. Proliferation of Presidential Primaries, 1968–1976

Party and Coverage	1968	1972	1976
Democratic Party			
Number of states using a primary for selecting or binding national convention delegates	17	23	29*
Number of votes cast by delegates chosen or bound by primaries	983	1,862	2,183
Percent of all votes cast by delegates chosen or bound by primaries	37.5	60.5	72.6
Republican Party			
Number of states using a primary for selecting or binding national convention delegates	16	22	28*
Number of votes cast by delegates chosen or bound by primaries	458	710	1,533
Percent of all votes cast by delegates chosen or bound by primaries	34.3	52.7	67.9

Source: Austin Ranney, *Participation in American Presidential Nominations, 1976* (Washington, D.C.: American Enterprise Institute for Public Policy Research, 1977), p. 6. The table was prepared from data appearing in the *Congressional Quarterly Weekly Report*, January 21, 1976, pp. 225–242.

*Does not include Vermont, which held a nonbinding presidential-preference poll but chose all delegates of both parties by caucuses and conventions.

system that appeared to be in accordance with the reform spirit. Moreover, the new rules of the Democratic party required extensive changes in caucus/convention systems if they were to be retained for the selection of delegates. Hence, to many legislators the adoption of primary legislation seemed to be an easier way to comply with national party rules than restructuring their existing systems; at the same time, this permitted states to keep intact their traditional convention systems for other party matters.[7]

Other forces were also at work. The turn toward primaries was in part a fall-out from Watergate. State politicians, like all others, were acutely aware of the growing public distrust of government and the rampant cynicism directed toward parties and politicians. In contrast to the convention system, the presidential primary promised a larger role for the public in the nominating process and a diminished role for professional politicians. And second, the attention lavished on primaries by the media did not escape the notice of certain presidential aspirants. They vigorously supported primary legislation in their home states, knowing that a primary would give them an opportunity to advertise their presidential wares before a national audience.

Prior to the 1970s, the manner in which national convention delegates were selected was left to the states. Today, their selection is tightly regulated by national party rules, especially in the Democratic party. The dimensions of national party control can best be appreciated by examining Table 10, which presents certain major rules in effect for the 1980 Democratic National Convention. In the selection of delegates, the rules make clear, not much is left to chance, not much to the discretion of individual state parties.

An amalgam of recommendations by three party study commissions,[8] stretching from 1969 to 1978, the rules were designed to serve several broad objectives: 1) to stimulate the participation of rank-and-file Democratic voters in the presidential nominating process; 2) to increase the representation of certain demographic groups (particularly women, blacks, and young people) in the convention through the use of guidelines on delegate selection; 3) to eliminate procedures held to be undemocratic (such as the unit rule); 4) to enhance the local character of delegate elections (by requiring 75 percent of the delegates in each state to be elected at the congressional district level or lower); and 5) to provide through "proportional representation" that elected delegates fairly reflect the presidential candidate preferences of Democratic voters in primary states and Democratic participants in caucus/convention states.[9]

For many members of the first commission, the McGovern–Fraser Commission, the underlying objective was to diminish the power of party professionals in the convention, while at the same time increasing that of rank-and-file members. They succeeded—in extraordinary degree. To some extent, party leaders have now been "readmitted" to the convention

TABLE 10. Leading Delegate Selection Rules for the 1980 Democratic National Convention

Rule 1A: State parties shall adopt explicit written rules and procedures covering all aspects of the delegate selection process . . . .

1B: Each state party shall adopt an Affirmative Action Plan and a Delegate Selection Plan which shall be submitted to the Compliance Review Commission for approval . . . . Such plans shall be consistent with national party rules . . . .

2A: Participation in the delegate selection process in primaries and caucuses shall be restricted to Democratic voters only who publicly declare their party preference . . . . [This rule, which prohibits open, cross-over primaries, cannot be waived under a Rule 20 exemption.]

3A: All official party meetings and events related to the national convention delegate selection process . . . shall be scheduled for dates, times, and public places which would be most likely to encourage the participation of all Democrats . . . .

6A: In order to encourage full participation by all Democrats, with particular concern for minority groups, Native Americans, women, and youth . . . the national and state Democratic parties shall adopt and implement Affirmative Action Programs with specific goals and timetables.

7C: Seventy-five percent of the national convention delegates . . . shall be elected at the congressional district level or lower. Twenty-five percent . . . shall be elected at large.

7D: After the election of congressional district (or lower) delegates and prior to the selection of at-large delegates, those national convention delegates or a state convention in each state shall elect party leaders and elected officials as national convention delegates provided, however, that the number of these delegates shall be 10 percent of the total number of publicly elected and at-large delegates.

9A: In all cases the election of an at-large delegation shall be used, if necessary, for purposes of achieving the representation goals established in the state party's Affirmative Action Plan.

10 A: No meetings, caucuses, conventions or primaries which constitute the first determining stage in the presidential nominating process . . . may be held prior to the second Tuesday in March or after the second Tuesday in June in the calendar year of the national convention. [States may apply to the Compliance Review Commission for exemptions.]

11A: All candidates for delegate in caucuses, conventions, committees, and on primary ballots shall be identified as to presidential preference or uncommitted status at all levels of a process which determines presidential preference.

TABLE 10   (Continued)

11H: All delegates to the national convention shall be bound to vote for the presidential candidate whom they were elected to support for at least the first convention ballot, unless released in writing by the presidential candidate.

Rule 12B: At all stages of the delegate selection process, delegates shall be allocated in a fashion that fairly reflects the expressed presidential preference or uncommitted status of the primary voters or if there is no binding primary, the convention and caucus participants, except that preferences securing less than the applicable percentage of votes cast for the delegates to the national convention shall not be awarded any delegates. The applicable percentage in presidential primary states shall be calculated by dividing the number of national convention delegates to be elected in that congressional district or other smaller delegate selection unit into 100, provided however, that the applicable percentage shall be no higher than 25 percent. In caucus states, at the level at which national convention delegates are selected, the applicable percentage shall be no lower than 15 percent and no higher than 20 percent . . . . The Compliance Review Commission shall adopt regulations to prevent winner-take-all outcomes at the congressional district or other smaller delegate selection unit. The CRC shall adopt regulations to govern the allocation of delegates in instances where no candidate reaches the applicable percentage.

13A: No petition requirements for participation at any level of the national convention delegate selection process shall exceed 1 percent or 1,000 signatures, whichever is less . . . .

16:   The unit rule, or any rule or practice whereby all members of a party unit or delegation may be required to cast their votes in accordance with a majority of the body, shall not be used at any stage of the delegate selection process.

19A: A Compliance Review Commission . . . shall be appointed . . . to administer and enforce affirmative action requirements [and to] review Affirmative Action and Delegate Selection Plans submitted by state parties and approve or recommend changes in such plans . . . .

20A: Wherever any part of any section contained in these rules conflicts with existing state laws, the state party shall take provable positive steps to achieve legislative changes to bring the state law into compliance with the provisions of these rules.

20C: A state party may be required to adopt and implement an alternative party-run delegate selection system which does not conflict with these rules, regardless of any provable positive steps the state may have taken.

Source: *Delegate Selection Rules for the 1980 Democratic National Convention* (Washington, D.C.: Democratic National Committee, 1978).

by the adoption of a provision in 1978 (recommended by the Winograd Commission) that expands each state delegation by 10 percent to include prominent party and elected officials.

The Republican party was much less active than the Democrats in the 1970s in restructuring its delegate selection rules, but it did make certain changes. Its rules now require open meetings for delegate selection, ban automatic (ex officio) delegates, and provide for the election rather than the selection of congressional district and at-large delegates (unless otherwise provided by state law). State Republican parties are not bound to develop action plans for increasing the participation of women, young people, minority, and other groups in the presidential nominating process, but they are urged to do so. The thrust to nationalize party rules, pronounced among Democratic reformers, finds only limited support among Republicans. Rather, Republicans continue to stress the federal character of their party: the basic authority to reshape delegate selection rules rests accordingly with state parties.[10]

Evaluating Presidential Primaries

The criticisms leveled against the presidential primary system are diverse. This primary, critics point out, occupies an anomalous position, at least in the public mind. On occasion, a single state's primary appears to govern the selection of the party's nominee. In the judgment of many observers, on the day that John F. Kennedy defeated Hubert H. Humphrey in the West Virginia presidential primary in 1960, he captured the Democratic nomination. In 1964, the critical Republican primary took place in California. In retrospect, it seems apparent that Barry Goldwater's narrow victory over Nelson Rockefeller in California assured his nomination, even though his performance in several earlier primaries had been disappointing. Similarly, in 1972, George McGovern's nomination seemed to be guaranteed following his victory in the California primary. Jimmy Carter's string of early primary victories in 1976, beginning with his narrow win in New Hampshire, gave him a commanding lead; his weakness in late primaries, marked by several losses to California Governor Jerry Brown, had only marginal impact on his bid for the nomination.

To the initiated voter, as well as the uninitiated, the presidential primary is a mass of oppositions and paradoxes. Unpredictability reigns. Victory in a single state has sometimes been the key to the nomination. Regional variations in candidate strength may be decisive. If the western primaries had been held at the beginning of the primary season instead of near the end of 1976, one study suggests, both Jimmy Carter and Ronald Reagan might have fared differently.[11]

Of the many other difficulties associated with presidential primaries,[12] two are particularly troublesome. One is the problem of raising campaign funds. Under the Federal Election Campaign Act, no individual can contribute more than $1000 to any one campaign. Moreover, candidates can qualify for matching federal funds only after they have raised $100,000 in small sums ($250 or less, $5000 per state) in 20 states. Hence, candidates need to develop a large network of small contributors, spread around the country—making fund-raising a chore for all candidates and a major obstacle for some. The press secretary to Fred Harris, whose campaign in 1976 sputtered from the outset, observed.

> You're caught in a kind of vicious circle. In order to raise money, especially money from more than twenty states, then you have to have national media attention, not just good local media that Fred has been able to generate.... But in order to raise that kind of money dispersed among twenty states then you need national media exposure. You need it because people do judge by national media exposure as to whether the campaign is serious or not and, believe me, they hesitate before they give money.... They're going to wait until they see Fred's smiling face on national television.[13]

Probably the most serious problem is that the results in early primary states (and in caucus/convention states as well) are overemphasized. Again, it is a matter of the media. Often speaking with greater finality than the voters themselves, the media create "winners" and "losers," "front runners" and "also-rans." An early victory is translated into a major political resource. The psychological impact is greater than the "body count" of delegates. The winner gains heightened visibility, an expanded and more attentive following in the journalist corps, and a "leg up" on the next contest.

The media are the new parties:

> The television news organizations in this country are an enormously dominant force in primary elections. They're every Tuesday night, not only counting the votes, but, in some cases, setting the tone.... (a member of the Jimmy Carter organization)

> ... [if] you're short of delegates, the real determining factor's going to be the psychological momentum the press creates. Is he a winner? Can he get the nomination? (a member of the Fred Harris organization)

> You go into a place like New Hampshire, and you've got two things in mind. Primarily is winning New Hampshire. Secondly is getting out the stories about your candidate and where he stands and all that to the rest of the country.... (a member of the Ronald Reagan organization)

> Everywhere we go, we're on a media trip; I mean we're attempting to generate as much free television and print, as much free radio, as we can get. Any angle can play.... (a member of the Morris Udall organization)[14]

At bottom, it is a matter of the interpretation of election results by the print and broadcast media. Christopher Arterton writes:

> Those who manage presidential campaigns uniformly believe that interpretations placed upon campaign events are frequently more important than the events themselves. In other words, the political contest is shaped primarily by the perceptual environment within which campaigns compete. *Particularly in the early nomination stages, perceptions outweigh reality in terms of their political impact.* Since journalists communicate these perceptions to voters and party activists and since part of the reporter's job is creating these interpretations, campaigners believe that journalists can and do affect whether their campaign is viewed as succeeding or failing, and that this perception in turn will determine their ability to mobilize political resources in the future: endorsements, volunteers, money, and hence, votes.[15]

The system of presidential primaries is that of a crazy quilt. Candidates fly from one end of the country to the other, then back again, emphasizing certain primaries, deemphasizing others, and avoiding still others. No candidate is very confident about how or where he should spend his time; no voter can be sure he understands what is taking place. But there is more to the system than its awkwardness and complexity.

In the first place, presidential primaries give rank-and-file voters a much larger role in the presidential nominating process. In 1976, nearly 29 million voters cast ballots in the presidential primary states; the mean turnout for these states was 28.2 percent of their *voting-age* populations and 42.9 percent of their *registered* voters. By contrast, in the caucus/ convention states the mean proportion of *voting-age* populations taking part in Democratic precinct caucuses (the first and most open stage in the process that culminates in a state convention) was only 1.9 percent.[16] Viewed in another way, about 29 million voters took part in the presidential nominating process in the primary states as contrasted with about 1.1 million (for both parties) in the nonprimary states.[17] Obviously, primaries induce far more popular participation than caucuses.

A major contribution of presidential primaries is that they present an opportunity for testing candidacies and policies in a number of states. The Vietnam war was the pivotal issue in both the 1968 and 1972 Democratic primaries. It contributed to President Johnson's decision not to seek reelection in 1968 and, four years later, was central to George McGovern's nomination. And when an "outsider," Jimmy Carter, won a large majority (17 of 26) of the Democratic primaries in 1976, everyone learned something of the intensity of voters' resentment toward the "Washington Establishment." There is merit to the argument that even though not all states hold presidential primaries, the media coverage they receive permits the nation as a whole to become familiar with the candidates and to take their measure as potential presidents.

What has been the overall impact of presidential primaries on the choice of candidates? The answer is that in recent years primaries have become decisive, sharply constricting the significance of the national conventions in the selection of presidential nominees. More than anything else, John F. Kennedy owed his nomination in 1960 to his successes in primary states; numerous state and local Democratic candidates would have preferred a "safer" candidate, but they found it impossible to withstand the surge of public support behind Kennedy. Democratic party professionals were again confounded in 1972 and 1976 when party outsiders, George McGovern and Jimmy Carter, won numerous primary victories and, coupled with their successes in nonprimary states, the nominations. On the Republican side, despite the advantage of the presidency, Gerald R. Ford barely escaped with the nomination in 1976 after an extraordinary preconvention challenge by Ronald Reagan, who won ten primaries. President Ford won 17.

In earlier years, leading candidates for their party's nomination often avoided the primaries, concentrating rather on the "cultivation" of state and local party leaders in numerous caucus/convention states. And because state delegations were frequently under the tight control of the leadership, this strategy was often effective. The proliferation of presidential primaries has rendered this approach obsolete. Even an incumbent president has reason to fear a challenge to his renomination. With roughly three-fourths of all delegates elected in primary states, no serious candidate for the presidential nomination can avoid taking the "primary route," entering most if not all of them. This does not mean, necessarily, that the preconvention struggle will settle the choice of a nominee. When the primaries fail to yield a clear-cut winner, the selection will turn on convention bargaining. A "brokered" convention, characterized by struggles between leading candidates, is thus still a possibility.

The Convention Delegates

The ramifications of political reforms are often much larger than anticipated. The new emphasis on popular participation in the delegate selection process, coupled with the requirements for affirmative action plans to promote the representation of disadvantaged groups, has sharply changed the composition of Democratic national conventions. Prior to the 1970s, Democratic delegates were preponderantly male, middle-aged, and white. And they were usually "party regulars"—officials of the party, important contributors, and reliable rank-and-file members. Public officeholders were prominent in all state delegations. The selection process itself was dominated by state and local party leaders.[18]

The reforms produced a new breed of delegate—overall, a "new presidential elite." Directly as a result of the guidelines adopted by the McGovern–Fraser Commission, the representation of women increased from 13 percent in 1968 to 40 percent in 1972, of blacks from 5.5 percent to 15 percent, and of younger voters (under age 30) from 3 percent to 22 percent. In 1976, under less restrictive delegate selection rules (affirmative action in lieu of "quotas") the percentages for these groups remained high: 33 percent for women, 11 percent for blacks, and 15 percent for younger voters. Under the new rules, the chief losers were party professionals and public officeholders. In 1976, only 18 percent of all Democratic U.S. senators, 15 percent of all Democratic House members, and 47 percent of all Democratic governors were selected as delegates. The percentages for these groups in 1968 had been 68, 39, and 83, respectively.[19]

"Issue and candidate enthusiasts" are dominant in the new Democratic presidential elite. They have few if any ties to the party organization. They are considerably more liberal than the average Democrat. Indeed, a study of the 1972 delegates by Jeane Kirkpatrick found that the policy preferences of rank-and-file Democrats (as shown by national surveys) were much closer to those of Republican delegates than they were to those of delegates of their own party.[20] The "open" processes of the party obviously do not guarantee that the delegates will represent the opinions and values of the average voters who identify with it.

In the Republican party changes have come more gradually. A larger proportion of women, blacks, and young people are being elected as Republican delegates than in the past. And amateur activists, firmly committed to candidates and issues, also show up in greater number in state delegations—political newcomers were especially numerous among the Reagan delegates in the 1976 convention. Overall, however, the degree of change is much less pronounced than on the Democratic side. Party leaders and public officials, for example, were more prominent in the Republican conventions of the 1970s than in those of the Democrats. The gradualism of the Republican party in terms of "reform" traces from the reluctance of the national party to impose comprehensive delegate selection requirements on state parties.[21] The Republican party is in fact as well as in form a federal structure.

THE POLITICS OF THE CONVENTION

Three practical aims dominate the proceedings of the national convention: to nominate presidential and vice-presidential candidates, to draft the party platform, and to lay the groundwork for party unity in the campaign. The way in which the party addresses itself to the tasks of drafting the platform and nominating the candidates is likely to determine how well it achieves its third objective, that of healing party rifts and forging a cohesive party. To put together a platform and a presidential ticket that satisfies the principal elements of the party is exceedingly difficult. The task of reconciling divergent interests within the party occupies the convention from its earliest moments until the final gavel—at least, in most conventions. By and large, convention leaders have been successful in shaping the compromises necessary to keep the national party, such as it is, from flying apart.

The Convention Committees

The initial business of the convention is handled mainly by four committees. The *committee on credentials* is given the responsibility for determining the permanent roll (official membership) of the convention. Its specific function is to ascertain the members' legal right to seats in the convention. In the absence of challenges to the right of certain delegates to be seated or contests between two delegations from the same state, each trying to be seated, the review is handled routinely and with dispatch. Most state delegations are seated without difficulty. When disputes arise, the committee holds hearings and takes testimony; its recommendations for seating delegates are then reported to the convention, where ordinarily (but not invariably) they are sustained. The *committee on permanent organization* is charged with the responsibility of selecting the permanent officers of the convention, including the permanent chairman, the clerks, and the sergeant at arms. The *committee on rules* devises the rules under which the convention will operate and establishes the order of business.

Ordinarily the most important of the convention committees is the *committee on resolutions,* which is in charge of the drafting of the party platform. The actual work of this committee begins many weeks in advance of the convention, so that usually there is a draft of the document by the time the convention opens and the formal committee hearings begin. When a president seeks reelection, the platform is likely to be prepared under his direction and accepted by the committee (and later by the floor) without major changes.

The struggle over the nomination may influence the drafting of the platform, since the leading candidates have an interest in securing planks that are compatible with their views. Indeed, the outcomes of clashes over planks may provide a good indication of which candidate will capture the nomination. In the 1968 Democratic convention, for example, it was all but certain that Hubert H. Humphrey would win the nomination when the convention, after a lengthy and emotional floor debate, adopted by a comfortable margin a plank that reflected the Johnson Administration's position on the war in Vietnam. His two principal opponents, Senators Eugene J. McCarthy and George S. McGovern, were the most prominent supporters of the losing (committee) minority plank, which called for an unconditional halt to the bombing of North Vietnam. In the 1976 Republican convention, intense committee struggles took place between the forces of President Ford and those of Ronald Reagan. In nearly all cases, the planks adopted represented victories for the supporters of Ford, thus auguring well for his nomination.

Selecting the Presidential Ticket

To at least some party leaders, the best convention is the one that opens with significant uncertainties and imponderables—a good, though not surefire, prescription for generating public interest in the convention, the party, and its nominees. In the usual convention, however, uncertainties are far from numerous. Doubts are much more likely to surround the choice of the vice-presidential nominee than the presidential nominee. So many presidential candidates are screened out by the primaries—to a lesser extent, by caucus/conventions—that by the time the convention opens the range of choice has become sharply narrowed, perhaps nonexistent.

Table 11, the work of Donald R. Matthews, establishes the significance of the *early* stages of the nominating process for the selection of presiden-

TABLE 11.   Continuity and Change in Presidential Nominating Politics, 1936–1976

Year	Leading Candidate at Beginning of Election Year	Nominee
Party in Power		
1936 (D)	Roosevelt	Roosevelt
1940 (D)	Roosevelt	Roosevelt
1944 (D)	Roosevelt	Roosevelt
1948 (D)	Truman	Truman
1952 (D)	Truman	Stevenson
1956 (R)	Eisenhower	Eisenhower
1960 (R)	Nixon	Nixon
1964 (D)	Johnson	Johnson
1968 (D)	Johnson	Humphrey
1972 (R)	Nixon	Nixon
1976 (R)	Ford	Ford
Party Out of Power		
1936 (R)	Landon	Landon
1940 (R)	?	Willkie
1944 (R)	Dewey	Dewey
1948 (R)	Dewey–Taft	Dewey
1952 (R)	Eisenhower–Taft	Eisenhower
1956 (D)	Stevenson	Stevenson
1960 (D)	Kennedy	Kennedy
1964 (R)	?	Goldwater
1968 (R)	Nixon	Nixon
1972 (D)	Muskie	McGovern
1976 (D)	Kennedy–Humphrey	Carter

Source: Donald R. Matthews, "Presidential Nominations: Process and Outcome," in James David Barber (ed.), *Choosing the President* (Englewood Cliffs, N.J.: Prentice-Hall, 1974), p. 54 (as updated).

tial candidates. In a typical presidential year, the candidate leading the public opinion polls at the start of the year (before the first delegate is even chosen) winds up with the nomination. The new opportunities that primaries in particular present for challenging leading candidates may, of course, alter this pattern. In both 1972 and 1976, the Democratic nomination was won by an outsider whose poll standings were unimpressive at the start of the year.

The experience of recent conventions is instructive. In the 1960, 1968, and 1972 Republican conventions, Richard M. Nixon's nomination occurred on the first ballot, without really significant opposition. In 1964, in the judgment of most party professionals, Barry Goldwater's nomination was assured by his victory over Nelson Rockefeller in the California primary. The great bulk of the Goldwater delegates had been captured earlier in state conventions. The Democratic experience is about the same. Lyndon Johnson's nomination in 1964 was a foregone conclusion, following the custom (at that time) that incumbent presidents were entitled to another term if they chose to run. In 1968, with the forces opposed to the Johnson Administration in disarray following the assassination of Robert F. Kennedy, there was scarcely any doubt but that Vice-President Hubert H. Humphrey would become the party standard-bearer. In 1972, George McGovern arrived at the Democratic convention with over twice as many delegate votes as any other candidate, and his nomination on the first ballot, though it could not have been predicted a few months earlier, was anything but a surprise at the convention. In 1976, Jimmy Carter came to the Democratic convention in Madison Square Garden with the nomination "locked up." Some months earlier, that feat could not have been predicted either.

The stark fact is that in only a few conventions over the last three decades has there been substantial doubt about the ultimate winner: both conventions in 1952 (Eisenhower versus Taft in the Republican convention and a wide-open contest in the Democratic convention), the Democratic convention in 1960 (John F. Kennedy, who won the presidential primaries, versus the field), and the 1976 Republican convention (Gerald R. Ford versus Ronald Reagan). The broad point is that it is unusual for a "front-runner"—the candidate holding the most delegate votes prior to the convention—to lose out at the convention. Often, in fact, his nomination occurs on the first ballot.

The final major item of convention business is the selection of the party's vice-presidential nominee. Here the task of the party is to come up with the right political formula—the candidate who can add the most to the ticket and detract the least. In all but rare cases the presidential nominee makes the choice himself, following rounds of consultation with various party and candidate organization leaders.[22] Although a great deal of suspense is usually created over the vice-presidential nomination, convention ratification comes easily once the presidential nominee has made up his mind and "cleared" the selection with key leaders. Unless the presidential nominee is inclined to take a major risk to serve the interest of his own faction or ideology (as Barry Goldwater did in choosing Republican National Chairman William E. Miller in 1964), he selects a candidate who can help to balance the ticket and unify the party.[23] Jimmy Carter's choice of Senator Walter F. Mondale in 1976 fits neatly into this category. The range of the presidential candidate's choice may be constricted by the necessity for rewarding a particular party element (for example, sectional or ideological), the support of which was critical to his own nomination.

A NATIONAL PRIMARY? REGIONAL PRIMARIES?

Dissatisfaction with the current system has led some politicians and analysts to prefer a single, one-day national primary. Under a typical proposal, to win the nomination a candidate would be required to obtain a majority of the popular vote cast in his party primary; if no candidate received a majority, a run-off election would be held between the top two finishers. A separate vote would be held for vice-presidential candidates. The national convention would be retained for writing the platform and fashioning party rules.

Another plan calls for regional primaries, under which all those states holding primaries within a region would be required to hold them on the same day.[24] A total of perhaps five regional primaries would be conducted, one each month from March through July in the presidential year, their order to be determined by lot. The national convention would continue, at least formally, to select the presidential candidate; when the primaries failed to produce a clear-cut winner, the actual choice would be made by the convention.

Still another proposal would require all states using primaries to choose one of four dates (in March, April, May, or June) for this election—thus bringing a measure of order to the system and diminishing the significance of a single state's early primary. Left to the decision of each state, a caucus/convention system could be used in place of a primary. The national convention would continue in its present form.

The adoption of a national primary law would represent the sharpest departure from the current system. It seems evident that it would favor well-known, well-financed candidates and would hurt "outsiders"—those lesser-known candidates who gain visibility and momentum through a win or an impressive showing in an early primary or caucus state. Inevitably, a national primary would have a destructive impact on the political parties, eliminating them from any role in the selection of presidential candidates. Austin Ranney writes:

> [The] clear gainers in influence from the dismantling of the party organizations would be the national news media—the national television and radio

networks, the major newspapers, and the wire services. . . . [Their] interpretations of the state primaries and caucuses, especially the early ones, already have a powerful influence on who wins or who loses. . . . In a national primary . . . the only preelection facts relevant to who was winning would be public opinion polls and estimates of the sizes of crowds at candidate meetings. The former are scientifically more respectable than the latter, but neither constitutes hard data in the sense that election returns do. And hard data of that sort would be available only after national primary day. Thus, a one-day national direct primary would give the news media even more power than they now have to influence the outcomes of contests for nominations by shaping most people's perceptions of how these contests were proceeding.[25]

POLITICAL CAMPAIGNS

It is difficult to bring political campaigns into articulate focus for one very good reason: campaigns come in an extraordinary variety of shapes and sizes. Whether there is such a thing as a typical campaign is open to serious doubt. It seems clear, for example, that campaigns will differ depending upon the office sought (whether executive, legislative, or judicial), the level of government (national, state, or local), the legal and political environments (partisan or nonpartisan election, competitive or noncompetitive constituency), and the initial advantages or disadvantages of the candidates (incumbent or nonincumbent, well-known or little-known), among other things.

The standards by which to measure and evaluate the effectiveness of campaigns are not easy to discover because of the vast number of variables that intrude both on campaign decisions and on voter choice. In the usual election, does the party that wins owe its victory to a superior campaign or would it have won in any case? Data with which to answer such a question obviously are elusive. What is evident is that strategies that are appropriate to one campaign may be less appropriate or even inappropriate to another. Tactics that work at one time or in one place may not work under other circumstances. Organizational arrangements that satisfy one party may not satisfy the other. Campaigns, in a word, are loaded with imponderables. There are numerous factors over which neither the party organizations nor the candidates have any control. Moreover, there is no way for parties and candidates to develop an immunity against campaign mistakes. Even so, in most cases it is not immediately clear when a miscalculation has been made, how serious it may have been, or how best to restore the damage.

Despite the variability and uncertainty that characterize political campaigns, there are a few general requirements imposed upon all candidates and parties. The candidate making a serious bid for votes must acquire certain resources and meet certain problems. Whatever his perspective of the campaign, he will have to come to terms with matters of organization, strategy, and finances.

Campaign Organization

Very likely the single most important fact to be known about campaign organization is that the regular party organizations are ill-equipped by themselves to organize and conduct campaigns. Of necessity, they look to outsiders for assistance in all kinds of party work and for the development and staffing of auxiliary campaign organizations. A multiplicity of organizational units are created in every major election for the promotion of particular candidacies. There will be businessmen organized to support the Republican nominee and businessmen organized to support the Democratic candidate. And the same will be true for educators, lawyers, pharmacists, advertising executives, and even independents, to mention but a few. At times these groups work in impressive harmony with the regular party organizations (perhaps to the point of being wholly dominated by them), and at other times they function as virtually independent units, seemingly oblivious to the requirements for communication or for coordination of their activities with those of other party or auxiliary units.

The regular party organizations share control of campaigns not only with the citizens groups but also with a variety of political action committees that operate under the sponsorship of certain interest groups. Among the best known of these groups are the AFL–CIO Committee on Political Education (COPE), the American Medical Association Political Action Committee, and the National Committee for an Effective Congress. Like other campaign groups, these committees raise campaign funds, endorse candidates, and otherwise support those candidates in sympathy with their positions and programs.

At the top of the heterogeneous cluster of party and auxiliary campaign committees are the campaign organizations created by the individual candidates. Virtually every candidate for an important, competitive office feels it obligatory to develop his personal campaign organization to counsel him on strategy and issues, to assist him with travel arrangements and speeches, to raise money, to defend his interests in party circles, and to try to coordinate his activities with those of other candidates and campaign units. The size of the candidate's personal organization is likely to vary according to the significance of the office and the competitiveness of the constituency. The congressman from a safe district, for example, habituated to easy elections, has less need of an elaborate campaign organization than a candidate from a closely competitive district. There are at least some congressional districts that are so safe (at least for the candidate, if not for the party) that were it not for certain district party and civic rites that the incumbent is obligated to attend, he could easily skip campaigning and remain in Washington.[26]

In some campaigns the regular party organization is reduced to being just another spectator. It is not unusual for candidates to employ professional management firms to direct their campaigns rather than to rely on the party organizations.[27] All facets of American politics today come under the influence of public relations specialists and advertising firms. Possessing resources which the party organizations cannot match, they raise funds, recruit campaign workers, develop issues, gain endorsements, write speeches, arrange campaign schedules, direct the candidate's television appearances, and prepare campaign literature, films, and advertising. Indeed, they sometimes create the overall campaign strategy and dominate day-to-day decision-making. Put baldly, their principal task is to build the candidate's "image" by controlling the way he appears to the general public. The observations of one of Richard M. Nixon's campaign advisers in the 1968 presidential election make the point:

> [Nixon] has to come across as a person larger than life, the stuff of legend. People are stirred by legend, including the living legend, not by the man himself. It's the aura that surrounds the charismatic figure more than it is the figure itself that draws the followers. Our task is to build that aura. . . .[28]

Campaign Strategy

The paramount goal of all major party campaigns is to bring together a coalition of sufficient size to bring victory to the candidate or party. Ordinarily, the early days of the campaign are devoted to the development and testing of a broad campaign strategy designed to produce a winning coalition. In the most general sense, strategy should be seen as "an overall plan for acquiring and using the resources needed for a campaign."[29] In developing a broad strategy, candidates, their advisers, and party leaders must take into consideration a number of factors. These include: 1) the principal themes to be developed during the campaign; 2) the issues to be emphasized and exploited; 3) the candidate's personal qualities to be emphasized; 4) the specific groups and geographical areas to whom appeals will be directed; 5) the acquisition of financial support and endorsements; 6) the timing of campaign activities; 7) the relationship of the candidate to the party organization and to factions within it; and 8) the uses to be made of the communications media, particularly television.

To the casual observer, it may appear that there are no limits to the number of major and minor strategies open to a resourceful candidate. In point of fact, however, there are a number of important constraints that serve to shape and define the candidate's options. It is reasonable to expect, for example, that campaign strategy will be affected by the political, social, and economic environments that are present. Among these factors which intrude on campaign strategy are the competitiveness of the district, the nature of the electorate, the quality and representativeness of the party ticket, the unity of the party, the presence of an incumbent, the election timetable (for example, presidential or off-year election), and the predispositions and commitments of political interest groups. And though it is difficult to weigh its significance, it seems clear that the temper of the times will also affect the candidate's broad plan of action. "In eras of general complacency and economic well-being," V. O. Key has written, "assaults against the interests and crusades against abuses by the privileged classes seem to pay small dividends. Periods of hardship and unrest move campaigners to contrive strategies to exploit the anxieties of people —or to insulate themselves from public wrath."[30] Whatever the impact of these constraints upon campaign strategy, it seems evident that most of them are beyond the control of the candidate; they are, purely and simply, conditions to which he must adjust and adapt. The overall strategy that the candidate fashions or selects must he consonant with the "givens" of the campaign environment.

Opportunities and constraints vary from campaign to campaign and from candidate to candidate. Although this results in great diversity, it is nevertheless possible to depict the three overarching strategies that serious candidates usually follow. The most important is for the candidate to get his *supporters out to vote.* A great many elections are won or lost depending on the turnout of the party faithful. In fact, there is good reason to believe that minority party candidates would win most elections if all they were to accomplish was to increase the rate of turnout of their own supporters (assuming turnout for the major party candidates remained the same). The second general strategy is to *activate latent support.* Successful campaigns often turn on the ability of the candidate to activate potential voters among those groups that ordinarily support his party. For the Democratic candidate, this means that special effort must be directed to activating such segments of the population as Catholics, Jews, blacks, blue-collar workers, union members, and urban residents; for the Republican candidate, this rule prescribes a similar effort to activate Protestants, whites, suburban and rural residents, and professional, business, and managerial elements. The third general strategy is to *change the opposition.* In recent years this strategy has been spectacularly successful. A large number of Democrats, for example, voted for Dwight D. Eisenhower in the elections of 1952 and 1956, and a large number of Republicans bolted their party to vote for Lyndon B. Johnson in 1964. Similarly, in 1972, Democrats in great numbers abandoned their party's candidate, George McGovern, to vote for Richard Nixon (though it is probable that they were not so much attracted to Nixon as repelled by McGovern). For most elections, perhaps especially at the state and local levels, this is the least promising of the three strategies. With limited resources at his disposal, the typical candidate is more likely to be elected by getting his supporters and latent supporters to the polls than by trying to convert members of the other party. The important point is that strategies—particularly those relating to manipulation of symbols and issues—will vary sharply according to the audience to whom appeals are directed.[31]

Myths and facts are mixed in about equal proportion in the lore of campaign strategy. Strategies are not easily devised, sorted out, or tested. Indeed, it is scarcely ever apparent in advance which strategies are likely to be most productive and which least productive or even counter-productive. However disciplined and well-managed campaigns may appear to those who stand on the outskirts, they rarely are in reality. As Stimson Bullitt has observed:

> A politician, unlike a general or an athlete, never can be invincible, except within a constituency which constitutes a sinecure. Furthermore, a candidate cannot even be sure that his campaigning will change the election result. . . . [A] politician must act on his hypotheses, which are tested only by looking backward on his acts. A candidate cannot even experiment. Because no one knows what works in a campaign, money is spent beyond the point of diminishing returns. To meet similar efforts of the opposition all advertising and propaganda devices are used—billboards, radio, TV, sound trucks, newspaper ads, letter writing or telephone committee programs, handbills, bus cards. No one dares to omit any approach. Every cartridge must be fired because among the multitude of blanks one may be a bullet. . . .

> A common mistake of post-mortems is to assert that a certain event or a stand or mannerism of a candidate caused him to win or lose. Often no one knows whether the election result was because of this factor or despite it. Spectacular events, whether a dramatic proposal, an attack, or something in the news outside the campaign, are like a revolving door. They win some voters and lose others. . . .[32]

The evidence of many studies suggests that campaign decisions are about as likely to be shaped by chance and by the ability of the candidate to seize upon events as they are by the careful formulation of a broad and coherent plan of attack. Consider the decision of John F. Kennedy in the 1960 presidential campaign to telephone Mrs. Martin Luther King to express his concern over the welfare of her husband, who had been jailed in Atlanta following a "sit-in" in a department store. There is no evidence that Kennedy's decision—perhaps as critical as any of the campaign—was based upon a comprehensive assessment of alternatives or possible consequences. Rather, according to Theodore H. White, the decision came about in this way:

> The crisis was instantly recognized by all concerned with the Kennedy campaign. . . . [The] suggestion for meeting it [was made by] Harris Wofford. Wofford's idea was as simple as it was human—that the candidate telephone directly to Mrs. King in Georgia to express his concern. Desperately Wofford tried to reach his own chief, Sargent Shriver, head of the Civil Rights Section of the Kennedy campaign, so that Shriver might break through to the candidate barnstorming somewhere in the Middle West. Early [the next] morning, Wofford was able to locate Shriver . . . and Shriver enthusiastically agreed. Moving fast, Shriver reached the candidate [as he] was preparing to leave for

a day of barnstorming in Michigan. The candidate's reaction to Wofford's suggestion of participation was impulsive, direct, and immediate. From his room at the Inn, without consulting anyone, he placed a long-distance telephone call to Mrs. Martin Luther King, assured her of his interest and concern in her suffering and, if necessary, his intervention. . . . The entire episode received only casual notice from the generality of American citizens in the heat of the last three weeks of the Presidential campaign. But in the Negro community the Kennedy intervention rang like a carillon.[33]

The development of critical issues is not invariably of great importance in designing campaign strategy. Although some voters are highly sensitive to the specific issues generated in a campaign, there are many others who are preoccupied with the candidate's image, personality, and style. Candidates often are judged less by what they say than by how they say it, less by their achievements than by their personality. Scandals in government, such as the incredible Watergate affair, typically have a major impact on the strategies of subsequent campaigns, serving to heighten the significance of the candidate's alleged personal virtues—especially those of "honesty" and "sincerity"—and to diminish the significance of issues. "I don't think issues mean a great deal about whether you win or lose," observes a newly-elected U.S. senator. "I think issues give you a chance to [demonstrate] your intellectual capacity. Issues are a vehicle by which voters determine your honesty and candor. I don't think a right or wrong answer on an issue makes up anyone's mind but the ideologues. . . ."[34]

Yet, in some elections issues lie at the center of campaign manipulations. And vogue appears in issues as in other things. The passage of Proposition 13 (a California referendum that reduced property taxes) had a dramatic impact on campaigns in 1978 as candidates at all levels sought to outstrip each other in their opposition to taxes, higher spending, and "big" government. Politicians know a good issue when they see it. Attacks against Washington, like those made by Jimmy Carter two years earlier, found their way into congressional campaigns throughout the country.

Increasingly, gimmickry is a key element in "creative" campaign strategy. Statewide walking tours have become commonplace since Lawton Chiles used this technique to win a Florida Senate seat in 1970. But the new vogue requires candidates to engage in different forms of blue-collar work, dutifully filmed, of course, by the media for news stories and by the candidate's public relations team for television advertising. A relatively unknown state senator who won the Democratic nomination for governor in Florida in 1978 (and later the election) worked at 100 different jobs in a period of over a year prior to the primary. His laboring experiences included work as a shrimp fisherman, a citrus fruit picker, a stable boy, a bellboy, a Tallahassee policeman, an airline attendant, and an orderly in a nursing home. Not surprisingly, wealthy candidates seem to find blue-collar work stunts an attractive campaign technique, undoubtedly because it permits them to develop their image as an "average, hard-working citizen."[35] Stunts are a matter of image-making. However ingenious and beguiling, they beg the question: can a public officeholder understand the problems of the shrimp industry without having labored as a shrimp fisherman or the problems of nursing homes without the learning that comes from dumping bedpans? The answer is yes.

Campaign Money

Of all the requirements for successful campaigns, perhaps none is more important than a strong infusion of money. Campaign costs have risen steadily over the years. In 1952, for example, expenditures for the nomination and election of public officials at all levels of government came to about $140 million. By 1968, the figure had climbed to $300 million. Candidates and parties spent about $425 million in 1972 and at least $500 million in 1976.

The spiraling costs of running for office are caused by a number of factors. The steady increase in the general price level is, of course, one reason; inflation affects campaign costs as well as everything else. To this must be added the costs that have accompanied utilization of new techniques in campaigning (particularly television and computerized mailings), the growth in population, and the enlargement of the electorate. The substitution of presidential primaries for caucus/convention systems in many states has undoubtedly increased campaign expenditures. And considerable sums are spent by candidates in hiring political consultants to direct their appeals for both campaign money and votes.

Whether campaign money is spent intelligently is problematical at the least. Candidates spend as heavily as they do because neither they nor their advisers know which expenditures are likely to produce the greatest return in votes. Lacking systematic information, they jump at every opportunity to contact and persuade voters—and every opportunity costs money.

Major campaigns are extraordinarily expensive. In 1976, the average candidate for the Senate spent nearly $600,000 in his campaign (including the primary). For the average House candidate the figure was roughly $71,000. But some campaigns were much more costly. Fifteen House candidates spent in excess of $250,000 in their campaigns and ten Senate candidates spent more than $1 million each.

An explosion of spending occurred in 1978. Total campaign expenditures for all House and Senate elections rose from about $100 million in 1976 to $150 million in 1978. The average Senate campaign cost about $920,000 and the average House campaign about $108,000. The campaign costs of the 35 winning Senate candidates averaged about $1.2 million. Jesse Helms, Republican candidate for the Senate in North Carolina, spent more than $7 million in his successful bid for reelection—this came to an expenditure of about $12.10 for every vote he received. Overall, Senate incumbents outspent their challengers by a margin of about two-to-one. On the House side, 120 candidates spent in excess of $200,000 each on their 1978 campaigns. Incredibly, two House candidates had campaign expenditures that exceeded $1 million.[36]

Political money poses problems for the politician no less than the public. The first problem is to raise it, the second to deal with those who contribute it. In recent years political interest groups have become a rich source of campaign money. Although banks, corporations, and labor organizations are prohibited from making political contributions from their own treasuries, they are permitted to establish political action committees (PACs) to which contributions may be made for utilization in campaigns. Pioneered by labor organizations, PACs today are employed by all kinds of interest groups. They bear such names as Voluntary Contributors for Better Government (International Paper Company), Realtors Political Action Committee (National Association of Realtors), Amoco Political Action Committee (Standard Oil of Indiana), Nonpartisan Committee for Good Government (Coca-Cola Company), Southern Railway Tax Eligible Good Government Fund (Southern Railway Company), and AFL–CIO Committee on Political Education. The Federal Election Commission reported that 1828 political action committees had received and contributed funds in the 1978 congressional elections.[37]

The public financing of presidential elections has led interest groups to concentrate on congressional races. Political action committees in 1974 made campaign contributions of about $12.5 million to congressional candidates. By 1976, their allocations had nearly doubled, reaching $22.6 million. And in the off-year election of 1978, PACs contributed in excess of $30 million to House and Senate candidates.[38] Of the $22.6 million contributed by interest groups in 1976, $7 million was furnished by business groups and $8 million by labor groups. The various political units of the American Medical Association made campaign gifts of nearly $1.8 million, a sum that made it the largest single contributor in that election.[39]

Interest groups "target" their contributions carefully. The Committee on Political Education of the AFL–CIO contributed nearly $1 million to congressional candidates in 1978, with over 95 percent of it given to Democratic candidates. At least two-thirds of the contributions of business and trade associations in 1978 were given to Republican candidates. Although some groups, such as the Gun Owners of America Campaign Committee, focus their contributions on "open" seats (those in which no incumbent is on the ballot), most are interested in protecting incumbents who are friendly to their legislative objectives. Committee chairmen and party leaders are especially likely to be major beneficiaries of interest-group largesse.[40] The following observations illustrate the pattern of interest-group contributions:

The main goal is to support our friends who have been with us most of the time. (An official of the UAW)

The prevailing attitude is that PAC money should be used to facilitate access to incumbents. (The director of governmental and political participation for the U.S. Chamber of Commerce)

We're inclined to support incumbents because we tend to go with those who support our industry. We are not out looking to find challengers. Our aim is not to change the tone of Congress. (A spokesman for the Lockheed Good Government Program)

We're looking especially for members who serve on key committees, and people who help us on the floor. (A spokesman for the Automobile and Truck Dealers Election Action Committee)[41]

Individuals contribute to political campaigns for a variety of reasons. Undoubtedly, some contributors give money out of a sense of civic duty or for the psychological satisfaction they receive from assisting a particular candidate or their party. Probably far more contributors donate to campaign coffers because they want to elect candidates of suitable ideological bent and because they hope to influence the course of public policy. What kinds of benefits accrue to those individuals who pay the costs of political campaigns? Is there in any sense a "payoff"? One expert on campaign finance argues:

What contributors buy is not as tangible as is often supposed. Mostly what they buy is "access." Politicians who get the money, along with solicitors who raise it and contributors themselves, state invariably that in return for his funds a contributor can get, if he seeks it, access to the party, legislative or administrative officials concerned with a matter of interest to him. One lobbyist called it "entree" and another called it "a basis for talking." Access may not give the contributor what he wants, as the number of disgruntled (and talkative) contributors indicates. And if he is eligible for what he wants, a government contract or a job, he will often get it anyway. The main result of access ... is to "speed things up." The number of cold bargains that are struck for campaign funds are negligible.[42]

The link between contributions and entree to the member's office is aptly described by a lobbyist who was formerly a congressional staff member: "A congressman has 30 times more requests for his time than he can grant. Who are you going to talk to—the contributor or someone else?"[43]

The Regulation of Campaign Finance

Public restiveness over the role of money in American politics has long been present. Dissatisfaction focuses around three main complaints. The first is simply that campaign costs have risen to such an extent that candidates with limited resources are seriously disadvantaged in the electoral process. The doubt persists that some talented people never seek public office because they lack financial support or are unwilling to solicit funds from others because of the risk of incurring political indebtedness and of compromising their independence.[44] Moreover, the high cost of elections may mean that the public hears only one side of the campaign, that of the candidate with access to "real" money.

The second complaint is that those individuals, families, and groups that contribute lavishly to parties and candidates are thought to be buying influence and gaining preferments of some kind in return for the money they channel into campaigns. Whether this is true may not be as important as the fact that the public believes it to be true. In some measure, public suspicion about campaign financing contributes to public suspicion of the government itself.

And finally, as a result of the Watergate exposé, there has been a heightened awareness of the potential for corruption and abuse when huge sums of money are collected and spent for political purposes.

To deal with a variety of maladies associated with the financing of federal political campaigns, Congress passed two comprehensive enactments in the 1970s. The first, the Federal Election Campaign Act of 1971, was an act of unusual importance, the first serious attempt to reform campaign financing since 1925. Adopted prior to the Watergate incident, the act anticipated public financing of federal election campaigns by providing that taxpayers could earmark $1 on their personal income tax returns for use in the 1976 presidential election. Of at least equal importance, the act provided for rigorous disclosure requirements concerning campaign contributions, expenditures, and debts. Finally, taking a different tack, a provision to stimulate *private* contributions to political campaigns was placed in the act. Under a tax incentive system, taxpayers were permitted to deduct small campaign contributions from their tax obligations. In retrospect, it seems clear that the extraordinary dimensions of the 1972 presidential election scandal never would have been uncovered without the disclosure requirements for political contributions and expenditures contained in the law.

Crisis is often a spur to legislative action. It was largely in response to Watergate that Congress passed a more comprehensive campaign financing law in 1974. Designed to curtail the influence and abuse of money in campaign politics, the enactment placed tight restrictions on contributions, expenditures, disclosure and reporting, and, most important, provided for at least partial public financing of presidential primaries, elections, and nominating conventions. The constitutionality of the new act was promptly tested in the courts. In *Buckley* v. *Valeo*,[45] decided in 1976, the Supreme Court held that the act's limitations on *individual expenditures* (either those of the candidate[46] or those of individuals spending *independently* on behalf of a candidate) were unconstitutional, since they interfered with the right of free speech under the First Amendment. Political money, in a sense, is political speech. The Court upheld the limitations on contributions to campaigns, the disclosure requirements, and the public funding provisions for presidential primaries and elections. The main features of the 1974 law, as modified by later amendments, are shown in Table 12.

Although the new law represents a profound political experiment, particularly in its provisions for public financing, it is hard to see that it harbors any coherent vision of competitive, party-oriented politics. In the first place, it is essentially a *candidate*-centered rather than a party-centered measure.[47] The public funds that are made available in presidential primaries and general elections are channeled to the candidates and their personal organizations rather than to the parties. In 1976, $24.1 million was allocated in matching funds to 15 presidential primary candidates (see provision III-C in Table 12). The leading beneficiaries of campaign subsidies under the matching formula were Ronald Reagan ($5.1 million), Gerald R. Ford ($4.7 million), Jimmy Carter ($3.5 million), George C. Wallace ($3.3 million), Henry M. Jackson ($2 million), and Morris K. Udall ($1.8 million).[48] In the general election, both major party candidates elected to accept public financing of their campaigns (see provision III-A in Table 12) and each received $21.8 million in subsidies. Accordingly, both the Carter and Ford campaigns were prohibited from accepting private contributions.

A second large characteristic of the campaign finance law is that it focuses on the presidency. No provision is made for the public financing of campaigns for Congress. For those who believe that what is good for the goose is good for the gander, the observations of Senator Edward M. Kennedy (D., Mass.) are especially appropriate:

> Abuses of campaign spending and private campaign financing do not stop at the other end of Pennsylvania Avenue. They dominate congressional elections as well. If the abuses are the same for the presidency and Congress, the reforms should also be the same. If public financing is good enough for presidential elections, it should also be good enough for Senate and House elections.[49]

Third, the absence of a provision for public financing of congressional campaigns represents a triumph for incumbent members of Congress. Past experience has shown that it is scarcely ever easy to defeat a member of Congress,[50] and the new law does nothing to make it easier. Incumbents invariably are much more successful than challengers in securing campaign contributions, particularly from the political action committees of interest groups. In 1976, for example, the political action committees of agricultural groups gave in excess of seven times as much money to incum-

TABLE 12. Major Provisions for the Regulation of Campaign Financing in Federal Elections

I. *Contribution Limits*

A. No individual may contribute more than $1000 to any candidate or candidate committee per election. (Primary, runoff, and general elections are considered to be separate elections.)

B. Individual contributions to a national party committee are limited to $20,000 per calendar year and to any other political committee to $5000 per calendar year. (The total contributions by an individual to all *federal* candidates in one year cannot exceed $25,000.)

C. A multicandidate committee (one with more than 50 contributors that makes contributions to five or more federal candidates) may contribute no more than $5000 to any candidate or candidate committee per election, no more than $15,000 to the national committee of a political party, and no more than $5000 to any other political committee per calendar year.

D. The national committee and the congressional campaign committee may each contribute up to $5000 to each House candidate, per election; the national committee together with the senatorial campaign committee may contribute up to a combined total of $17,500 to each Senate candidate for the entire campaign period (including a primary election).

E. Political action committees formed by businesses, trade associations, or unions are limited to contributions of no more than $5000 to any candidate in any election. No limits apply to their aggregate contributions.

F. Banks, corporations, and labor unions are prohibited from making contributions from their treasuries to federal election campaigns. Government contractors and foreign nationals are similarly restricted. Contributions may not be supplied by one person but made in the name of another person. Contributions in cash are limited to $100.

II. *Expenditure Limits*

A. Candidates are limited to an expenditure of $10 million each plus COLA (cost-of-living adjustment) in all presidential primaries.

B. Major party presidential candidates may spend no more than $20 million plus COLA in the general election (a total of $21.8 million each in 1976).

C. Presidential and vice-presidential candidates who accept public funding may spend no more than $50,000 of personal funds in their campaigns.

D. Each national party may spend up to 2 cents per voter on behalf of its presidential candidate (about $3.2 million for each in 1976).

TABLE 12 (Continued)

II. *Expenditure Limits* (continued)

    E. In addition to making contributions to candidates, the national committee, together with congressional and senatorial campaign committees, may make expenditures on *behalf* of House and Senate candidates. For each House member—in states with more than one district—the sum is $10,000 plus COLA. (In 1978, the limit for these "party-coordinated expenditures" was $12,290 for House candidates.) For each Senate candidate the sum is $20,000 plus COLA or 2 cents for each person in the state's voting-age population, whichever is greater. (Under the second formula, party committees in 1978 could have spent, for example, $384,111 on behalf of a California Senate candidate, $215,640 on behalf of a Texas Senate candidate, and $24,580 on behalf of a Wyoming Senate candidate.) State party committees may make expenditures on behalf of House and Senate candidates up to the same limits.

    F. As a result of the *Buckley* v. *Valeo* decision, there are no limits on how much House and Senate candidates may collect and spend in their campaigns (or on how much they may spend of their own or their family's money).

    G. Also in the wake of *Buckley* v. *Valeo*, there are no limits on the amount that individuals and groups may spend on behalf of any presidential or congressional candidate so long as the expenditures are *independent*—that is, not arranged or controlled by the candidate.

III. *Public Financing*

    A. Major party candidates for the presidency qualify for full funding ($20 million plus COLA) prior to the campaign, the money to be drawn from the federal income-tax dollar checkoff. Candidates may decline to participate in the public funding program and finance their campaigns through private contributions. Candidates who accept public funding may not accept private contributions.

    B. Minor party and independent candidates qualify for lesser sums, provided their candidates received at least 5 percent of the vote in the previous presidential election. New parties or parties that received less than 5 percent of the vote four years earlier qualify for public financing *after* the election, provided they drew 5 percent of the vote.

    C. Matching public funds of up to $5 million (plus COLA) are available for presidential primary candidates, provided that they first raise $100,000 in private funds ($5000 in contributions of no more than $250 in each of 20 states). Once that threshold is reached, the candidate receives matching funds up to $250 per contribution. No candidate is eligible for more than 25 percent of the total available funds.

TABLE 12   (Continued)

III. *Public Financing* (continued)

  D. Presidential candidates who receive less than 10 percent of the vote in two consecutive presidential primaries become ineligible for additional campaign subsidies.

  E. Optional public funding of presidential nominating conventions is available for the major parties, with lesser amounts for minor parties. (In 1976, each major party was given $2.2 million under this provision.)

IV. *Disclosure and Reporting*

  A. Each federal candidate is required to establish a single, overarching campaign committee to report on all contributions and expenditures on behalf of the candidate.

  B. Frequent reports on contributions and expenditures are to be filed with the Federal Election Commission.

V. *Enforcement*

  A. Administration of the law is the responsibility of a six-member, bipartisan Federal Election Commission. The Commission is empowered to make rules and regulations, to receive campaign reports, to render advisory opinions, to conduct audits and investigations, to subpoena witnesses and information, and to seek civil injunctions through court action.

bents as to challengers. Among business PACs, the ratio was four-to-one in favor of incumbents. Overall, campaign money given to incumbents by PACs was more than three times greater than that given to challengers.[51] For the most part, the record makes clear, interest groups put their eggs in the baskets of incumbents.

Fourth, the law places third or minor parties, especially those newly created, at a severe disadvantage. Minor parties can qualify for some public funding only if their candidates received 5 percent of the vote in the previous election. New parties or parties that failed to receive at least 5 percent of the vote in the previous election cannot qualify for public funds until *after* the election has been held and then only if they reach the 5 percent threshold. On the other hand, a third party that qualifies for funding in one election will automatically qualify for funding in the next, contributing perhaps to the institutionalization of a multiple party or, more accurately, a multiple *candidate* system of presidential elections— an anomaly worth pondering by those concerned about the fragmentation of American politics.

Attempts since 1974 to extend public financing to congressional elections have been unsuccessful. The chief opponents of this legislation have been Republicans and southern Democrats, joined by some northern, big-city Democrats. In general, Republicans profess to see proposals for public financing of congressional elections as designed to protect incumbents—which translates into the safeguarding of heavy Democratic majorities. Prospects for the Republican party, they may reason, will be better under the present system of private financing. In contrast, some Democrats who oppose this legislation worry that the public funds made available to challengers would heighten competitiveness in their states and districts and thus threaten their reelection. (Doubtlessly some Republicans share their anxieties.) As a Democratic congressman from New York has observed, "the more of a challenger's bill public financing gets to be, the harder it is to pass it."[52] The strongest supporters of public financing, not surprisingly, have been the newer, reform-minded members, particularly in the Democratic party. Some of them were first elected with pledges to support public financing. But another reason for their support may be equally important: as newcomers, many undoubtedly have found the raising of large sums of campaign money difficult, time-consuming, and frustrating. Public financing would remove some of the "hassle" from their political lives.

Whatever the motives that underlie members' attitudes toward public financing, it is plain that this legislation bears peculiarly on congressional careers. The temptation will be strong for members to evaluate it in personal and political terms, favoring or opposing it in light of its probable impact, first, on their electoral security, and second, on the welfare of their party. At the same time, the pressure for some form of public financing of congressional campaigns, linked to tighter restrictions on total spending, is likely to become more intense in view of the runaway campaign costs of recent years.

Although experience with the new campaign finance law has been limited, certain observations concerning its impact appear warranted:

1. *Restrictions on spending have led to less costly presidential campaigns.* Under the public financing provisions of the Federal Election Campaign Act, $21.8 million was made available to the presidential campaign of each major party in 1976—a total of $43.6 million. Campaign subsidies in the form of matching·funds to presidential candidates in the primaries and grants to the major parties for their national conventions brought the total public outlay to $72 million. In 1972, by contrast, the private funding of the presidential election (including prenomination campaigns) came to an estimated $137.8 million. Even though private spending on behalf of the presidential candidates in 1976 involved millions of dollars, the total cost was substantially below that of 1972.

To many observers, it should be mentioned, the limits on campaign spending in the presidential election were set at an unrealistically low level. One result was that, with limited funds and seeking to reach the largest number of voters in 1976, the candidates focused on television appeals.[53] The Carter–Ford contest was perhaps more of a media event, reflecting personalities and styles, than any previous presidential election.

2. *Spending in congressional and senatorial primaries and elections has increased.* The 1976 ruling of the Supreme Court in *Buckley* v. *Valeo* that restrictions on the personal and total expenditures of candidates for Congress were unconstitutional led to an explosion of spending in these elections. H. John Heinz spent nearly $2.5 million of personal funds in winning a Pennsylvania Senate seat in 1976. Several candidates in 1978 spent in excess of $500,000 of their own funds in Senate campaigns.[54] But personal spending has been only part of the story. Shut out of the presidential campaign when the presidential candidates accept public funding, interest groups have turned to congressional campaigns. Political action committees gave nearly twice as much money to congressional candidates in 1976 as they had in 1974. In 1978, they spent nearly three times as much on House and Senate elections as they had only four years earlier. Million-dollar campaigns for the Senate have become commonplace.

3. *The influence of "fat cats" (wealthy contributors) on electoral politics has declined, at least at the national level.* The contributions of an individual to federal candidates are limited to $1000 for each election and to a total of $25,000 in a calendar year.

4. *The importance of raising large amounts of money in small sums has become apparent to all candidates, and particularly to those seeking the presidential nomination.* As provided by the Federal Election Campaign Act, matching federal funds become available for presidential primary candidates who first raise $100,000 in small sums—obtaining $5000 in contributions of $250 or less in each of 20 states. Once a candidate has reached the $100,000 threshold, the government matches the first $250 of any gift. For the 15 presidential primary candidates who qualified for matching funds in 1976, the average matched contribution was roughly $35.[55] One incidental result of the new emphasis on small gifts is that firms that engage in direct mail solicitations, working with computerized mailing lists, have assumed even greater importance in the fund-raising efforts of candidates. In fund-raising as in certain other respects, the party organizations have been shunted aside.

5. *Opportunities for persons to engage in corrupt practices in the use of campaign money in federal elections have been constricted.* The risks of detection are greater as a result of timely and comprehensive disclosure provisions, requirements for centralized accounting of contributions and expenditures, curbs on cash contributions, and the existence of a full-time agency, the Federal Election Commission, to administer the law and to investigate alleged infractions of it. At the same time, the campaign finance act has served to make candidates and party organizations exceedingly cautious in raising and spending funds so as to avoid allegations of financial improprieties. Reportedly, the Carter organization in 1976 hired about 100 accountants and 150 lawyers around the country simply to

monitor campaign financing to keep within the limits of the law.[56] Bookkeeping has become a major feature (and expense) of political campaigns.

6. *The price of financial purity, or what passes as that, has been high.* Already weak national parties have been further weakened. The party role in national fund-raising is now minimal. In broad view, the parties appear more as bystanders than as participants in presidential elections. The reality is that the struggle for the presidency takes place between candidates and their organizations, carried on via television, refereed and explained by the news celebrities of that industry, and judged by a fidgety public waiting for the campaign to end in order that normal programming can return to the tube.

7. *Obvious to most observers, the new rules of the 1970s did not solve all problems of financing politics.* Inequity continues to be the major dilemma. Money still "talks." As a result of the Supreme Court's ruling, wealthy candidates have a sharp advantage in the struggle for office: they can spend as much of their own and their family's money as ambition, leavened by prudence, dictates. Interest groups, moreover, are spending with a vengeance, undoubtedly gaining improved access to policy-makers, if not in fact securing questionable preferments. For their part, candidates may worry over from whom to accept money, but they usually accept it, caught amid the escalating costs of running for office. And finally, there are all the inequities that distinguish congressional incumbents from their challengers. Indeed, so large are the campaign benefits of incumbency that, under ordinary circumstances, the typical member of Congress has only himself or herself to blame for losing office.

The preeminent objectives of those who struggle to reform campaign financing are to increase public confidence in the political process by curbing the abusive uses of political money, to enhance the opportunitites for citizens to participate in politics by running for public office, and to reduce the vulnerability of candidates and public officials to the importunities and pressures of wealthy contributors. The campaign finance legislation of the 1970s contributed in varying measure to the achievement of these objectives. But it also created new problems, accentuated certain old ones, conferred advantages on some politicians and disadvantages on others and, most important, by stressing candidates over parties, contributed to the further enfeeblement of the party system. In truth, not a great many more changes are needed to "reform" the parties out of business.

NOTES

1. Despite its dominant position, the primary is not the exclusive method for making nominations in the states. In a few states, conventions are still used to make nominations for certain statewide offices, such as governor or U.S. senator. Also, because competition for nominations within the Republican party in southern states is ordinarily not very great, the party is permitted to use conventions rather than primaries to make its nominations. Finally,

a number of states continue to use a combination caucus/convention system for the selection of delegates to the national party conventions.

2. Laws in a few states make specific provisions for the parties to hold *preprimary conventions* for the purpose of choosing the "organization slate." The candidates selected by these conventions will usually appear on the ballot bearing the party endorsement. In the great majority of states, however, slating is an informal party process; the party depends on its organizational network and the communications media to inform the voters as to which candidates carry party support.

3. These themes appear in Frank J. Sorauf, *Party Politics in America* (Boston: Little, Brown, 1968), pp. 210–211.

4. V. O. Key, Jr., *American State Politics: An Introduction* (New York: Knopf, 1956); William H. Standing and James A. Robinson, "Inter-Party Competition and Primary Contesting: The Case of Indiana," *American Political Science Review*, LII (December 1958), pp. 1066–1077; and Malcolm E. Jewell, "Party and Primary Competition in Kentucky State Legislative Races," *Kentucky Law Journal*, XLVIII (Summer 1960), pp. 517–535.

5. Denis G. Sullivan, Jeffrey L. Pressman, and F. Christopher Arterton, *Explorations in Convention Decision Making* (San Francisco: Freeman, 1976), p. 17. Reprinted by permission.

6. Sullivan, Pressman, and Arterton, *Explorations in Convention Decision Making,* pp. 20–21.

7. Austin Ranney, *Curing the Mischiefs of Faction: Party Reform in America* (Berkeley, Calif.: University of California Press, 1975), p. 206.

8. The commissions were as follows: the Commission on Party Structure and Delegate Selection (mandated by the 1968 convention and established in 1969, known as the McGovern–Fraser Commission); the Commission on Delegate Selection (established in 1972, known as the Mikulski Commission); and the Commission on Presidential Nomination and Party Structure (established in 1975, known as the Winograd Commission).

9. The proportional representation rule (12B) is perhaps the most important of all the delegate selection rules. It provides that each candidate who achieves a certain threshold in votes receives a proportionate share of the delegation, based on his percentage of the total vote cast for all candidates who reach the threshold. In 1976, the threshold was 15 percent —that is, any candidate who received at least 15 percent of the vote in a caucus or proportional representation primary was entitled to a proportionate share of delegates. In 1978, the Democratic National Committee (acting on the recommendation of the Winograd Commission) approved a system of flexible thresholds, varying between 15 and 25 percent, for the 1980 election. Where the threshold in a delegate selection district is 25 percent (a district with 4 delegates), a candidate who fails to achieve this percentage will not be entitled to any delegates (except under certain limited circumstances). Under regulations adopted by the Compliance Review Commission in 1979, winner-take-all is almost completely eliminated. A candidate will win all the delegates in a district only if he receives more than 90 percent of the vote. To return to the main point, *the broad effect of high thresholds is to diminish the fragmentation effects of proportional representation.* Votes for candidates who trail badly are simply "wasted."

10. William J. Crotty, *Political Reform and the American Experiment* (New York: Crowell, 1977), pp. 255–260.

11. William R. Keech and Donald R. Matthews, "Patterns in the Presidential Nominating Process, 1936–1976," in Jeff Fishel (ed.), *Parties and Elections in an Anti-Party Age* (Bloomington, Ind.: Indiana University Press, 1978), p. 216.

12. Through its party reform commissions, the Democratic party has taken steps to remedy two nagging problems of the primary. First, a new rule reduces the length of the primary season, a change that will help to ease the physical strain on candidates. Another rule designed to give the party greater control over its nominating process outlaws "crossover" primaries—those open systems in which Republicans were able to vote in Democratic primaries.

13. F. Christopher Arterton, "Campaign Organizations Confront the Media-Political Environment," in *Race for the Presidency: The Media and the Nominating Process,* edited by James David Barber, © 1978 The American Assembly, Columbia University. Reprinted by permission of Prentice-Hall, Inc., Englewood Cliffs, New Jersey, p. 9.

14. F. Christopher Arterton, "Campaign Organizations Confront the Media-Political Environment," in *Race for the Presidency: The Media and the Nominating Process,* edited by James David Barber, © 1978 the American Assembly, Columbia University. Reprinted by permission of Prentice-Hall, Inc., Englewood Cliffs, New Jersey, p. 5.

15. F. Christopher Arterton, "Campaign Organizations Confront the Media-Political Environment," in *Race for the Presidency: The Media and the Nominating Process,* edited by James David Barber, © 1978 The American Assembly, Columbia University. Reprinted by permission of Prentice-Hall, Inc. Englewood Cliffs, New Jersey, p. 10 (emphasis added).

16. Austin Ranney, *Participation in American Presidential Nominations, 1976* (Washington, D.C.: American Enterprise Institute for Public Policy Research, 1977), pp. 15–20. The participation rates are for 26 primary states and 21 caucus/convention states.

17. Austin Ranney, "The Political Parties: Reform and Decline," in Anthony King (ed.), *The New American Political System* (Washington, D.C.: American Enterprise Institute for Public Policy Research, 1978), p. 219.

18. This section is based mainly on Ranney, "The Political Parties: Reform and Decline," pp. 230–236; and Jeane Kirkpatrick, *The New Presidential Elite* (New York: Russell Sage Foundation and The Twentieth Century Fund, 1976).

19. As noted earlier, a rule adopted by the Democratic National Committee in 1978 provides for enlarging state delegations by 10 percent to include party and elected officials. In creating this party contingent, preference will be given to Democratic governors, state party chairpersons and vice-chairpersons, other members of the Democratic National Committee, U.S. senators, and members of the House of Representatives—in that order. Another rule adopted in 1978 requires state delegations to be divided equally between men and women.

20. See Kirkpatrick, *The New Presidential Elite,* especially Chapter 10.

21. Accordingly, there are great variations in delegate selection procedures among Republican state parties. For example, although winner-take-all primaries are generally outlawed by the Democratic party's proportional representation rule, the Republican party uses them in a number of states, including California, where Reagan defeated Ford in 1976 (by a margin of nearly two to one) and won all 167 delegates.

22. An exception to this "rule" occurred in 1956 when Adlai Stevenson, the Democratic presidential nominee, created a stir by declining to express a preference for his vice-presidential running mate. Left to its own devices, the convention quickly settled on a choice between Senators Estes Kefauver and John F. Kennedy. Kefauver, who had been an active candidate for the presidency, won a narrow victory. Kennedy came off even better—he launched his candidacy for the presidential nomination in 1960.

23. The preference of party professionals for a balanced ticket grows out of their instinct for the conservation of the party and their understanding of the electorate. The ticket should be broadly appealing, in their view, rather than narrowly ideological or sectional. The factors that ordinarily come under review in the consideration of balance are geography, political philosophy, religion, and factional recognition.

24. A variation of this regional plan would *require* all states to hold a presidential primary.

25. Austin Ranney, *The Federalization of Presidential Primaries* (Washington, D.C.: The American Enterprise Institute for Public Policy Research, 1978), pp. 36–37. This monograph provides a comprehensive analysis of the proposals discussed in this section.

26. Two House Democratic incumbents, one from Ohio and the other from Massachusetts, reported that they spent less than $100 in campaign funds in 1978. At the other end of the scale, eight House candidates (including six incumbents) spent more than $500,000 each. *The New York Times,* January 18, 1979, p. A19.

27. For an analysis of the new style of campaigning, particularly in terms of the role of campaign management firms, see Robert Agranoff, *The New Style in Election Campaigns* (Boston: Holbrook Press, 1972).

28. Quoted by Joe McGinniss, *The Selling of the President, 1968.* © 1969 by Joemac, Incorporated. Reprinted by permission of Trident Press, division of Simon & Schuster, Inc.

29. David A. Leuthold, *Electioneering in a Democracy* (New York: Wiley, 1968), p. 3. Leuthold's study of congressional campaigns shows that "the problems of acquisition are more significant than the problems of using the resources. As a result, the decision on making an appeal for the labor vote, for example, will depend not only on the proportion of the constituency which is labor-oriented, but also on the success that the candidate has had in acquiring such resources as the support of labor leaders, the money and workers needed to send a mailing to labor union members, and information about issues important to labor people."

30. V. O. Key, Jr., *Politics, Parties, and Pressure Groups* (New York: Crowell, 1964), p. 464.

31. Lewis A. Froman, Jr., "A Realistic Approach to Campaign Strategies and Tactics," in M. Kent Jennings and L. Harmon Zeigler (eds.), *The Electoral Process* (Englewood Cliffs, N.J.: Prentice-Hall, 1966), pp. 7–8.

32. Stimson Bullitt, *To Be a Politician* (Garden City, N.Y.: Doubleday, 1961), pp. 72–73.

33. From *The Making of the President, 1960* by Theodore H. White. Copyright © 1961 by Atheneum House, Inc. Reprinted by permission of the author and Atheneum Publishers, pp. 322–323. For analysis of the major models of campaign decision-making, see Karl A. Lamb and Paul A. Smith, *Campaign Decision-Making: The Presidential Election of 1964* (Belmont, Calif.: Wadsworth, 1968).

34. "Campaign Consultants: Pushing Sincerity in 1974," *Congressional Quarterly Weekly Report,* May 4, 1974, p. 1105.

35. *Congressional Quarterly Weekly Report,* October 21, 1978, pp. 3060–3061.

36. The data on congressional campaign expenditures are drawn from the *Congressional Quarterly Weekly Report,* October 29, 1977, pp. 2299–2311, and *The New York Times,* issues of March 7, 1977, January 9, 1979, and January 18, 1979.

37. *Congressional Quarterly Weekly Report,* November 11, 1978, pp. 3260–3262.

38. *Congressional Quarterly Weekly Report,* November 11, 1978, p. 3260.

39. *Congressional Quarterly Weekly Report,* April 16, 1977, p. 710.

40. For example, consider the sums given by PACs to party leaders for their 1978 campaigns. Senator Howard Baker (minority leader) spent $1,874,000 in his campaign; $336,000 (18 percent) was contributed by political action committees. The comparable figures for the other leaders were: Senator Ted Stevens (Republican deputy leader) $329,000 and $177,000 (54 percent); Thomas P. O'Neill, Jr. (Speaker) $14,000 and $23,000 (100 percent); Congressman Jim Wright (majority leader) $232,000 and $79,000 (34 percent); Congressman John Brademas (majority whip) $230,000 and $75,000 (32 percent); Congressman John Rhodes (minority leader) $191,000 and $123,000 (67 percent); Congressman Robert Michel (minority whip) $81,000 and $33,000 (41 percent); and Congressman John Anderson (chairman of minority policy committee) $231,000 and $81,000 (35 percent). Contributions to Speaker O'Neill's campaign by political action committees exceeded his campaign expenditures; his total expenditures ($14,000) were, of course, exceptionally low. *The New York Times,* January 4, 1979, p. A16.

41. *Congressional Quarterly Weekly Report,* issues of April 8, 1978, pp. 850–851, and November 11, 1978, pp. 3260–3262.

42. Alexander Heard, *Money and Politics* (New York: Public Affairs Pamphlet No. 242, 1956), p. 15.

43. *U.S. News & World Report,* January 29, 1979, p. 24.

44. Consider the observation of a New York congressman: "When I ran for Congress, the first question asked me was whether I could finance my own campaign. If I had said 'no, I cannot,' I would not have been the candidate. When you mention candidates for public office, you are only mentioning men of affluence." *Congressional Quarterly Weekly Report,* December 5, 1969, p. 2434.

45. 424 U.S. 1 (1976).

46. Struck down by the Court were provisions that limited the spending of *personal* funds by candidates ($35,000 for Senate candidates and $25,000 for House candidates) and those that limited *total* expenditures. Senate candidates were to be limited to total expenditures of no more than $100,000, or 8 cents per eligible voter (whichever is greater) in primaries, and $150,000, or 12 cents per voter (whichever is greater) in general elections. Fund-raising costs of up to 20 percent of the spending limit could be added to these amounts. House candidates were to be limited to no more than $70,000 in primaries and $70,000 in general elections (plus fund-raising costs of up to 20 percent of the spending limit).

47. Two thrusts in the law can be described as proparty. One provides for optional public funding of presidential nominating conventions. The other provides that national party committees can make certain contributions to House and Senate candidates and certain expenditures on behalf of these candidates and its presidential candidate. Consult Table 12 for the details.

48. Herbert E. Alexander, *Financing Politics: Money, Elections and Political Reform* (Washington, D.C.: Congressional Quarterly Press, 1976), p. 248.

49. *Congressional Quarterly Weekly Report,* October 12, 1974, p. 2865.

50. Among the incumbent's advantages are the franking privilege, visibility gained through the media, a public record, a network of political allies, a structure of opportunities for helping constituents with their problems ("casework"), an established system for soliciting campaign funds, and a staff and offices.

51. *Congressional Quarterly Weekly Report,* January 21, 1978, p. 119.

52. *Congressional Quarterly Weekly Report,* August 5, 1978, p. 2029.

53. Ranney, "The Political Parties: Reform and Decline," p. 243.

54. *Congressional Quarterly Weekly Report,* October 28, 1978, pp. 3113–3114.

55. Alexander, *Financing Politics,* p. 248.

56. *Congressional Quarterly Weekly Report,* April 16, 1977, p. 709.

POLITICAL PARTIES
AND THE
ELECTORATE

It is a nagging fact of American life that for a large proportion of the population politics carries no interest, registers no significance, and excites no demands. A vast array of evidence shows the political role of the typical citizen to be that of a spectator, occasionally aroused by political events but more often inattentive to them. However tarnished this commonplace, it comes close to being the chief truth to be known about the political behavior of American citizens. Much less certain, however, is what this means. Whether it is necessary to have greatly interested and active citizens to have strong and responsible political institutions is by no means clear. No neat or simple formula exists for assessing public support for political institutions. Does the presence of a large nonvoting population reflect substantial disillusionment with the political system and its processes, or does it reflect a general satisfaction with the state of things? The answer is elusive.[1]

Whatever the consequences of low or modest turnouts for the vitality of a democratic political system, it is obvious that some American citizens use their political resources far more than others. Their political involvement is reflected not only in the fact that they vote regularly but also in the fact that they participate in politics in various other ways—perhaps by attempting to persuade other voters to support their candidates or party, by making campaign contributions, or by contributing time and energy to political campaigns. The net result of differential rates of participation is that some citizens gain access to political decision-makers and influence over their decisions, while other citizens are all but excluded from the political process.

An important element in understanding the political behavior of the active members of the American electorate is the political party. More than any other agency, the party provides cues for the voters and gives shape and meaning to elections. Some voters, of course, elude party labeling, preferring the role of the independent. Their number has grown dramatically in recent years. Even though their importance cannot be minimized, especially in presidential elections, their consistent impact on politics is less than that of party members. The reason for this is partly a matter of numbers: about two out of three voters classify themselves as members of one or the other of the two major parties. Before examining the behavior of partisans and nonpartisans, however, it is appropriate to consider the broad characteristics of citizen participation in politics.

TURNOUT: THE DIMINISHED ELECTORATE

There are few facts about American political behavior that stand out more sharply than the comparatively low level of citizen involvement in politics. And there are clear signs that popular participation is in fact declining.

Atrophy of the Electorate

Figure 7 depicts the shape of the active American electorate over the last century. In presidential elections during the last quarter of the nineteenth century, turnout was regularly high; in the presidential election of

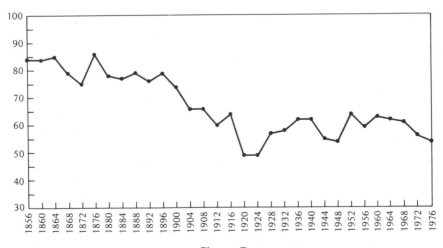

Figure 7.
PERCENTAGE OF VOTING-AGE POPULATION CASTING VOTES FOR THE OFFICE OF PRESIDENT, 1856–1976
Source of data: Paul Allen Beck, "The Electoral Cycle and Patterns of American Politics," *British Journal of Political Science* (forthcoming, 1979).

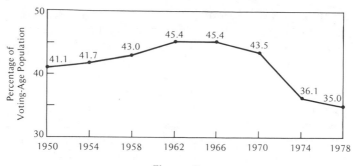

Figure 8.

THE PUBLIC'S DIMINISHING INVOLVEMENT: OFF-YEAR TURNOUT FOR ELECTIONS TO
THE U.S. HOUSE OF REPRESENTATIVES, 1950–1978
Source of data: U.S. Bureau of the Census, *Statistical Abstract of the United States,* 98th ed.
(Washington, D.C.: U.S. Government Printing Office, 1977), p. 508. Estimated turnout for 1978.

1876, for example, over 85 percent of the eligible voters cast ballots.
Beginning around the turn of the century, however, a sharp decline in
voting set in, reaching its nadir of 44 percent in 1920. A moderate increase
in turnout took place during the next several decades, with participation
hovering around 60 percent during the 1950s and 1960s. But participation
declined again in the 1970s, dropping to 54 percent in 1976, the lowest
level since 1948 and one of the lowest in history.

Although these data on American voting participation are far from
complimentary, they may conceal more of the problem than they un-
cover. The hard truth is that turnout is even less impressive in nonpresidential elections. In off-year congressional elections from 1950 to 1970,
turnout percentages ranged between 41 and 45 percent of the eligible
voters. In the mid-term election of 1974, turnout dropped to 36 percent.
And in 1978, it fell even lower—to 35 percent. It is a startling fact that,
for whatever reasons, nearly two-thirds of all eligible voters have come to
ignore off-year elections. (See Figure 8.)

Turnout in state and local elections is more of the same story. Figure 9
shows recent turnout percentages for the office of governor in the 50 states
in off-year (that is, nonpresidential) and presidential years. Several conclusions can be drawn from the figure. In the first place, the states differ
sharply in their turnout patterns. The relation of region to participation
is shown by the higher voter participation rates in western (especially
plains and mountain) and New England states, and the lower rates of
participation in most southern states. The industrialized states of the
North (for example, Michigan, New Jersey, New York, Ohio, and Pennsylvania) rank near the middle in turnout levels. Second, and not unexpect-
edly, those states that elect governors in presidential years nearly always
have higher turnouts than those whose gubernatorial elections occur in off
years.[2] Third, notwithstanding major variations among the states, overall
citizen performance is far from impressive. The *median* turnout for the

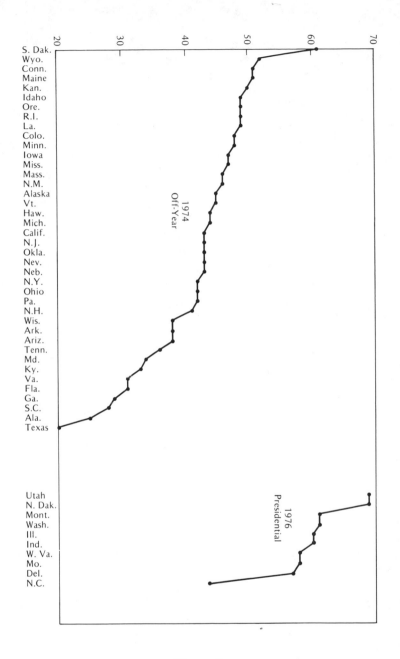

Figure 9.

PERCENTAGE OF VOTING-AGE POPULATION CASTING VOTES FOR THE OFFICE OF
GOVERNOR,* OFF-YEAR AND PRESIDENTIAL ELECTIONS, 1974 and 1976**
*Data derived from U.S. Bureau of the Census, *Statistical Abstract of the United States,* 98th ed.
(Washington, D.C.: U.S. Government Printing Office, 1977), pp. 505 and 510.
**For New Jersey and Virginia, the gubernatorial election is that of 1973; for Kentucky and Missis-
sippi, the election is 1975.

40 states that elected governors in 1974 was only 43 percent; in 1970, the median turnout for these states had been 51 percent.

It remains to be observed that the low point in participation is ordinarily plumbed in primary elections—a total primary vote of only 20 to 25 percent of the potential electorate is not unusual. In the one-party Democratic states of the South, however, participation in primary elections—often the "real" elections in that region—is about as high as it is in general elections.[3] (See Table 13.) In sum, it is a large and uncomfortable fact of American political life that a great many citizens—comprising almost half of the eligible electorate even in presidential years—are almost wholly detached from the political system and the processes through which its leaders are selected.

There are a number of reasons for the poor performance of twentieth-century American electorates. In the case of the southern states, it is plain that the limitations placed on black suffrage shortly before the turn of the century drastically curtailed their participation. A variety of legal abridgments and strategies, buttressed by social and economic sanctions of all kinds, effectively disfranchised all but the most persistent and resourceful black citizens. The ingenuity of southern white politicians during this era can scarcely be exaggerated. Poll taxes, literacy tests, understanding-the-constitution tests, white primaries,[4] stringent residence and registration requirements, and discriminatory registration administration—all were consciously employed by dominant elites to maintain a white electorate and thus to settle political questions within the white community.

Another prime reason for the sharp contraction of the active electorate stems from the advent of one-party politics throughout large sections of the country. Democratic domination of the South began shortly after the Civil War Reconstruction governments were terminated. Nevertheless, even in the 1880s, the Republican presidential vote was at least half of the Democratic vote in all but a few southern states. The election of 1896, one of the most decisive elections in American history, culminated in the virtual disappearance of the Republican party in the South and in a precipitate drop in Democratic strength in the North. E. E. Schattschneider's analysis of this election is instructive:

> The 1896 party cleavage resulted from the tremendous reaction of conservatives in both major parties to the Populist movement, a radical agrarian agitation that alarmed people of substance all over the country. . . . Southern conservatives reacted so strongly that they were willing to revive the tensions and animosities of the Civil War and the Reconstruction in order to set up a one-party sectional southern political monopoly in which nearly all Negroes and many poor whites were disfranchised. . . . The northern conservatives were so badly frightened by the Bryan candidacy that they adopted drastic measures to alarm the country. As a matter of fact, the conservative reaction to Bryanism in the North was almost as spectacular as the conservative reaction to Populism in the South. As a result the Democratic party in large areas

TABLE 13. Mean Percent Voting Turnout in Primary and General Elections for Governor and U.S. Senator, 1962–1972

Type of State	For Governor			For U.S. Senator		
	Primary Elections	General Elections	Difference	Primary Elections	General Elections	Difference
One-party Democratic	36.7	37.7	+1.0	27.5	34.9	−7.4
Modified one-party Democratic	29.9	52.0	−22.1	23.3	48.9	−25.6
Two-party	25.8	57.1	−31.3	25.1	58.8	−33.7
Modified one-party Republican	27.0	63.4	−36.4	22.3	61.6	−39.3

Source: From Austin Ranney, "Parties in State Politics," in Herbert Jacob and Kenneth N. Vines, eds., *Politics in the American States: A Comparative Analysis*, 3rd Ed., p. 71, copyright © 1976, Little, Brown and Company (Inc.). Reprinted by permission.

of the Northeast and Middle West was wiped out, or decimated, while the Republican party consolidated its supremacy in all of the most populous areas of the country. The resulting party lineup was one of the most sharply sectional political divisions in American history. . . . Both sections became more conservative because *one-party politics tends strongly to vest political power in the hands of the people who already have enormous power.* Moreover, in one-party areas (areas of extreme sectionalism) votes decline in value because the voters no longer have a valuable party alternative.[5]

The smothering effect of a noncompetitive environment on participation can be seen in election turnouts following the realignment of the 1890s. Consider this evidence: between 1884 and 1904, turnout in Virginia dropped 57 percent; in Mississippi, 51 percent; and in Louisiana, 50 percent. Part of the explanation for these drop-offs undoubtedly can be associated with the success of southern efforts to disfranchise blacks, but it is also clear that one-party politics had a decisive impact on the electorate. In the first place, the drop in participation was too large to be accounted for merely by the disappearance of black votes. Second, the impact of the new sectionalism was not confined simply to the South. Despite their growing populations, some 14 northern states had smaller turnouts in 1904 than they did in 1896.[6]

It seems clear that the lower rate of turnout in the South in the twentieth century is partially attributable to diminished competition between the parties. If the outcome of an election is predictable, there is scant inducement for voters to pay the time, energy, and other costs that voting requires. Changes in the turnout of southern voters, however, are under way. Today, elections in the South (especially presidential) are substantially more competitive than they were a generation ago, and voter turnout rates have been increasing, here and there dramatically. Undoubtedly, the elimination of legal barriers to registration and voting (such as the poll tax and the literacy test) has also contributed to the expansion of southern electorates. In presidential elections, voters in southern states now participate at a level only marginally lower than voters in other parts of the country.

Still other reasons have been advanced for the decline in mass political involvement in this century. One concerns woman suffrage. Although women were given the vote in 1920, large numbers of them were indifferent to their new right and did not use it immediately. In subsequent decades, a significantly larger proportion of women entered the active electorate; today, their rate of participation is only slightly lower than that of men.

In the past, stringent registration laws undoubtedly served to keep many citizens away from the polls. During the latter part of the nineteenth century, when turnout was regularly between 75 and 85 percent of the eligible electorate, there were many parts of the country where voters were not required to register or where automatic registration was in effect. During the early twentieth century, registration laws became much more restrictive, making voting more difficult. Provisions were adopted, for example, to require voters to register annually in person, to purge voters' names from the registration rolls if they failed to vote within a particular period of time, and to require voters to reside within a state at least a year (and sometimes two) before becoming eligible to register. In addition, poll taxes and literacy tests were used, particularly in the South, to disfranchise prospective voters. The effect of these legal barriers was, of course, to diminish turnout.

Major changes in the 1960s and 1970s, however, greatly relaxed registration laws. Poll taxes and literacy tests were eliminated. Periodic registration gave way virtually everywhere to permanent registration. As a result of an act passed by Congress in 1970, the residency requirement for *federal* elections is now limited to a *maximum* of 30 days before the election; moreover, for other elections, only a handful of states have closing dates earlier than 30 days. In about one-third of the states, in fact, registration is possible up to 20 days before the election. Finally, all states must now meet certain minimum national standards for absentee registration.[7]

Although states vary as to their requirements, registration laws are no longer generally burdensome. Nonetheless, a study by Rosenstone and Wolfinger has shown that if all states had registration laws as permissive as those found in the most permissive states, turnout would increase. Had permissive laws been in effect everywhere in the 1972 presidential election, turnout would have been about 9 percent higher. Their study shows that late closing dates have the largest impact on voting participation. Facilitative provisions for absentee registration also encourage turnout, as do provisions for registration during normal business hours, evenings, and Saturdays. What it comes down to is that in states where registration laws are permissive, the costs of voting in time, energy, and information are lower. It is simply easier to vote. Less restrictive provisions are particularly likely to increase the participation of persons with limited education and limited interest in politics.[8]

The evidence is plain that legal bars to participation no longer are an important explanation for nonvoting. Yet nonvoting persists at a high level, and in fact is growing. A partial explanation is that the number of potential voters has increased as a result of lowering the voting age to 18 and of enfranchising blacks through legislation and court decisions. Since neither group has an impressive rate of turnout, the overall level of participation suffers. Even so, one study has shown that no more than one-fourth of the loss in turnout between 1968 and 1972 could have occurred as a result of the enfranchisement of young voters.[9] And further complicating the explanation for nonvoting is the fact that turnout rates have apparently declined for *all* major demographic groups. Fewer white, well-

TABLE 14.   The Decline in Voting, Presidential Elections, 1964–1976

Group	Percentage of Persons Reporting That They Voted			
	1964	1968	1972	1976
Nation	69.3	67.8	63.0	59.2
Men	71.9	69.8	64.1	59.6
Women	67.0	66.0	62.0	58.8
White	70.7	69.1	64.5	60.9
Black	58.5	57.6	52.1	48.7
Spanish origin	*	*	37.4	31.8
18–20 years of age	39.2	33.3	48.3	38.0
21–24	51.3	51.1	50.7	45.6
25–34	64.7	62.5	59.7	55.4
35–44	72.8	70.8	66.3	63.3
45–64	75.9	74.9	70.8	68.7
65 and over	66.3	65.8	63.5	62.2
Metropolitan	70.8	68.0	64.3	59.2
Nonmetropolitan	66.5	67.3	59.4	59.1
North and West	74.6	71.0	66.4	61.2
South	56.7	60.1	55.4	54.9
8 years of school or less	59.0	54.5	47.4	44.1
9–11 years	65.4	61.3	52.0	47.2
12 years	76.1	72.5	65.4	59.4
More than 12	84.8	81.2	78.8	73.5
Employed	73.0	71.1	66.0	62.0
Unemployed	58.0	52.1	49.9	43.7
Not in labor force	64.6	63.2	59.3	56.5

Source of data: U.S. Bureau of the Census, *Statistical Abstract of the United States*, various eds. (Washington, D.C.: U.S. Government Printing Office, 1965–1977). *Actual* turnout is, of course, lower than *reported* turnout. For elections prior to 1972, voting participation for persons 18–20 was confined to four states: Georgia and Kentucky (18 and over), Alaska (19 and over), and Hawaii (20 and over).

* Not available.

educated, and older voters are voting today than in the past. (See Table 14.)

Surveys show that the vast majority of the public believes that citizens should vote. In 1976, for example, nine out of ten persons *disagreed* with the statement, "So many other people vote in the national elections that it doesn't matter much to me whether I vote or not."[10] The reality of voting obviously does not match well with that statistic: what people profess and what they do are two different things.

Some portion of the explanation for nonvoting undoubtedly lies in the public's attitudes toward politics. It is likely, for example, that participation has declined because a growing number of citizens care less which party or which candidate wins, because they believe that their votes will not make much difference, because they believe that public officials do not care what voters think, or because they think that politicians cannot be trusted.[11] Indifference and cynicism, mixed with a generalized distrust of government, may thus take a toll on participation. For many citizens, it seems likely, "voting simply isn't worth the effort."[12]

THE REGULATION OF VOTING

The phrasing of the U.S. Constitution makes it clear that control over suffrage was a matter to be left to the states. The basic reference to suffrage in the Constitution appears in Article I, Section 2, which provides that for elections to the House of Representatives ". . . the electors [that is, voters] in each state shall have the qualifications requisite for electors of the most numerous branch of the state legislature." As a result of this settlement, until recently the major national intrusions involving suffrage came in the form of constitutional amendments. The Fifteenth Amendment (1870) forbade the states to deny citizens the right to vote on the grounds of race, and the Nineteenth Amendment (1920) provided that states could not deny citizens the ballot on account of sex. More recently, the Twenty-fourth Amendment (1964) outlawed poll taxes, while the Twenty-sixth Amendment (1971) lowered the voting age in all elections to 18.

In the last two decades, the tradition of state control over suffrage has been significantly challenged by Congress through the passage of a series of civil rights acts (1957, 1960, 1964, and 1965). The acts of 1957 and 1960 were designed primarily to prevent discrimination against blacks seeking to register to vote. Individuals who were denied the right to register by local registrars could seek relief from the federal government through the Attorney General and the federal court system. Where discriminatory practices affecting registration were found to exist, the court was empowered to appoint federal voting referees to enroll black voters. Although the overall impact of these early acts on black voting was marginal, due largely to the cumbersome procedural requirements involved in jury trials and in establishing patterns of discrimination, they were important for establishing the power of the federal government, through a legislative enactment, to intervene in state election systems.

Of much greater substantive significance have been the Civil Rights Act of 1964 and the Voting Rights Act of 1965. In its provisions concerning voting, the 1964 Act made a sixth-grade education presumptive evidence of literacy and required that all literacy tests be administered in writing. In addition, registrars were required to administer registration procedures fairly and were forbidden to reject registration applications because of immaterial errors on registration forms.

A year later, with the support of strong majorities of both parties, Congress passed the Voting Rights Act of 1965, undoubtedly the most important civil rights act in American history. Under its terms, literacy tests or other voter qualification devices used for discriminatory purposes were suspended in any state or county in which less than 50 percent of the voting age residents were registered to vote in November 1964 or did not vote in the 1964 presidential election. Augmenting the federal government's power to supervise elections, the act authorized the appointment of federal voting examiners with the authority to register persons who have been unable to register even though they meet state requirements for voting. Finally, the act provided that if a state or local governmental unit decides to change its voting regulations, the U.S. Attorney General or the U.S. District Court for the District of Columbia must first certify that the new rules will not serve the purposes of racial discrimination. In 1975, this act was extended for another seven years, with its coverage expanded to include "language minorities" (including Spanish-speaking populations, American Indians, Alaskan natives, and Asian-Americans). The extension also placed a permanent ban on voter qualifying tests.

In its most important respects, the regulation of voting is today as much a matter of federal law as it is of state law. Had it not been for the civil rights movement in the 1950s and 1960s, it is doubtful that such fundamental changes would have occurred in the regulation of suffrage. What has been the impact of the new role of the national government in protecting the right to vote? In the case of black political participation, the results have been dramatic, as Table 15 shows. In 1960, only 29 percent of the blacks of voting age were registered to vote in the 11 states of the South. By 1976, the number had grown to 63 percent, almost as large a proportion as that for white voters. In Mississippi, there were nearly 12 times as many blacks registered to vote in 1976 as there had been in 1960. The vast majority of these new voters in Mississippi and elsewhere were enrolled following the passage of the Voting Rights Act of 1965.

Under the aegis of Congress and the President, and buttressed in the law courts, widespread black political participation is now a reality in southern politics. To be sure, registration and voting will not solve all the problems of the black citizen. But they do afford him substantially greater leverage on the political system. It is surely not happenstance that prominent white politicians throughout the South have abandoned race-baiting campaign ploys and, indeed, now pay much more attention to the interests and aspirations of their black constituents. Nor is it an accident that

TABLE 15. Percentage of Voting-Age Population Registered to Vote in 11 Southern States, by Race, 1960 and 1976

State	1960		1976	
	White	Black	White	Black
Alabama	63.6	13.7	79.3	58.4
Arkansas	60.9	38.0	62.6	94.0
Florida	69.3	39.4	61.3	61.1
Georgia	56.8	29.3	65.9	74.8
Louisiana	76.9	31.1	78.4	63.0
Mississippi	63.9	5.2	80.0	60.7
North Carolina	92.1	39.1	69.2	54.8
South Carolina	57.1	13.7	58.4	56.5
Tennessee	73.0	59.1	73.7	66.4
Texas	42.5	35.5	69.1	65.0
Virginia	46.1	23.1	61.6	54.7
Total	61.1	29.1	67.9	63.1

Source of data: U.S. Bureau of the Census, *Statistical Abstract of the United States*, 98th ed. (Washington, D.C.: U.S. Government Printing Office, 1977), p. 507.

the number of black elected officials has increased dramatically in recent years, especially in the South.[13] The southern state electorates of today are vastly different from those of the 1950s. It seems inevitable that whatever the future shape of southern politics, black voters and black politicians will play a more important role in political decision-making than at any time since the Reconstruction Era.[14]

FORMS OF POLITICAL PARTICIPATION

The act of voting is an appropriate point of departure for exploring the political involvement of American citizens, but it is not the only form of participation. Table 16, drawn from a comprehensive survey of political participation in America by Sidney Verba and Norman H. Nie, shows the range and dimensions of citizen activities in politics. Several findings should be emphasized. Perhaps of most importance, the only political activity in which a majority of American citizens participates is voting in presidential elections. Voting regularly in local elections follows as a rather distant second.[15] The survey discloses that as political activity requires more time, initiative, and involvement on the part of the citizen—working to solve a community problem, attempting to persuade others how to vote, working for a party or candidate, contributing to political campaigns —participation levels drop even lower.

The impression most sharply conveyed by the data as a whole is that a relatively small group of citizens performs most of the political activities

TABLE 16.   A Profile of the Political Activity of American Citizens

Form of Activity	Percent of Citizens
Report regularly voting in presidential elections	72
Report always voting in local elections	47
Acting in at least one organization involved in community problems	32
Have worked with others in trying to solve some community problems	30
Have attempted to persuade others to vote as they were	28
Have ever actively worked for a party or candidates during an election	26
Have ever contacted a local government official about some issue or problem	20
Have attended at least one political meeting or rally in last three years	19
Have ever contacted a state or national government official about some issue or problem	18
Have ever formed a group or organization to attempt to solve some local community problem	14
Have ever given money to a party or candidate during an election campaign	13
Presently a member of a political club or organization	8

Source: Sidney Verba and Norman H. Nie, *Participation in America: Political Democracy and Social Equality* (New York: Harper & Row, 1972), p. 31.

of the nation.[16] There is obviously much more than a germ of truth to this. Yet, to some extent, the data underrepresent the political activity of citizens, since those citizens who perform one political act are not necessarily the same as those who perform another act. In fact, the authors indicate that, excluding voting from the analysis, less than a third of their sample reported engaging in *no* political activities.[17] Even so, this is a fairly large lump of the citizenry.

Cumulative Involvement in Politics

The evidence from a number of studies of political participation is that people do not participate randomly in politics. Rather, there is a hierarchy of political involvement, as suggested in Figure 10, drawn from a study by Lester W. Milbrath.[18] Individuals who are actively involved in politics engage in a wide variety of political acts. A notable characteristic of their participation is that it tends to be cumulative. The active members of a political party, for example, are likely to be found soliciting political funds, contributing time and money to campaigns, attending meetings, and so on. Individuals who are minimally involved in politics typically engage

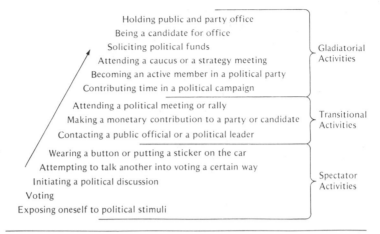

Figure 10.
HIERARCHY OF POLITICAL INVOLVEMENT
Source: Lester W. Milbrath, *Political Participation* (Chicago: Rand McNally, 1965), p. 18.

only in such limited activities as those grouped near the base of the hierarchy. At the very bottom are those persons who stand on the outskirts of the political world, scarcely, if at all, aware of the political forces that play upon them or of the opportunities open to them to use their resources (including the vote) to gain political objectives.

Some portion of the explanation for the passivity of American citizens may lie with the parties themselves. There is little evidence that the parties are active in clearing the road for popular participation. One survey has shown that only a small proportion of citizens are contacted (either called upon personally or telephoned) by party workers in an effort to get them to vote for the candidates of their party. Immediately prior to the 1968 presidential election, for example, only 8 percent of a national sample reported that they had been contacted by Democratic party workers, and only 12 percent were contacted by Republican workers. The individuals most likely to come into contact with the electioneering activities of the parties are those with high socioeconomic status—in particular, those with a college education, a professional or business background, and a high income.[19] For most Americans, the party organization, *qua* organization, is all but invisible. The passivity of the ordinary citizen is almost matched by the passivity of the party organizations.

The Active and Passive Citizenry

A number of social, demographic, and political variables are related to the act of voting. Table 17 provides a profile of those citizens who are more likely to turn out at elections and those who are less likely to turn out.

Some of these factors, it will be seen, are closely related—for example, high income, high occupational status, and college education. Nevertheless, it should be pointed out that the high rate of participation by citizens of higher socioeconomic status is not simply a function of status. Rather, the explanation lies in the civic orientations that are linked to upper-class status and environment. Upper-status citizens, for example, are more likely than citizens of lower status to belong to organizations and to participate in their activities, more likely to possess the resources and skills to be effective in politics, and more likely to be attentive to political problems and to feel efficacious in dealing with them.[20]

How much the factors that influence participation at the individual level can account for the differences among the states in voter turnout is not altogether clear.[21] What is clear is that of all the sections of the country, the South not only ranks lowest in turnout but also lowest in terms of family income, levels of education, and other measures of economic well-being. In addition, the legal structures (for example, election laws) in southern states typically are less encouraging toward voting than those of northern states. To the extent that participation is influenced by these variables, it is reasonable to expect that the level of participation in southern states will increase as their sociodemographic characteristics change (for example, an improved economic position) or as their legal structures become more facilitative.[22]

TABLE 17.   A Profile of the More Active and Less Active Citizenry*

More Likely to Vote	Less Likely to Vote
High income	Low income
High occupational status	Low occupational status
College education	Grade school education
Male	Female
Middle-aged	Young or old
Urban resident	Rural resident[†]
Metropolitan area resident	Small town resident
White	Black
Northern state resident	Southern state resident
Resident in competitive party environment	Resident in noncompetitive party environment
Union member	Nonunion labor
Homeowner	Renter
Jews and Catholics	Protestants

*These findings result from a large number of studies of the American electorate. For a summary and analysis of this literature, see Lester W. Milbrath, *Political Participation* (Chicago: Rand McNally, 1965).

†There is conflicting evidence on the voting participation of rural and urban residents. A study of Illinois voters finds that, contrary to the usual pattern, turnout is much higher in rural areas than in urban areas—despite the fact that rural voters rank lower in education, income, and socioeconomic status. See Alan D. Monroe, "Urbanism and Voter Turnout: A Note on Some Unexpected Findings," *American Journal of Political Science*, XXII (February 1977), pp. 77-78.

For all their interest, the distinctions drawn in Table 17 cannot be taken at face value. In the first place, the differences between voters and nonvoters are less apparent today than in the past. There is not much difference now between the participation rates of men and women or between rural and urban dwellers. Turnout in the South is on the rise while in the North it has been decreasing. A noticeable decline in voting by middle-aged persons has occurred.[23] What stands out most clearly is that participation has declined along a broad demographic front.

The lower turnout of Protestants is also deceptive. It is undoubtedly due in part to the lower levels of participation of southern and of rural voters, who happen to be largely Protestants.

Finally, it should be stressed that the variables are not of equal importance. The best social indicators of voting participation are those that reflect socioeconomic status: education, income, and occupation. And of these, clearly the most important is education.[24] The close relationship between education and turnout is shown in Figure 11.

Citizens who show enthusiasm for voting and who participate regularly in elections can be distinguished by their psychological makeup as well as by their social and economic backgrounds. The prospect that a person will vote is heavily influenced by the intensity of his partisan preference: the more substantial his commitment to a party, the stronger the probability that he will vote. The person who has a strong partisan preference and who perceives the election as likely to be close is virtually certain to vote.

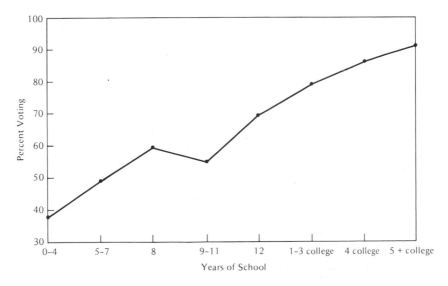

Figure 11.
EDUCATION AND PARTICIPATION IN THE 1972 PRESIDENTIAL ELECTION
Source: Adapted from data in Raymond E. Wolfinger and Steven J. Rosenstone, "Who Votes?" a paper delivered at the Annual Meeting of the American Political Science Association, Washington, D.C., September 1–4, 1977, p. 13.

TABLE 18.   Relation of Sense of Political Efficacy to Voting Turnout, 1976

Sense of Political Efficacy	Voted	Did Not Vote
Low*	62.1%	37.9%
High	79.8	20.2

Source of data: *Presidential Election Series*, Center for Political Studies, University of Michigan. *Respondents classified as "low" in sense of political efficacy *agreed* with this statement: "People like me don't have any say about what the government does." Those persons with a "high" sense of political efficacy *disagreed* with it. Number of cases: low—982, high—1,348.

The voter can also be distinguished by other indices of psychological involvement in political affairs. Survey research data show him to be more interested in campaigns and more concerned with election outcomes. He is also more likely than the nonvoter to possess a strong sense of political efficacy—that is, a disposition to see his own participation in politics as important and effective. (See Table 18.) Finally, in contrast to the nonvoter, the voter is more likely to accept the norm that voting is a civic obligation. In sum, the evidence suggests that psychological involvement —marked by interest in elections, concern over their outcome, a sense of political efficacy, and a sense of citizen duty—increases the probability that a person will pay the costs in time and energy that voting requires.

PARTY IDENTIFICATION IN THE ELECTORATE

Figure 12, showing the distribution of party identification in the electorate over a 38-year period, is an interesting study in stability and change. Over most of this period, the proportion of individuals identifying themselves as Democrats has been remarkably consistent. In the typical survey, between 42 and 48 percent of the respondents have identified themselves as Democrats, with the remainder (at least until 1971) about evenly divided between Republicans and independents. At various intervals during the 1960s and 1970s, Democratic identifiers outnumbered Republican identifiers by a margin of two to one.

Of perhaps greater interest are the changes that have occurred in party identification. Not since 1960 have as many as 30 percent of the voters classified themselves as Republicans. In 1975, only 22 percent of the electorate identified itself as Republican, the smallest percentage since the first surveys were taken in 1940. The percentage stood at 24 in 1978. Compounding the party's problems, among younger voters (ages 18–29) only 15 percent classified themselves as Republicans in 1978—a percentage so low as to raise genuine doubts concerning the future of the party.[25]

The other noteworthy change in affiliation is the marked growth in the number of individuals who perceive themselves as independents. In 1940,

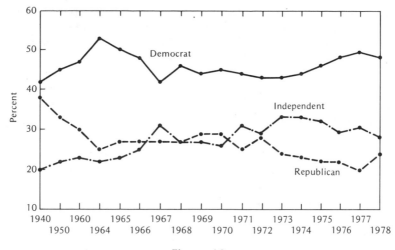

Figure 12.
THE DISTRIBUTION OF PARTY IDENTIFICATION IN THE ELECTORATE, 1940–1978
Source: *The Gallup Opinion Index.*

only one out of every five persons was classified as an independent; currently, the proportion is nearly one out of three. Increasingly, these independents have been at the decisive center of American elections, holding the balance of power between the major parties. This large bloc of voters is not only a prime target of the parties but also volatile in its behavior. Independents voted strongly Democratic in the 1940s, strongly Republican in the 1950s, and alternated between the parties in the 1960s. In 1972, they voted about two to one for Richard M. Nixon, the Republican candidate.[26] In 1976, they favored Gerald R. Ford over Jimmy Carter by a margin of 55 to 45 percent.[27] In all elections over this period except 1960 and 1976, a majority of the independents supported the winning presidential candidate, always by a margin in excess of his national average.

The Significance of Party Identification

When the distribution of underlying loyalties in the electorate is understood, there is less mystery as to the Democratic party's successes in national elections in recent decades. The Democratic party launches each campaign with about two out of every three partisans affiliated in one degree or another with its candidates. If it can assemble the support of most of those who identify themselves as Democrats and make a reasonable showing among independents, it is certain to win. By contrast, the task of the Republican party is much more formidable. Not only must it retain and mobilize its own partisans, but it must also carry a major share of the independents and attract a significant number of Democratic partisans as well. Republican prospects would be thin at best were it not for the fact that the turnout rate of Democratic partisans is much lower than that of Republicans.[28] The effect of this lower level of participation, one study suggests, is to reduce the normal Democratic proportion of the two-party popular vote to about 53 or 54 percent.[29]

The distribution of party allegiance in the electorate places the Republican party at a substantial disadvantage. It can win national elections only if it offers candidates or issues of sufficient appeal to offset the normal Democratic majority. As recent experience shows, however, this has not been especially difficult to achieve. Consider the following examples of Republican *presidential* success despite its minority following in the electorate. The 1952 Republican victory appears to have resulted from the convergence of three factors: disenchantment with the Truman Administration, the personal magnetism of Eisenhower, and widespread public frustration over the Korean war. Four years later, the Republican majority was due principally to candidate appeal—to the public's high regard for President Eisenhower as a person.[30] In the 1956 election, Eisenhower lost the votes of only a small fraction of Republican identifiers and received the support of about three out of four independents and about one out of four Democrats.[31] Despite the exceptional appeal of Eisenhower, the underlying support for the Democratic party was sufficient to permit it to capture both houses of Congress.

"Short term" forces again were of critical importance in the victory of Richard M. Nixon in the 1968 presidential election. Although the underlying distribution of party loyalties remained about the same as in 1964, a "sense of cumulative grievance" with the Johnson Administration led many Democrats to abandon their party. The disillusionment of voters over the administration's handling of the Vietnam war, the racial crisis, and the "law and order" issue was so great that a full 30 percent of all white voters (both Democrats and Republicans) who supported Lyndon Johnson in 1964 switched to Richard Nixon or George Wallace in 1968 (with Nixon the beneficiary by a four-to-one ratio). Very probably the polarization of the races has never been greater than in 1968, when nearly 90 percent of the black voters voted for the Democratic nominee, Hubert Humphrey, as contrasted with less than 35 percent of the white voters. Despite the substantial shift of Democratic identifiers to Nixon or Wallace in the presidential race, there was little change at other levels of government. The Republican party gained only four seats in the U.S. House of Representatives and only five seats in the Senate. At the state legislative level the Democratic proportion of seats declined hardly at all—from 57.7 percent of the seats to 57.5 percent. Democratic dominance in the electorate thus remained firm at all but the presidential level.[32]

The 1972 presidential election is of equal interest in terms of the significance of "short term" forces. Even though Democratic identifiers greatly outnumbered Republican identifiers (43 percent to 28 percent at the time of the election), the Republican candidate, Richard M. Nixon, defeated the Democratic candidate, George McGovern, by more than 17 million votes.

Although McGovern was not a personally appealing candidate, a more important reason for his extraordinary defeat was that numerous traditionally Democratic voters perceived his positions on major policy issues —for example, the Vietnam war, amnesty, military spending, urban unrest, government aid to minorities, abortion—as far to the left of the mainstream of their party. "Above all else," one study suggests, "the outcome of the election was the result of the ideological polarization within the Democratic ranks that pitted the left wing Democrats against those on the right."[33]

There is no doubt that there have been major changes in the behavior of the American electorate in recent years. Far more voters now profess to be independents than ever in the past. An independent stance is especially fashionable among younger voters—an important explanation, incidentally, for the overall growth in the proportion of independents. Allegiance to the Republican party has declined to an all-time low. Ticket-splitting has become increasingly common, with the result, among other things, that it has become more difficult for one party to win a range of offices in the same election. (See the evidence of Table 19.)

Figure 13 presents a closer look at the phenomenon of ticket-splitting. In the 1976 presidential election, more than half of all voters split their tickets. As would be expected, self-styled independents led all other groups in this practice. More instructive are the data on split- and straight-ticket voting arrayed in terms of race, education, and age. Sixty percent of all white voters split their tickets as compared with only 24 percent of nonwhite voters. The educational level of voters also affects their willing-

TABLE 19. Split Party Victories in States Electing Governor and U.S. Senator at Same Time, 1950–1954, 1970–1978

Year	Number of States Electing Both Governor and Senator at Same Time	Number of States Electing Governor and Senator of Different Parties	Percentage of Split Victories
1950	19	3	16
1952	20	6	30
1954	25	5	20
1970	23	11	48
1972	12	6	50
1974	26	11	42
1976	10	3	30
1978	24	10	42

Source: Data drawn from Richard M. Scammon (ed.), *America Votes 1* (New York: Macmillan, 1956); and various issues of the *Congressional Quarterly Almanac* and the *Congressional Quarterly Weekly Report*.

ness to split their votes between the parties. College-educated voters were twice as likely as those with a grade-school education to split their tickets. An especially weak attachment to party was shown by voters under the age of 30; only about one-quarter voted straight tickets. Interestingly, the erosion of party loyalty also appears in the behavior of older voters; there were as many ticket splitters in 1976 in the "50 and over" age group as there were straight-ticket voters.

In three respects, party identification is less important than previously. First, fewer individuals now choose to identify with a party. As recently as 1964, 78 percent of all voters classified themselves as either Democrats or Republicans. By 1978, only 72 percent of all voters indicated a partisan attachment. Second, the proportion of *strong* party identifiers has declined in each party. And third, party regularity in voting has declined even among partisans. The defection rate (proportion voting for the opposite party) among *strong* partisans in each party was twice as great in national elections between 1962 and 1972 as it was in national elections between 1952 and 1960. Even in 1976, when party identification regained significance, 8.4 percent of strong Democrats and 3.2 percent of strong Republicans voted for the opposing party's presidential candidate.[34]

Although party identification is clearly less significant than earlier in explaining voter decisions, especially in presidential elections, it is never-

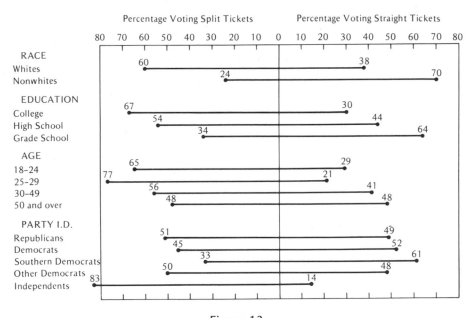

Figure 13.
SPLIT- AND STRAIGHT-TICKET VOTERS IN 1976 PRESIDENTIAL ELECTION*
*Source of data: *The Gallup Poll: Public Opinion, 1976–1977* (Wilmington, Del.: Scholarly Resources, 1978), pp. 922–923. The percentages do not total to 100 because a few voters are reported as "Don't Know."

theless important in other respects. First, party identification continues to be the best single explanation for the vote decision on candidates for offices less visible than the presidency. The persistent capacity of the Democratic party to win congressional elections, for example, is due principally to its dominant electoral advantage. Second, it remains true that strong partisan loyalty is closely associated with certain aspects of political involvement. Strong partisans are more likely than weak partisans or independents to be interested in political campaigns, to vote, and to express concern over election outcomes. Third, despite the overall decline in party identification, it continues to be salient for a great many voters, serving to orient them to candidates, issues, and political events and to simplify and order their electoral choices.

It seems clear that the growth in the number of independents will have a major impact upon the shape of American politics. Although it is still too early to forecast the demise of the parties, it is not too early to observe their enfeeblement. The immediate effect of the easing of the parties' grip on the electorate is that, in jurisdiction after jurisdiction, the value of party endorsements has declined. Perhaps taking their cues from the voters, candidates for office at all levels increasingly have staked out their independence from party, either ignoring the "machine" or decrying its existence. From the vantage point of the candidate, the politics of independence is "good" campaign politics—apparently, in most places, more likely to attract than to repel voters. About the most that can be said is that the next decade or two should tell us whether the heady independent politics of recent years was vogue or precursor.

Party Identification and Presidential Elections

Presidential elections can be classified in broad contour by examining the relationship between election outcomes and the pattern of party loyalties present in the electorate. Three basic types of elections can be identified: maintaining, deviating, and realigning.[35] A *maintaining* election is described as one in which the pattern of party attachments in the electorate fixes the outcome; the winning party owes its victory to the fact that more voters identify with it than with any other party. A *deviating* election, by contrast, is one in which existing party loyalties are temporarily displaced by short-term forces, enabling the minority (or second) party to win the presidency. In a *realigning* election the majority party in the electorate not only loses the election but also finds that many of its previous supporters have abandoned their loyalties and moved into the ranks of the other party. So fundamental is the transformation of partisan attachments that the second party becomes the majority party.

The most common form of presidential election is that in which the party dominant in the electorate wins the presidency—that is, a maintaining election. The dynamics of a maintaining election are furnished by the majority party; the minority party loses because it has been unable to develop either issues or candidates sufficiently attractive to upset the prevailing pattern of party affiliation. Most of the Republican victories during the last half of the nineteenth century and the first quarter of the twentieth century would be classified as maintaining elections. Recent elections of this type occurred in 1948, 1960, 1964, and 1976.[36] The 1976 election is of special interest. After a period of decline, party identification assumed much of its earlier importance, as a significantly larger proportion of party identifiers cast votes in accordance with their partisan predispositions. As Miller and Levitin observe, "the 1976 election was as much a party election as those elections from the 1950s or early 1960s in which party was acknowledged to be a major determinant of voters' decisions."[37]

It is not surprising that on occasion party loyalties fail to hold and that the party that occupies minority status in terms of electoral preferences wins the presidential office. Although the Republicans clearly held an electoral majority in the early twentieth century, Woodrow Wilson was twice elected president—in 1912, when the Republican party was split between Roosevelt and Taft, and in 1916, when his incumbency and the war issue were sufficient to give him a slight edge. More recent examples are the elections of 1952, 1956, 1968, and 1972. Both victories of Dwight D. Eisenhower in the 1950s were achieved in the face of heavy Democratic majorities in the electorate, as were Richard Nixon's victories in 1968 and 1972. Taken as a group, deviating elections tend to be characterized by dramatic issues, charismatic personalities, or sharp factional conflict within the majority party. Ticket splitting becomes the order of the day. Despite the appeal of the minority party's presidential candidate, his coattails have rarely been strong enough to give his party control of Congress. Hence, deviating elections are likely to result in one party's controlling the presidency and the other party's controlling the Congress.

The familiar terrain of American politics is sharply changed as a result of realigning elections. These elections are episodic and drastic. Large numbers of voters move out of the majority party and into the minority party, switching not only their vote at that election but also their long-term party allegiance. The most recent examples of realigning elections are those of 1896 and 1932. In the case of the former, a great many Democrats left their party following the financial panic of 1893, voted for McKinley in 1896, and became part of the strong Republican majority that dominated the country until 1932. An even sharper upheaval in the electorate occurred in the election of 1932, when the normal Republican majority collapsed as a result of the Great Depression. Franklin D. Roosevelt was swept into office, and millions of Republicans shifted, more or less permanently, into the ranks of the Democratic party. Realigning elections are the products of major crises, of disturbances so severe that not even traditional party loyalties can survive.

THE VOTING BEHAVIOR OF SOCIAL GROUPS

The role of social groups should not be overlooked in explaining the behavior of the American electorate. It has long been known that the voting behavior of individuals is influenced not only by their personal values and predilections (often derived from family party attachment) but also by their affiliations with social groups.[38] Table 20 indicates the relationships between social categories and voting behavior in seven presidential elections between 1952 and 1976.

The most notable conclusion to be drawn from the table is that each party enjoys within the electorate a set of relatively loyal followings. In election after election, the Democratic party has received strong, sometimes overwhelming, support from members of the working class, blacks, Catholics, Jews, voters with limited formal education, and younger voters. In contrast, the Republican party has ordinarily attracted a disproportionate number of voters with college educations and professional and business backgrounds. Moreover, white-collar workers, farmers, Protestants, and older voters have more often voted Republican than Democrat. On a regional basis, voters in the South and the East have leaned slightly to the Democratic presidential ticket, whereas voters in the Midwest and West have been somewhat more attracted to the Republican one.

Although voters with professional occupations typically are strongly aligned with the Republican party, there is at least one influential profession whose members are much more likely to vote Democratic than Republican. This group is the professoriate: the men and women who are members of college and university faculties. Table 21, drawn from a study by Everett Ladd and Seymour Martin Lipset, contrasts the presidential vote of academics with that of the electorate as a whole. Since 1952, professors have given the Democratic presidential candidate a proportion of their vote at least 10 percentage points higher than he obtained from the entire electorate; in the elections between 1964 and 1976, the Democratic vote cast by academics exceeded the party's national vote by between 13 and 17 points.

The evidence on the voting behavior of social groups must be treated warily. The tendency of Catholics to vote Democratic, for example, is undoubtedly due more to their historical association with Democratic politics (particularly in Eastern cities) and to their socioeconomic status than it is to any factors associated with their religion. One study has shown that when the "life situation" of Catholics—for example, their socioeconomic status, education, or place of residence—is controlled, the distinctiveness of their voting behavior virtually disappears; in other words, Catholic voters are not much more likely to vote Democratic than other voters who have similar social characteristics. By contrast, union members, blacks, and Jews vote significantly more Democratic than other indi-

TABLE 20. Vote by Groups in Presidential Elections, 1952–1976

	1952		1956		1960		1964		1968			1972		1976	
	Dem.	Rep.	Dem.	Rep.	Dem.	Rep.	Dem.	Rep.	Dem.	Rep.	Wallace	Dem.	Rep.	Dem.	Rep.
	%		%		%		%		%			%		%	
National	44.6	55.4	44.2	57.8	50.1	49.9	61.3	38.7	43.0	43.4	13.6	38	62	50	48
Men	47	53	45	55	52	48	60	40	41	43	16	37	63	53	45
Women	42	58	39	61	49	51	62	38	45	43	12	38	62	48	51
White	43	57	41	59	49	51	59	41	38	47	15	32	68	46	52
Nonwhite	79	21	61	39	68	32	94	6	85	12	3	87	13	85	15
College	34	66	31	69	39	61	52	48	37	54	9	37	63	42	55
High school	45	55	42	58	52	48	62	38	42	43	15	34	66	54	46
Grade school	52	48	50	50	55	45	66	34	52	33	15	49	51	58	41
Professional and business	36	64	32	68	42	58	54	46	34	56	10	31	69	42	56
White collar	40	60	37	63	48	52	57	43	41	47	12	36	64	50	48
Manual	55	45	50	50	60	40	71	29	50	35	15	43	57	58	41

Farmers	33	67	46	54	48	52	53	47	29	51	20	—	—	—	—
Under 30	51	49	43	57	54	46	64	36	47	38	15	48	52	53	45
30–49 years	47	53	45	55	54	46	63	37	44	41	15	33	67	48	49
50 years and older	39	61	39	61	46	54	59	41	41	47	12	36	64	52	48
Protestant	37	63	37	63	38	62	55	45	35	49	16	30	70	46	53
Catholic	56	44	51	49	78	22	76	24	59	33	8	48	52	57	42
Republicans	8	92	4	96	5	95	20	80	9	86	5	5	95	9	91
Democrats	77	23	85	15	84	16	87	13	74	12	14	67	33	82	18
Independents	35	65	30	70	43	57	56	44	31	44	25	31	69	38	57
East	45	55	40	60	53	47	68	32	50	43	7	42	58	51	47
Midwest	42	58	41	59	48	52	61	39	44	47	9	40	60	48	50
South	51	49	49	51	51	49	52	48	31	36	33	29	71	54	45
West	42	58	43	57	49	51	60	40	44	49	7	41	59	46	51
Members of labor union families	61	39	57	43	65	35	73	27	56	29	15	46	54	63	36

Source: *Gallup Opinion Index*, December 1976, pp. 16–17.

TABLE 21.   Presidential Vote of Faculty and General Public, 1948–1976 (all data presented as row percentages)

	Faculty			National Electorate		Percentage Margin Between Faculty Vote and National Vote	
	Demo-cratic	Third party	Repub-lican	Repub-lican	Demo-cratic	Repub-lican	Demo-cratic
1948*	50	11	39	45	50	− 6	0
1952*	54	2	44	55	44	−11	+10
1956*	60	2	38	57	42	−19	+18
1960†	—	—	—	—	—	—	—
1964‡	77	1	22	39	61	−17	+16
1968‡	58	4	39	43	43	− 4	+15
1972§	56	1	43	61	39	−18	+17
1976§§	63	4	33	48	50	−15	+13

Source: Everett Carll Ladd, Jr., and Seymour Martin Lipset, *Academics, Politics, and the 1972 Election* (Washington, D.C.: American Enterprise Institute for Public Policy Research, 1973), p. 70.

*Lawrence C. Howard, "The Academic and the Ballot," *School and Society*, 86 (November 22, 1958), pp. 415–419.

†No national survey.

‡Carnegie faculty survey, 1969; number of respondents—60,028.

§ Ladd–Lipset faculty survey, 1972; number of respondents—472.

§§ Ladd–Lipset faculty survey, 1976; number of respondents—4,383.

viduals who occupy essentially the same life situation. For individuals in these groups, it is clear that membership exerts an important influence on voting behavior—in this case, promoting the likelihood that they will vote Democratic.

In yet another respect the significance of group voting behavior is easy to misinterpret. The party strategist who leans too heavily on the data showing group performance may be tempted to play martial airs designed mainly to stir the followings ordinarily loyal to his party. There are, after all, a number of groups strongly identified with one or the other of the two parties. However, candidates and strategists seldom make the mistake of concentrating their appeals on narrow sectors of the electorate, no matter how attractive the possibilities may seem. The other great truth in Table 20 is that, despite the special orientations of certain groups and interests toward the parties, the parties as a whole are remarkably heterogeneous. Although manual workers are dominantly Democratic, they are not exclusively Democratic. Typically, in recent presidential elections, at least one-third of the manual workers have voted Republican. (In 1972, an unusual election, over 50 percent of the manual workers cast ballots for the Republican candidate.) A similar story can be told of those voters with professional and business backgrounds; although they are much more likely to vote Republican than Democratic, they cannot be taken for granted. In a typical presidential election, from one-third to two-fifths of this group will support the Democratic candidate.

And so it goes. Every social group has a mix of some sort. For this reason, more than any other, both parties set great store on fashioning campaigns that will have appeal for all social groups. The conventional wisdom that each party should appeal in at least some measure to all groups contributes to an untidy sort of politics, one in which the differences between the parties are often blurred. At the same time, however, it helps to keep conflict between the parties within tolerable limits, thereby contributing to the general stability of the political system.

NOTES

1. Among the studies that can be consulted on the meaning of modest rates of turnout are the following: E. E. Schattschneider, *The Semisovereign People* (New York: Holt, Rinehart and Winston, 1975), especially Chapter 6; Heinz Eulau, "The Politics of Happiness," *Antioch Review*, XVI (September 1956), pp. 259–264; Arthur T. Hadley, *The Empty Polling Booth* (Englewood Cliffs, N.J.: Prentice-Hall, 1978); William H. Flanigan and Nancy H. Zingale, *Political Behavior of the American Electorate* (Boston: Allyn and Bacon, 1979), especially Chapter 1; and, of a different order, Everett Carll Ladd, Jr., *Where Have All the Voters Gone?* (New York: Norton, 1978).

2. A few states, such as Arkansas and New Hampshire, elect their governors for two-year terms. Turnout figures for these states are shown for 1974, a nonpresidential year, since this better reflects popular involvement in state politics.

3. The explanation for this is well known: often the only significant choice among candidates available to southern voters is to be found in Democratic primaries. As the Republican party gains competitive strength in the South, participation in general elections is virtually certain to increase.

4. The white primary in southern states resulted from the exclusion of blacks from membership in the Democratic party, which was held to be a "private" organization. Since the real election at this time in most southern states occurred in the Democratic primaries, there was little opportunity for blacks to make their influence felt. After many years of litigation, the Supreme Court in 1944 held that the white primary was in violation of the Fifteenth Amendment. The Court's position in *Smith* v. *Allwright* was that the primary is an integral part of the election process and that political parties are engaged in a public rather than a private function in holding primary elections. After the white primary was held unconstitutional, southern states turned to the development of literacy and understanding tests, along with discriminatory registration systems, in order to bar black access to the polls.

5. From *The Semisovereign People* by E. E. Schattschneider. Copyright © 1975 by E. E. Schattschneider. Reprinted by permission of Holt, Rinehart and Winston, Inc., pp. 78–80.

6. Schattschneider, *The Semisovereign People*, p. 84.

7. Steven J. Rosenstone and Raymond E. Wolfinger, "The Effect of Registration Laws on Voter Turnout," *American Political Science Review*, LXXII (March 1978), especially pp. 25–30. The most facilitative laws on closing dates, apart from North Dakota which has no registration, are those of Idaho and Vermont. Voters in these states may register up to three days before the election. Maine provides for eight days and New Hampshire for nine.

8. Rosenstone and Wolfinger, "The Effect of Registration Laws on Voter Turnout," pp. 31–36.

9. Raymond E. Wolfinger and Steven J. Rosenstone, "Who Votes?" a paper delivered at the Annual Meeting of the American Political Science Association, Washington, D.C., September 1–4, 1977, p. 48.

10. Richard A. Brody, "The Puzzle of Political Participation in America," in Anthony King (ed.), *The New American Political System* (Washington, D.C.: American Enterprise Institute for Public Policy Research, 1978), p. 302.

11. But see a study which shows that persons who have low levels of trust in government vote at about the same level as those persons who have high trust in government. Jack Citrin, "Comment: The Political Relevance of Trust in Government," *American Political Science Review*, LXVIII (September 1974), pp. 973–988.

12. Brody, "The Puzzle of Political Participation in America," p. 306.

13. As of 1977, there were 4311 black elected officials in the United States as compared with only 1472 in 1970. Of the 4311, 2568 were from the South. Less than 6 percent were from western states. See U.S. Bureau of the Census, *Statistical Abstract of the United States*, 98th ed. (Washington, D.C.: U.S. Government Printing Office, 1977), p. 507.

14. The introduction of black voters on a large scale into southern electorates is not, of course, the only new force at work in that region. A surprising number of white southerners, especially among the younger generation, now regard themselves as independents rather than as partisans. There is reason to believe that many of those voters who declare themselves independents are dissatisfied with the party system, because neither party is sufficiently antiblack or segregationist in tone and policy. The lack of partisan moorings among a large sector of the electorate seems to promise that southern politics, at least in the short run, will remain turbulent and factionalized. See Paul Allen Beck, "Partisan Dealignment in the Postwar South," *American Political Science Review*, LXXI (June 1977), pp. 477–496.

15. Actual turnout is clearly somewhat lower than the voting percentages reported in Table 16. Survey respondents sometimes forget whether or not they voted or else exaggerate their participation.

16. The conventional wisdom concerning participation in *campaign activities* (such as attending campaign meetings or rallies, attempting to persuade others to vote a certain way, or displaying buttons or bumper stickers) holds that older voters participate more than younger ones and that conservatives participate more than liberals. During the turbulent years of the late 1960s and early 1970s, marked by the civil rights movement and protests against the Vietnam war, this pattern was sharply reversed. Young persons were considerably more active than their elders, while the most vigorous activists among both youthful and older groups were liberals. See Paul Allen Beck and M. Kent Jennings, "Political Periods and Political Participation," *American Political Science Review*, LXXIII (forthcoming, September 1979).

17. The findings of these paragraphs are drawn from Sidney Verba and Norman H. Nie, *Participation in America: Political Democracy and Social Equality* (New York: Harper & Row, 1972), pp. 25–43.

18. Lester W. Milbrath, *Political Participation* (Chicago: Rand McNally, 1965), pp. 17–21. The holding that political participation involves a hierarchy of political acts—under which the citizen who performs a difficult political act, such as forming an organization to solve a local community problem, is virtually certain to perform less demanding acts—can be overstated. See Verba and Nie, *Participation in America*, especially Chapters 2 and 3. Their general position is that "the citizenry is not divided simply into more or less active citizens. Rather there are many types of activists engaging in different acts, with different motives, and different consequences." Quotation on p. 45.

19. *Gallup Opinion Index, Report No. 41*, November 1968, pp. 2–3. A variety of studies has shown that personal contact by a party worker is one of the principal stimulants to political participation. It not only increases the probability that the person contacted will vote but also that he will undertake certain activities on behalf of the party. See Milbrath, *Political Participation*, pp. 99–101.

20. See Verba and Nie, *Participation in America*, pp. 133–137.

21. For recent, instructive analyses of voting participation in the states, see Jae-On Kim, John R. Petrocik, and Stephen N. Enokson, "Voter Turnout Among the American States: Systemic and Individual Components," *American Political Science Review*, LXIX (March 1975), pp. 124–131.

22. Milbrath, "Individuals and Government," pp. 43–44.

23. See Hadley, *The Empty Polling Booth*, especially Chapter 1.

24. See the impressive evidence of Wolfinger and Rosenstone, "Who Votes?" especially pp. 10–32.

25. *Gallup Opinion Index*, December 1977, p. 30.

26. Flanigan and Zingale, *Political Behavior of the American Electorate*, p. 62.

27. *Presidential Election Series*, Center for Political Studies, University of Michigan.

28. A disposition to participate in elections is related to high interest, information, and involvement. The Democratic vote regularly suffers from the fact that citizens who might be expected to vote Democratic—those in the lower socioeconomic strata—are often not sufficiently interested or involved in the election to turn out on election day.

29. Philip E. Converse, Angus Campbell, Warren E. Miller, and Donald E. Stokes, "Stability and Change in 1960: A Reinstating Election," *American Political Science Review*, LV (June 1961), p. 274.

30. Angus Campbell, Philip E. Converse, Warren E. Miller, and Donald E. Stokes, *The American Voter* (New York: Wiley, 1960), pp. 525–527.

31. Angus Campbell, "A Classification of the Presidential Elections," in Angus Campbell et al. (eds.), *Elections and the Political Order* (New York: Wiley, 1966), p. 72.

32. Philip E. Converse, Warren E. Miller, Jerrold G. Rusk, and Arthur G. Wolfe, "Continuity and Change in American Politics: Parties and Issues in the 1968 Election," *American Political Science Review*, LXIII (December 1969), pp. 1083–1105.

33. Arthur H. Miller, Warren E. Miller, Alden S. Raine, and Thad A. Brown, "A Majority Party in Disarray: Policy Polarization in the 1972 Election," *American Political Science Review*, LXX (September 1976), p. 778.

34. The average voting defection rate for strong Democrats was 4.3 percent in the 1950s and 8.0 percent in the 1960s; for strong Republicans, the percentages were 3.7 and 7.2, respectively. Warren E. Miller and Teresa E. Levitin, *Leadership & Change: Presidential Elections from 1952 to 1976* (Cambridge, Mass.: Winthrop, 1976), p. 37. The 1976 data are from the *Presidential Election Series*, Center for Political Studies, University of Michigan.

35. These categories are drawn from Campbell et al., *The American Voter*, pp. 531–538.

36. The elections of 1960 and 1976 can also be described as *reinstating* elections. In these cases, the normal Democratic majority was returned to power following the deviating elections of 1952 and 1956 (the Eisenhower victories) and 1968 and 1972 (the Nixon victories). As in maintaining elections, party identification comes to the fore in reinstating elections.

37. Miller and Levitin, *Leadership & Change*, p. 211.

38. Studies of electoral behavior that bear too heavily on the group as the unit of analysis may do some injustice to the individual voter, making him appear as an object to be managed by skillful propagandists or as the victim of social determinants (for example, his occupation, race, or education). Preoccupation with the gross characteristics of voters may lead the analyst to minimize the individual's awareness and concern over issues. V. O. Key, Jr., has argued that "... the electorate behaves about as rationally and responsibly as we should expect, given the clarity of the alternatives presented to it and the character of the information available to it." By and large, in Key's study, the American voter emerges as a rational and responsible person concerned over matters of public policy, governmental performance, and executive personality. See V. O. Key, Jr. (with Milton C. Cummings), *The Responsible Electorate* (New York: Vintage Books, 1966), p. 7.

Chapter 5

THE CONGRESSIONAL PARTY AND THE FORMATION OF PUBLIC POLICY

The tasks that confront the American major party are formidably ambitious. From one perspective, the party is a wide-ranging electoral agency organized in such a way as to make a credible bid for power. Here and there a party organization is so stunted and devitalized that it is seldom able to organize an authentic effort to win office. Elections may go by default to the dominant party as the second party struggles merely to stay in business. But throughout most of the country the parties compete on fairly even terms—if not for certain offices or in certain districts, at least for some offices or in the state at large. Presidential elections, of course, are vigorously contested virtually everywhere. As electoral organizations, the parties recruit candidates, organize campaigns, develop issues, and mobilize voters. The typical voter gets his best glimpse of the workings of party when he observes the "party-in-the-electorate" during political campaigns.

From another perspective, the party is a collection of officeholders who share, in some measure, common values and policy orientations. In the broadest sense, its mission is to take hold of government, to identify national problems and priorities, and to work for their settlement or achievement. In a narrower sense, the task of the "party-in-the-government" is to consolidate and fulfill promises made to the electorate during the campaign. How it is organized to do this and how it does it is the concern of this chapter. The focus centers on the party in Congress.

PARTY REPRESENTATION IN CONGRESS

The critical variable in the election of members of Congress is their party affiliation. As discussed in Chapter 2, a substantial majority of House and Senate seats ordinarily are not competitive, with the result that the same party wins election after election in the district or state. It is not uncommon, in fact, for House and Senate elections to go uncontested because one party is so thoroughly dominant. Throughout much of the country, Democratic districts produce Democratic legislators and Republican districts produce Republican legislators—ordinarily without much regard for the qualifications of the candidates or without the intrusion of startling issues or events. Who wins and who loses in American legislative elections is influenced more by the party affiliation of candidates than by any other factor.

Figures 14 and 15 depict the fortunes of the parties in congressional races over the last half century, from 1920 to 1978. Two central conclusions emerge. First, with few exceptions since 1932, the Democratic party has held comfortable majorities in Congress. The high point of Democratic dominance occurred in 1936 when over 75 percent of the members of both houses were Democrats. Second, the capacity of the Republican party to win presidential elections has not extended to Congress. The Republican party controlled the House by a slim margin from 1952 to 1954 and broke even in the Senate during the same period. During the remaining six years of the Eisenhower Administration, both houses of Congress were held by the Democrats, at times by lopsided margins.

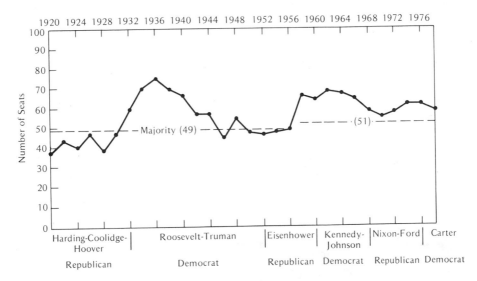

Figure 14.
DEMOCRATIC STRENGTH IN THE U.S. SENATE, 1920–1978

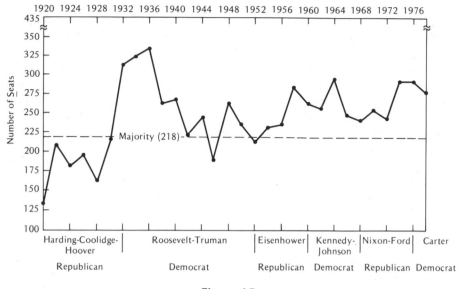

Figure 15.
DEMOCRATIC STRENGTH IN THE U.S. HOUSE OF REPRESENTATIVES, 1920–1978

Democratic control of Congress continued during the 1960s and 1970s. Given the prevailing pattern of party allegiance in the electorate (see Chapter 4), the prospects are strong that Republican presidents will be faced with Democratic majorities in Congress. As a result, their success in getting their legislative programs adopted is likely to depend on their ability, and that of the legislative leaders of their party, to forge and maintain effective biparty coalitions.

Party membership is not only the most important variable in determining who is elected to Congress but also the most important variable in governing members' behavior once they have taken office. The fact that party lines collapse on certain kinds of issues that come before Congress does not alter the general proposition that party affiliation is the principal determinant of legislative voting. This matter will be considered following an analysis of the character and quality of party organization in Congress.

PARTY ORGANIZATION IN CONGRESS

Party Conferences

In the broadest sense, the governing agency of each party in each house is the conference or caucus. Each member elected to Congress automatically becomes a member of his party's caucus. For a short period during the early twentieth century—notably during the Wilson Administration—the majority party caucus was extraordinarily powerful. Members were expected to be loyal to their party, and caucus decisions to bind the members occurred frequently on major legislation. After World War I, disillusionment with the caucus became manifest as members increasingly questioned the right of the caucus to bind them to a course of action. The power of the caucus declined sharply, and its functions became limited to the selection of party leaders such as the Speaker of the House, the floor leaders and whips, and the leadership of the policy committees.

In recent years, however, the House Democrats have significantly strengthened their caucus. In 1969, after years of somnolence, the Democratic caucus began to hold regular monthly meetings to examine proposals for reforming the House. In the early 1970s, the caucus made several modifications of the seniority system, the most important of which provided for secret ballots on nominees for committee chairmen. A Steering and Policy Committee was created by the caucus in 1973 to formulate legislative programs and to participate in the scheduling of legislation for floor consideration.

The power of the Democratic caucus was dramatically demonstrated at the opening of the Ninety-fourth Congress in 1975 when, among other things, the caucus voted to remove three committee chairmen from their positions, transferred the power to make committee assignments from the Democratic members of the Ways and Means Committee to the Steering and Policy Committee, and made a number of changes involving committee nominations and subcommittee procedures. Included in these changes was a provision to empower the Speaker, subject to caucus approval, to nominate the Democratic members of the powerful Rules Committee. In filling vacancies on this committee, the key test now appears to be the prospective member's allegiance to the Speaker.

The revitalization of the Democratic caucus has weakened the hold of the seniority system and strengthened the positions of party leaders, particularly the Speaker. But the central question involves the extent to which the caucus can influence the behavior of party members on major policy proposals. It is in this domain that caucus power collides with the nagging reality of all legislative politics: the individual member's electoral security, and thus his or her primary interest, lies in the constituency. For many members of the House, the attractions of a cohesive party are not nearly so great as the attractions of independence, with all the opportunities it affords the legislator to concentrate on constituency interests and problems. Moreover, party leaders as well as committee leaders usually take a dim view of caucus involvement in policy questions. "I don't like any of these [policy] matters coming from the caucus on a direct vote," Speaker Thomas P. O'Neill, Jr., has observed. Congressman Richard Bolling (D., Mo.) offers a similar evaluation: "I think [members] would have an awful time if they tried [to set party policy in the caucus]. It's better left to the committee system."[1] Hence, despite the growing influence of the caucus in matters involving committee assignments and House rules, it is difficult to foresee a return to anything resembling the earlier days when "King Caucus" reigned over the House and dominated its affairs.

The Speaker of the House

The most powerful party leader in Congress is the Speaker of the House.[2] In the early twentieth century, the Speaker's powers were virtually beyond limit, the House virtually his private domain. It is scarcely an exaggeration to say that legislation the Speaker favored was adopted and that legislation he opposed was lost. The despotic rule of Speaker "Uncle Joe" Cannon eventually proved his undoing. A coalition of Democrats and rebellious Republicans was formed in 1910 to challenge the leadership of Cannon. After a struggle of many months, they succeeded in instituting a number of rules changes to curb the Speaker's powers. He was removed from membership on the Rules Committee (of which he had been chairman), his power to appoint and remove members and chairmen of the standing committees was eliminated, and his power to recognize (or not to recognize) members was limited. Although the "revolution of 1910–1911" fundamentally altered the formal powers of the Speaker, it did not render the office impotent. Since then, a succession of Speakers—men disposed to negotiate rather than to command—has helped to rebuild the powers of the office. What a Speaker like Joseph G. Cannon (1903–1911) secured through autocratic rule, today's Speakers secure through persuasion and the astute exploitation of the bargaining advantages that are inherent in their positions.

Each Speaker leaves his imprint on the office. Changes in the times and in the character of politics also help to shape the speakership. Thomas P. ("Tip") O'Neill, elected Speaker in the Ninety-fifth Congress (1977–1978), comments:

> Old Sam Rayburn [Speaker for 17 years between 1940 and 1961] couldn't name 12 new members of Congress, and he was an institution that awed people. Only on the rarest of occasions could a Congressman get an appointment to see him. And when he called the Attorney General and said, "You be in my office at 3 in the afternoon," that Cabinet officer was there at 3 in the afternoon. Politics has changed. I have to deal in dialogue, in openness; if someone wants to see me, they see me. And of course they're highly independent now. You have to talk to people in the House, listen to them. The whole ethics question has changed. Years ago you'd think nothing of calling Internal Revenue and saying that this case has been kicking around for a couple of years, and it ought to be civil instead of criminal. You'd think nothing of calling a chairman of a committee and saying, "Put this project in, put this dam in." Well, you can't do that now.[3]

The Speaker's formal powers are wide-ranging, though not especially significant in themselves.[4] He is, of course, the presiding officer of the

House; in this capacity he announces the order of business, puts questions to a vote, refers bills to committees, rules on points of order, interprets the rules, recognizes members who desire the floor, and appoints members to select and conference committees. In addition, he has the right to vote and enter floor debate; ordinarily he exercises these opportunities only in the case of major, closely contested issues.

Although difficult to delineate with precision, the informal powers of the Speaker are far more impressive. As the foremost leader of his party in Congress, he is at the center of critical information and policy-making systems. No one is in a better position than the Speaker to obtain and disseminate information, to shape strategies, or to advance or frustrate the careers of members. Perhaps the principal "tangible preferment" the Speaker has at his disposal is the influence he can exert to secure favorable committee assignments for members of the majority party. Having the good will of the Speaker is important to members of his party anxious to move ahead in the House. The following analysis by Randall Ripley describes the structure of the Speaker's influence:

His personal traits influence his ability to deal with members of his party. The one constant element is the importance of his showing trust in and respect for individual members of his party. A smile or nod of the head from the Speaker can bolster a member's ego and lead him to seek further evidences of favor. Being out of favor hurts the individual's pride, and may be noticed by his colleagues. Most Speakers have had an instinct for knowing their loyal followers on legislative matters. Others have either kept records themselves or made frequent use of whip polls and official records to inform themselves about the relative loyalty of their members. Speakers have been able to convey critical information to members on a person-to-person basis, often with the help of the Parliamentarian. They have also encouraged their floor leaders and whip organizations to become collectors and purveyors of information on a larger scale. Particularly useful to a number of Speakers has been an informal gathering of intimates and friends of both parties to discuss the course of business in the House. Through such discussions, Speakers have been able to keep themselves informed of developments in the House and, at the same time, convey their desires to other members invited to attend.[5]

The Floor Leaders

In addition to the Speaker of the House, the key figures in the congressional party organizations are the House and Senate floor leaders, who are chosen by party caucuses in their respective chambers. The floor leaders serve as the principal spokesmen for party positions and interests and as mediaries in both intraparty and interparty negotiations. The floor leaders of the party that controls the presidency also serve as links between the president and his congressional party. Because the floor leader is obliged to play several roles at the same time—for example, as a representative of both the congressional party and the president—it is not surprising that role conflicts develop. Serving the interests of his congressional party colleagues or perhaps those of his constituents is anything but a guarantee that he will be serving presidential interests.

The floor leader has a potpourri of informal, middling powers. Their availability does not insure that he can, in fact, lead his colleagues or strongly shape the legislative program. By and large, his influence is based upon his willingness and talent to exploit these powers steadily and imaginatively in his relations with other members. He can, if he chooses: 1) influence the allocation of committee assignments (not only rewarding individual members but also shaping the ideological makeup of the committees); 2) help members to advance legislation of particular interest to them; 3) assist members in securing larger appropriations for their committees or subcommittees; 4) play a major role in debate; 5) intercede with the president or executive agencies on behalf of members (perhaps to assist their efforts to secure a federal project in their state or district); 6) make important information available to members; 7) help members to secure campaign money from a congressional campaign committee; 8) campaign on behalf of individual members; and 9) focus the attention of the communications media on the contributions of members. Much of the influence of the floor leader, like that of the Speaker, is derived from informal powers, in particular from opportunities afforded him to advance or protect the careers of party colleagues. In solving problems for them and in making their positions more secure, he increases the prospects of gaining their support on critical questions. By the same token, the floor leader can in some measure hamper the careers of those members who continually refuse to go along with him. At the center of the active floor leader's powers is the capacity to manipulate rewards and punishments.

An important function and a major source of power for the majority floor leader, particularly in the Senate, is that of controlling the scheduling of bill consideration on the floor. In the House, the Rules Committee dominates the process of controlling the agenda. However pedestrian the scheduling function may sound, it is a surprisingly important source of power. The majority leader who fails to keep his lines of communication clear, who misjudges the sentiments of members, who neglects to consolidate his majority by winning over undecided members or by propping up wavering members, or who picks the wrong time to call up a bill, can easily go down to defeat. Prospective majorities are much more tenuous and much more easily upset than might be supposed. Support can be lost rapidly as a result of poor communications, missed opportunities for negotiation and compromise, and bad timing. The effective leader builds his power base by tending to the shop, by ordering priorities, by having a sense of detail that overlooks nothing, by taking account of the demands placed upon members, by sensing the mood of congressional opinion (especially that of key members), and by exhibiting skill in splicing together the legislative elements necessary to fashion a majority.

The principal power of the floor leader is the power of persuasion. As a former Democratic leader of the Senate, Lyndon Johnson, once observed, " . . . the only real power available to the leader is the power of persuasion. There is no patronage; no power to discipline; no authority to fire Senators like a President can fire his members of Cabinet."[6] The current majority leader of the House, Jim Wright (D., Tex.) has described the leader's role in a similar vein: "The majority leader is a conciliator, a mediator, a peacemaker. Even when patching together a tenuous majority he must respect the right of honest dissent, conscious of the limits of his claims upon others."[7]

To be effective in persuasion, a leader must know the members well, know what they want and what they will settle for, and what concessions they can make and what concessions they cannot make, given their constituencies. The critical importance of such information requires the leader to develop a reliable communications network within his party. But more than that, he requires good lines of communication into the other party in order to pick up support here and there when elements of his own party appear likely to wander off the reservation. Other things being equal, members prefer to support their leader and the party position rather than the opposing forces. The task of the leader is to find reasons for them to do so and conditions under which they can.

The development of a legislative program requires the majority leader to work closely with the key leaders in his party, particularly the chairmen of the major committees. As Lyndon Johnson observed during his tenure as Senate majority leader, "You must understand why the committee took certain actions and why certain judgments were formed."[8] His successor, Mike Mansfield, observed: "I'm not the leader, really. They don't do what I tell them. I do what they tell me. . . . The brains are in the committees."[9] The effective leader works with the resources available—in essence, the power of persuasion. Relations between the leader and the committee chairmen are never characterized by a one-way flow of mandates. On the contrary, the leader must be acutely sensitive to the interests of the chairmen, adept at recognizing their political problems, and flexible in his negotiations with them. Bargaining is the key characteristic of the relationships between the majority leader and the committee chairmen.

Party management in Congress has become increasingly difficult in recent years. Several reasons help to explain this situation. In the first place, the adoption of "sunshine" rules in both houses has made Congress a much more "open" institution; for the most part, committee, subcommittee, and even party caucus meetings are now open to the public. Second, combined with the new visibility of congressional actions, the growing power of interest groups, particularly those organized around single issues (for example, abortion, gun control, tax relief, nuclear power), has made members more vulnerable to outside pressures and, at the same time, increasingly resistant to the influence of party leaders. Third, the weakening of the electoral parties has been accompanied by an extraordinary growth in candidate-centered campaigns; members who are elected to Congress largely on their own efforts have less reason to concern themselves with party objectives, less reason to defer to the wishes of party leaders. "Independence" and "free-wheeling" have become the *modus vivendi* of many members of Congress. Finally, internal changes have contributed to the further decentralization of congressional power. Subcommittees have grown both in number and in independence.[10] The influence of committee chairmen has declined while that of subcommittee chairmen has grown. In addition, both chambers now limit the number of committee and subcommittee chairmanships that a member may hold, the effect of which has been to spread leadership positions (and thus power) among more members. Singly and in combination, these changes have diminished the capacity of the parties to build majorities and to mobilize their members for concerted action.

A prominent New York member who served 50 years in the House (nearly 25 years as Chairman of the Judiciary Committee), Emanuel Celler, comments on the devolution of congressional power:

> When I was in Congress, we had strong chairmen. . . . They ruled the roost. . . . Then came along the so-called young Turks, insisting upon lessening the power of the chairmen. And you have all these youngsters clamoring for power and more power and more help, so that there's a tremendous proliferation of [staff] assistants to the subcommittees. And they are yammering and hollering for more and more power, which results in the combined efforts of Congress shouting and trying to make itself heard above the power of the president. . . . [11]

What has been said thus far suggests that there are several important constraints that shape the position of the floor leader. The leader is not free to fashion his role as he might like to see it. The limited range of powers available to him, his personality, his relationship to the president, and his skills in bargaining all affect in some measure the definition of his role. Moreover, no two leaders are likely to perceive the leader role in exactly the same light. In addition, the nature of the leader's position is strongly influenced by the nature of the legislative parties. The evidence is that the persistent cleavages present within both parties make it necessary for the leaders to occupy the role of middleman. The leader is a middleman in the sense that he is more or less steadily involved in negotiations with all major elements within the party, and also in terms of his voting record.[12] In the passage of much legislation the test is not so much the wisdom of the decision but its political feasibility. A leader identified with an extreme group within his party would find it difficult to work out the kinds of compromises necessary to put together a majority. The leader is first and foremost a broker. Candidates for leadership positions whose voting records place them on the ideological edges of their party are less likely to be elected than those whose voting records fall within the central range of party opinion.

The Whips

Another unit in the party structure of Congress is the whip organization. Party whips are selected in each house by the floor leaders or by other party agencies. A number of assistant whips are required in the House of Representatives because of the large size of the body. Working to enhance the efforts of the leadership, the whips carry on a number of important functions. They attempt to learn how members intend to vote on legislation, relay information from party leaders to individual members, work to insure that a large number of "friendly" members will be present at the time of voting, and attempt to win the support of those party members who are in opposition, or likely to be in opposition, to the leadership. The influence of the Speaker and the majority leader supplements the pressure of the whips. As described by the chief staff assistant to the majority whip, they apply "the heavy party loyalty shtick. Then it's more personalities than issues. There are some members who can only be gotten by the Speaker or the majority leader."[13]

The whips are also charged with discovering why members are opposed to certain legislation and how it could be changed to gain their support. The central importance of the whip organization is that it forms a communications link between the party leadership and rank-and-file members. The intelligence and leverage the whips supply is sometimes the difference between victory and defeat on a major issue. The relatively decentralized character of congressional party organization has made the whip function indispensable to all efforts to achieve party unity.[14] On some issues, of course, no amount of activity on the part of the leadership can bring recalcitrant members into the fold. If the outlook for a bill looks unpromising following a whip check of members' sentiments, the leadership will often postpone its floor consideration.

The Policy Committees

There have been few proposals for congressional reform that have received as much attention as those designed to strengthen the role of political parties in the legislative process. The Joint Committee on the Organization of Congress recommended in its 1946 report that policy committees be created for the purpose of formulating the basic policies of the two parties. Although this provision was later stricken from the reorganization bill, the Senate independently created such committees in

1947. The House Republicans established a policy committee in 1949, though it did not become fully active for another decade.[15] Rounding out the list, the rejuvenated House Democratic caucus voted to establish a policy committee in 1973.

The high promise of the policy committees as agencies for enhancing party responsibility for legislative programs has never been realized. Neither party leaders nor rank-and-file members have been agreed on the functions of the policy committees. There is not much exaggeration in the observation that the policy committees are "policy" committees in name only. The policy committees in the Senate " . . . have never been 'policy' bodies, in the sense of considering and investigating alternatives of public policy, and they have never put forth an overall congressional party program. The committees do not assume leadership in drawing up a general legislative program . . . and only rarely have the committees labeled their decisions as 'party policies.' "[16]

It is not surprising that the policy committees have been unable to function effectively as agencies for the development of overall party programs. An authoritative policy committee would constitute a major threat to the scattered and relatively independent centers of power within Congress. The seniority leaders who preside over the committee system would undoubtedly find their influence over legislation diminished if the policy committees were to assume a central role in defining party positions. Not only would the independence of the committee system be affected adversely, but many individual members would suffer an erosion of power. Had the policy committees functioned as planned, a major reshuffling of power in Congress would have resulted. To the men who hold the keys to congressional power, this is scarcely an appealing idea. However attractive the proposal for centralized committees empowered to speak for the parties in Congress, they are altogether unlikely to emerge so long as the parties themselves are decentralized and fragmented, composed of members who represent a wide variety of constituencies and ideological positions.

Although the lack of internal party agreement prevents the policy committees from functioning in a policy-shaping capacity, it does not render them useless. Both parties require forums for the discussion of issues and for the negotiation of compromises, and for these activities the policy committees are well designed. Moreover, the staffs of the committees have proved helpful for individual members seeking research assistance. Most important, the policy committees have served as a communications channel between the party leaders and their memberships. The policy committees are an ambitious attempt to come to terms with the persistent problem of party disunity. If generally they have failed in this respect, they have nonetheless succeeded in other respects. As clearinghouses for the exchange of party information and as agencies for the reconciliation of at least some intraparty differences, they have made useful contributions.

Informal Party Groups

In addition to the formal party units in Congress, there are several informal party organizations that meet more or less regularly to discuss legislation, strategy, and other questions of common interest. Among these organizations are the Democratic Study Group, the Chowder and Marching Club (Republican), the Acorns (Republican), the S.O.S. (Republican), and the Wednesday Club (Republican)—all House groups. The best-known, largest, and most effective of these organizations is the Democratic Study Group. Formed in 1959 by liberal Democrats as a counterbloc to the southern wing of the party, the DSG has grown steadily in numbers and in influence. In recent Congresses the DSG has had a membership of over 200, elected leaders, a whip system, a full-time staff, and a campaign unit to assist in fund-raising and campaign development. The distinguishing features of the DSG are its preoccupation with issues and its liberal bias.[17]

Factors Influencing the Success of Party Leaders

The cohesiveness of the parties in Congress can never be taken for granted. The independence of the committees and their chairmen, the rudimentary powers of elected leaders, the importance of constituency pressures, the influence of political interest groups, and the disposition of members to respond to parochial impulses—all, at one time or another, contribute to the fragmentation of power in Congress and to the erosion of party unity. The member who ignores leadership cues and requests or is oblivious to them, or who in fact builds a career as a party maverick, is far more common than might be supposed. There are few weapons in the leadership arsenal that can be used to bring refractory members into line.

Research on the Democratic party in the House of Representatives by Lewis Froman and Randall Ripley identifies a number of conditions under which leadership influence on legislative decisions will either be promoted or inhibited.[18] In the first place, leadership success is likely to be contingent upon a high degree of agreement among the leaders themselves. Ordinarily the Speaker, majority leader, and whip will be firm supporters of their president's legislative program; frequently, however, other key leaders, such as committee chairmen, will be allied with opponents. When unity among the leaders breaks down, prospects for success fall sharply. Second, leadership success in gathering the party together tends to be affected by the nature of the issue under consideration—specifically, whether it is procedural or substantive. On procedural issues (for example, election of the Speaker, adoption of rules, motions to adjourn), party cohesion is ordinarily much higher than on issues that involve substantive policy. Third, the efforts of party leaders are most likely to be successful on issues that do not have high visibility to the general public. In the usual pattern, conflicting pressures emerge when issues gain visibility, and the leaders must commit greater resources to keep their ranks intact.

In the fourth place, the visibility of the action to be taken will have bearing on the inclination of members to follow the leadership. Not all forms of voting, for example, are equally visible. Roll call votes on final passage of measures are highly visible—the member's "record" on a public question is firmly established at this point. Voting with the leadership at this stage may seem to the member to pose too great a risk. On the other hand, supporting the leadership in committee or on a key amendment is less risky because the actions are not as easily brought into public focus. Fifth, and perhaps most important, members are most likely to vote with their party when the issue at stake does not stir up opposition in their constituencies. Party leaders know full well that they cannot count on the support of members who feel that they are under the thumb of constituents on a particular issue—for example, southern members on certain questions relating to civil rights. Finally, support for the leadership is likely to be dependent upon the activity of the state delegations. Leadership victories are more likely to result when individual state delegations are not involved in bargaining with leaders over specific demands.

These conditions, then, comprise the background against which leadership efforts to mold their party as a unit take place. Party loyalty, it should be emphasized, is more than a veneer. By and large, members prefer to stay "regular," to go along with their party colleagues. But they will not queue up in support of their leaders if the conditions appear "wrong," if apparently there is more to be lost than gained by following the leadership. Members guard their careers by taking frequent soundings within their constituencies and among their colleagues and by making careful calculations as to the consequences that are likely to flow from their decisions.

NATIONAL PARTY AGENCIES AND THE CONGRESSIONAL PARTIES

In theory, the supreme governing body of the party between one national convention and the next is the national committee, which is composed of representatives from each of the states. In the best of all worlds, from the perspective of those who believe in party unity and responsibility, there would be close and continuing relationships between the national committee of each party and fellow party members in Congress. Out of such associations, presumably, would come coherent party policies and a heightened sense of responsibility among congressmen for developing a legislative program consistent with the promises of the party platform. In point of fact, however, the tone and mood that dominate relations between the national committees and the congressional parties are as likely to be characterized by suspicion as by cooperation. Congressional leaders in particular are little disposed to follow the cues that emanate from the national committees or, for that matter, from any other national party agency.

Not only do national party leaders have a minimal impact on congressional decision-making, but they are also largely excluded from the nominating process for congressional candidates. They seldom engage in negotiations with state and local party leaders on matters relating to congressional nominations. The reason for this is simply that state and local leaders, with considerable power in their own right, resent national interference in what is regarded as a state or local party function. Occasionally an intrepid president has sought to influence congressional nominations, as Franklin D. Roosevelt did in 1938. Disturbed by mounting opposition to his program in Congress, Roosevelt publicly endorsed the primary opponents of certain prominent anti-New Deal incumbent Democrats. As it turned out, nearly all of the lawmakers marked for defeat won easily, much to the chagrin of the president. Twelve years later President Harry S Truman met the same fate when he endorsed a candidate in the Democratic senatorial primary in Missouri; the state party organization rallied to the other side, and the president lost. Although a few presidential "purges" have succeeded, most attempts have failed. The lesson seems evident: congressional nominations are regarded as "local" matters, and the president who attempts to influence these nominations runs a good risk of suffering both public embarrassment and sharp congressional criticism.

The national party is concerned with the election of congressmen who are broadly sympathetic to its traditional policy orientations and its party platform. In counterpoise, local party organizations aim to guarantee their own survival as independent units. Occasional conflict between the two is predictable. The principal consequence of local control over congressional nominations is that all manner of men and women get elected to Congress, those who find it easy to accept national party goals and those who are almost wholly out of step with the national party. The failure of party unity in Congress is due as much as anything to the folkway that congressional nominations are local questions to be settled by local politicians and voters according to preferences they alone establish.

DO THE PARTIES DIFFER ON PUBLIC POLICIES?

Party affiliation is the cutting edge of congressional elections. Ordinarily there are few surprises on election day: Democratic candidates win where they are expected to win, and Republican candidates win where they are expected to win. The public at large may continue to believe that each election poses an opportunity for the "outs" to replace the "ins," but in fact this happens infrequently. The chief threat to an incumbent legislator is a landslide presidential vote for the other party, one so great that congressional candidates on the winning presidential ticket are lifted into office on the strength of the presidential candidate's coattails. Even landslide votes, however, do not disturb the great majority of congressional races.

If party affiliation largely determines which men and women go to Congress, does it also significantly influence their behavior once in office? The answer for most legislators—for majorities within each party—is yes. Party affiliation, we noted earlier, is the most important single variable in predicting how members will respond to questions that come before them. Indeed, the key fact to be known about any member is the party to which he belongs—it influences his choice of friends, his membership in groups, his relations with lobbies, his relations with other members and the leadership, and most important, his policy orientations. Party loyalty does not govern the behavior of members, but neither is it a factor taken lightly.

The proportion of roll call votes in Congress in which the parties are firmly opposed to each other is not particularly large. A study of selected congressional sessions between 1921 and 1967 shows that the number of "party votes" that occur in the House of Representatives has declined markedly over the years. Between 1921 and 1948, about 17 percent of the House roll call votes were "party votes"—votes in which 90 percent of the voting membership of one party opposed 90 percent of the voting membership of the other party. In the usual House sessions since 1950, party votes have numbered about 6 or 7 percent of the total. The "90 percent versus 90 percent" standard is, of course, an exceedingly rigorous test of party voting. If the standard is relaxed to "50 percent versus 50 percent" the proportion of party votes rises sharply. Typically, during the 1950s and 1960s, about one-half of the session roll call votes found party majorities arrayed against each other.[19]

A major explanation for the decline in party voting can be found in the behavior of the "wings" of each of the major parties. A study of voting patterns in the House of Representatives during the Eighty-sixth through the Ninety-first Congress finds not only a sharp decline in party voting but also a growing tendency for eastern Republicans to join forces with northern Democrats against an alliance of noneastern Republicans and southern Democrats. Throughout this period the majority elements of the two parties—northern Democrats and noneastern Republicans—steadily opposed each other on issues involving some degree of controversy. The increasing defection rate among the minority segments of each party— eastern Republicans and southern Democrats—seems likely to be the result of a growing responsiveness among these legislators to constituency preferences.[20]

Although party voting is less common today than in earlier periods, important issues are often at stake when party lines form. In general, Democrats have been much more likely than Republicans to support a low tariff, federal programs to assist agriculture, expanded health and welfare programs, legislation advantageous to labor and low-income groups, government regulation of business, and a larger role for the federal government.

The Parties and Liberal–Labor Legislation

The policy orientations of the parties in Congress are not markedly different from those they held during the New Deal–Fair Deal periods of the 1930s and 1940s. Figures 16 and 17 depict the positions of the parties (and the wings within them) on proposals of interest to the AFL–CIO in the first session of the Ninety-fifth Congress. A member voting in accordance with AFL–CIO positions would have supported proposals to: 1)

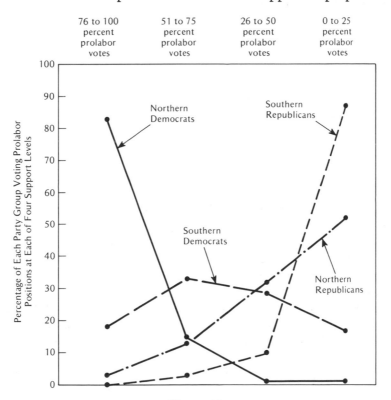

Figure 16.
SUPPORT FOR LABOR LEGISLATION BY PARTY AND SECTION, U.S. HOUSE OF REPRESENTATIVES, NINETY-FIFTH CONGRESS, FIRST SESSION
Source of data: *Congressional Quarterly Weekly Report,* April 15, 1978, pp. 914–915. Each member of the House is ranked in terms of the percentage of votes which he cast in accord with the positions of the AFL–CIO Committee on Political Education. The "South" is defined as the 11 states of the Confederacy plus Kentucky and Oklahoma.

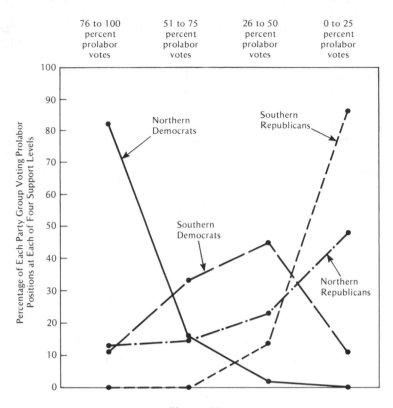

Figure 17.
SUPPORT FOR LABOR LEGISLATION BY PARTY AND SECTION, U.S. SENATE, NINETY-FIFTH
CONGRESS, FIRST SESSION
Source of data: *Congressional Quarterly Weekly Report,* April 15, 1978, p. 916. Each member of
the Senate is ranked in terms of the percentage of votes which he cast in accord with the positions
of the AFL–CIO Committee on Political Education. The "South" is defined as the 11 states of the
Confederacy plus Kentucky and Oklahoma.

provide greater protection for consumers; 2) raise the minimum wage; 3)
strengthen health and safety standards for mines; 4) give cargo preference
to American ships carrying oil; 5) halt the importation of Rhodesian
chrome; 6) increase assistance for low-income housing programs; 7) increase appropriations for community development programs; 8) continue
various water projects that the president had marked for elimination; and
9) provide for common-site picketing (which would permit a labor union
with a grievance against one contractor to picket all contractors on that
construction site). Similarly, a member would have opposed legislation to:
1) permit employers to pay young workers less than the minimum wage;
2) exempt small retail and service enterprises from minimum wage and
overtime requirements; 3) limit the availability of food stamps for striking
workers; 4) end federal price controls for natural gas; 5) reduce appropriations for public service job programs; 6) limit spending on the Clinch River

breeder reactor project; and 7) reduce appropriations for various health, education, elderly, and occupational safety programs.[21]

A glance at Figures 16 and 17 will reveal two broad characteristics of congressional voting on legislation of central interest to organized labor. First, it is plain that the parties are not cohesive units in voting on liberal–labor legislation. Second, notwithstanding serious intraparty splits, there are substantial differences between the parties. The two largest groups in each house—northern Democrats and northern Republicans—view liberal–labor legislation from vastly different perspectives. While only a few northern Republicans in each house (3 percent in the House and 13 percent in the Senate) are found at the highest support level—voting in agreement with AFL–CIO positions between 76 and 100 percent of the time—over 80 percent of the northern Democrats are at this level. Moreover, only a handful of northern Democrats are markedly out of step with labor objectives, voting less than half the time with the AFL–CIO. Interestingly, most of the northern Republicans who side most frequently with organized labor represent eastern states.

The most steadfast opponents of liberal–labor legislation are southern Republicans. Over 85 percent of the southern Republicans in each chamber are grouped at the lowest support level (0 to 25 percent). Many southern Democrats and northern Republicans similarly take a dim view of the objectives of organized labor. Nonetheless, it is worth noting that southern Democrats are more likely to support labor than are northern Republicans.

Figure 18 offers another way of looking at the policy orientations of the congressional parties. This figure shows the range of attitudes in the Senate in the Ninety-fifth Congress (first session) on issues deemed important by the liberal-oriented Americans for Democratic Action and the conservative-oriented Americans for Constitutional Action.[22] Each senator is located on the diagram according to the percentage of votes that he cast in agreement with the positions of each political interest group. Senators Edward M. Kennedy (D., Mass.), Gary Hart (D., Colo.), Dick Clark (D., Iowa), and Gaylord Nelson (D., Wis.) emerge as the most liberal members of the upper house. At the conservative pole, Barry Goldwater (R., Ariz.) and Jesse Helms (R., N.C.) scored 100 percent ACA and 0 percent ADA.

Figure 18 reinforces our earlier conclusions. Despite the party-in-disarray quality that appears in the Senate scattergram, it is nevertheless clear that significant differences separate the majorities of the two parties. A majority of the Republican senators are found on the right-hand side of the diagram, indicating their agreement with the ACA, while a majority of Democratic senators are lodged on the left-hand side, showing their support of the ADA. The "deviant" behavior of party members is largely confined to certain "wings" in each party. A strong majority of southern Democrats is clustered well over on the ACA side of the diagram; similarly, a group of Republicans from populous eastern and midwestern states

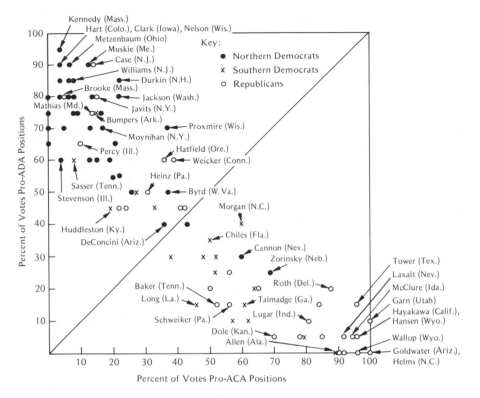

Figure 18.
SUPPORT OF POSITIONS HELD BY AMERICANS FOR DEMOCRATIC ACTION AND BY
AMERICANS FOR CONSTITUTIONAL ACTION BY EACH SENATOR, IN PERCENTAGES,
NINETY-FIFTH CONGRESS, FIRST SESSION
Source: Data are derived from the *Congressional Quarterly Weekly Report,* April 15, 1978, p. 916.

is shown to be more supportive of ADA than ACA positions. Viewed in
overall perspective, the Senate emerges as an institution more likely to
support liberal public policies than conservative ones.[23]

Biparty Coalitions

Of all the problems that confront the legislative party, none is more
persistent or difficult than that of maintaining party unity. There are
members who assiduously ignore the requests and entreaties of leaders,
others who cling tenaciously to constituency lines without pausing to consider the requirements of party, and still others who seek to tailor party
measures to the specifications of those parochial interests to which they
respond. The party is a repository for divergent claims and preferences.
Getting it to act as a collectivity is no mean feat.

The disruption of party lines leads to the formation of biparty coalitions. The most durable biparty coalition in the history of Congress has been the so-called conservative coalition—an informal league of southern Democrats and northern Republicans. Table 22 provides a statistical picture of the power held by the coalition in 18 congressional sessions since 1961. In recent years, the coalition has come to life on about one-fourth of the roll-call votes held during a session. More important, the coalition's successes often have been spectacular. In only two sessions over this period (1965 and 1966, the first two years of Lyndon Johnson's "Great Society") did the coalition win less than 50 percent of the roll calls on which it appeared. In nine out of the 18 sessions, the "batting average" of the coalition exceeded 60 percent.

The conservative coalition is a potent force in Congress. A wide range of issues occupy its attention. Ordinarily, it can be counted on to: 1) resist new federal spending on education and welfare or to attempt to cut the

TABLE 22.   The Conservative Coalition in Congress, Appearances and Victories, 1961–1978

Year	Percentage of Roll Calls in Which the Coalition Appeared— Both Houses*	Percentage of Coalition Victories		
		Both Houses	House	Senate
1961	28	55	74	48
1962	14	62	44	71
1963	17	50	67	44
1964	15	51	67	47
1965	24	33	25	39
1966	25	45	32	51
1967	20	63	73	54
1968	24	73	63	80
1969	27	68	71	67
1970	22	66	70	64
1971	30	83	79	86
1972	27	69	79	63
1973	23	61	67	54
1974	24	59	67	54
1975	28	50	52	48
1976	24	58	59	58
1977	26	68	60	74
1978	21	52	57	46

Source: *Congressional Quarterly Weekly Report*, December 16, 1978, p. 3442.

*A "coalition roll call" is defined as any roll call on which the majority of voting southern Democrats and the majority of voting Republicans are opposed to the majority of voting northern Democrats. The Congressional Quarterly includes these states in the southern wing of the Democratic party: Ala., Ark., Fla., Ga., Ky., La., Miss., N.C., Okla., S.C., Tenn., Tex., and Va. The other 37 states are classified as "northern" in this analysis.

level of this spending; 2) support proposals to transfer federal programs to the states; 3) support the military and the Department of Defense; 4) support major business sections (for example, oil and gas tax depletion allowances); 5) oppose legislation that would strengthen the position of organized labor; 6) favor military rather than economic aid to foreign countries; and 7) oppose certain kinds of civil rights legislation (for example, strict federal controls over voting or the busing of school children for desegregation purposes).

THE PRESIDENT AND THE CONGRESSIONAL PARTY

Presidential power appears more awesome at a distance than it does at close range. Although the Constitution awards the president a number of formal powers—for example, the power to initiate treaties, to make certain appointments, and to veto legislation—his principal day-in, day-out power is simply the power to persuade. The president who opts for an active role in the legislative process, who attempts to persuade members of Congress to accept his leadership and his program, runs up against certain obstacles in the structure of American government. Foremost among these is the separation of powers. This arrangement of "separated institutions sharing powers"[24] not only divides the formal structure of government, creating independent centers of legislative and executive authority, but it also contributes to the fragmentation of the national parties. The perspectives of those elements of the party for whom the president speaks are not necessarily the same as those for whom members of his congressional party speak. Policy that may suit one constituency may not suit another. Indeed, the chances are high that the presidential constituency and the constituencies of individual members of his party in Congress will differ in many important respects, making a certain amount of conflict between the branches inevitable.

The separation of powers is not the only constraint that faces the activist president who hopes to move Congress to adopt his program. The lack of centralized party leadership in Congress, the relatively independent position of committees and their chairmen, the paucity of sanctions to apply to wayward legislators, and the parochial cast in congressional perceptions of policy problems all converge to limit presidential influence. Moreover, electoral arrangements and electoral behavior may make executive leadership difficult. Off-year elections are nearly always more damaging to the president's party than they are to the out-party. In off-year elections from 1926 to 1978, for example, the president's party gained seats in only one House election (1934) and in only three Senate elections (1934, 1962, and 1970). Losses are often severe; the Democratic party emerged from the 1966 election with 47 fewer seats in the House, and the Republican party lost 43 House seats in the 1974 election. By contrast, the Democrats lost only 12 seats in the House and 3 in the Senate in 1978.

Finally, the root of the president's legislative difficulties may lie with the voters themselves. The election that produces a president of one party may yield a Congress dominated by the other party or one influenced by a different ideological coloration. James Sundquist's analysis of John F. Kennedy's congressional miseries is instructive:[25]

> [It] is neither fair nor accurate to blame the failure of the Kennedy domestic program in the Eighty-seventh Congress primarily upon congressional organization or procedure—the power of the reformed House Rules Committee, the seniority system, or any other of Congress' internal processes. The failure of Congress to enact the Kennedy program is chargeable, rather, to the simple fact that the voters who elected Kennedy did not send to Congress enough supporters of his program. His razor-thin popular majority was reflected in a Congress formally Democratic but actually narrowly balanced between activists and conservatives. If the machinery of both houses had been entirely controlled by supporters of the Kennedy program, that in itself would not have changed the convictions of the members so as to produce a dependable administration majority. The machinery might have been used more effectively to coerce Democratic congressmen into voting in opposition to their convictions—but that is another matter.[25]

So many words have been written about the role of the president as "chief legislator" that it is easy to lose sight of the fact that members of Congress have power in their own right. Although it is clear that in recent decades the initiative in the generation of legislation has shifted to the president, it is also true that Congress remains one of the world's most powerful legislative bodies. There are a good many conditions that are inimical to presidential domination of Congress. Congress may adopt what the president proposes, but in the process change its accent and scope. Sometimes it merely disposes of what he proposes. Nothing in the president's plans is inviolable. No certainty exists that Congress will share his perceptions or succumb to his influence. The careers of individual legislators are not tightly linked to the president's, except perhaps in the case of those congressmen from marginal districts, and even here the link is firm only when the president's popularity is high.[26] Indeed, some members of Congress have made their careers more secure through the visibility that comes from opposing the president and his program. Notwithstanding the worldwide trend toward executive supremacy, Congress remains a remarkably independent institution—a legislature almost as likely to resist executive initiatives as to embrace them.

The president and Congress get along as well as they do because of one element which the president and some members of Congress have in common: party affiliation. In substantial measure, party provides a frame of reference, an ideological underpinning, a rallying symbol, a structure for voting, and a language for testing and discussing ideas and policies. The congressman's constituency has never been the only valid criterion for assessing the wisdom of public policies. Congressmen prefer to ride along with their party if it is at all possible, if the costs do not loom too large. Moreover, the president and his legislative leaders are not at liberty to strike out in any direction they feel may be immediately popular with the voters. They are constrained by party platforms, by previous policy commitments, by interest group involvement, and by the need to consult with party officials and members at all levels, particularly with those who compose the congressional wing. Consensus politics is the essence of party processes.

President and Legislative Leaders

A study of majority party leadership in Congress indicates that a variety of alternatives are open to the president and party leaders in Congress in structuring their relations with one another. Typically, when the president and the majority leadership in Congress are of the same party, and the president assumes the role of "chief legislator," relations between the two branches have been characterized by cooperation. Within this pattern leaders tend to see themselves as lieutenants of the president, of necessity sensitive to his initiatives and responsible for his program. On the other hand, even though his party controls Congress, the president may decline to play a central role in the legislative process. In this situation, relations between the president and congressional leaders tend to be mixed and nonsupportive. Collegial rather than centralized leadership usually emerges as Congress generates its own legislative program instead of relying on presidential initiative. Finally, when the president and the majority in Congress (at least in one house) are of opposing parties (a so-called truncated majority), relations between the president and congressional leaders are often characterized by conflict and opposition. Leadership tends to be highly centralized, but legislative successes are usually few in number. "The leader of a truncated majority has great room for maneuver in the tactics of opposition and embarrassment on the domestic front, if his followers are willing to go along with him, but he must necessarily remain partially frustrated by his inability to accomplish much of his program domestically."[27]

David Truman has described the relationship between the president and the elective leaders of his congressional party as one of "functional interdependence." There are mutual advantages in this interdependence. The president needs information in order to make intelligent judgments, and the leaders can supply it. Moreover, they can offer him policy guidance. At the same time, the leaders can do their jobs better if bolstered by the initiatives and leverage of the president. They have no power to give orders. They can only bargain and negotiate, and their effectiveness in doing this, in notable measure, is tied to the president's prestige and political assets. The nature of their jobs makes it important for the president's program to move through Congress. If he wins, they win; if he loses, they lose.[28]

The Role of the Minority Party in Congress

A study by Charles O. Jones identifies a number of political conditions that individually and in combination help to shape the role that the minority party plays in mobilizing congressional majorities and in shaping public policy. Some of these conditions originate outside Congress while others manifest themselves inside Congress. The principal external forces are the temper of the times (for example, the presence of a domestic or international crisis), the relative political strength of the minority party in the electorate, the degree of unity within the parties outside Congress, and the power of the president and his willingness to use the advantages that are inherent in his office. Conditions within Congress that affect minority party behavior are legislative procedures, the majority party's margin over the minority, the relative effectiveness of majority and minority party leadership, the length of time of the party in a minority status (perhaps contributing to a "minority party mentality"), and the relative strength of the party in the other house.[29]

The important point to recognize about the behavior of the minority party is that the strategies open to it are determined not simply by the preferences of the leadership or the rank-and-file members, by idiosyncratic circumstances, or by opportunities thrust up from time to time. Rather, what it does is influenced to a significant extent by conditions of varying importance over which it has little or no control. By and large, the conditions most likely to affect the minority party's behavior and shape its strategies are, among the external group, party unity and presidential power, and among the internal group, the size of the margin and the effectiveness of party leaders in both parties. Although restrictive political conditions depress the range of alternatives available to the minority party, a resourceful minority leadership can occasionally overcome them, enabling the minority party to assume an aggressive, creative role in the legislative process. Among twentieth-century Congresses, however, this has been the exception, not the rule.[30]

THE PARTY IN CONGRESS

It is about as difficult to write about congressional parties without revealing uncertainty as it is to pin a butterfly without first netting it. The party is hard to catch in a light that discloses all its qualities or its basic significance. Party is the organizing mechanism of Congress, and Congress could not do without it. It is hard to imagine how Congress could assemble itself for work, process the claims made upon it, lend itself to majority coalition-building, or be held accountable in any fashion without a wide range of party activities in its midst. Moreover, there are some sessions of Congress in which the only way to understand what Congress has done is to focus heavily on the performance of the majority party. But that is only part of the story. In the critical area of policy formation, majority party control often slips away, to be replaced by enduring biparty alliances or coalitions of expediency. Party counts, in other words, but not altogether predictably—hence the reason for the uncertainty in assessing the role of the congressional party.

Summary arguments may help to establish a perspective in the analysis. The indifferent success that sometimes characterizes party efforts in Congress, in fact, is not hard to explain. The odds are stacked against the party. In the first place, members of Congress are elected under a variety of conditions in a variety of constituencies: they are elected in environments where local party organizations are powerful and where they are weak; where populations are homogeneous and where they are heterogeneous; where competition is intense and where it is absent; where the level of voter education is relatively high and where it is relatively low; where income is relatively high and where it is relatively low; and where one or a few interests are dominant and where a multiplicity of interests compete for the advantages government can confer. The mix within congressional parties is a product of the mix within the nation's constituencies. It could scarcely be otherwise. The net result of diversity is that the men and women who make their way to Congress see the world in different ways, stress different values, and pursue different objectives. A vast amount of disagreement inevitably lurks behind each party's label.

In the second place, the salient fact in the life of the legislator is his career. If he fails to protect it, no one else will. The congressman knows that his party can do very little to enhance his security in office or, conversely, very little to threaten it. As a member of Congress puts it,"If we depended on the party organization to get elected, none of us would be here."[31] The truth of the matter is that the congressman is on his own. Whether he is reelected or not will depend more on the decisions he makes than on those his party makes, more on how he "cultivates" his constituency than on how his party "cultivates" the nation, more on the credit he is able to claim for "desirable" governmental action than on the credit his party is able to claim,[32] more on the electoral coalition he puts together or benefits from than on the electoral coalition his party puts together or benefits from. A sweeping electoral tide may, of course, carry him out of office. Though this is to be feared from time to time, there is not much he can do about it. Hence, the typical congressman concentrates on immediate problems. He takes his constituency as it is; if he monitors and defends its interests carefully he stands a good chance of having a long career in Congress, no matter what fate deals to his party.

Third, party efforts are confounded by the fragmentation of power within Congress. The seniority leaders who chair major committees and subcommittees are as likely to have keys to congressional power as the elected party leaders. Committees go their separate ways, sometimes in harmony with the party leadership and sometimes not. Powerful committees are sometimes under the control of party elements that are out of step with the leadership and with national party goals. No power to command rests with the party leadership, and there is not a great deal it can do to bring into line those members who steadily defy the party and oppose its objectives. The observations of two prominent members of the House illuminate the problems of party leaders:

> In order for the Speaker to twist arms he has to have power, and we haven't recovered from the revolt against Uncle Joe Cannon which stripped power from a dictatorial speaker nearly 65 years ago.

> We Democrats are all under one tent. In any other country we'd be five splinter parties. Years ago we had patronage. The Speaker doesn't have any goodies to hand out. The President can promise judgeships, public works and fly [congressmen] around in airplanes. There's nothing like having the White House.[33]

In addition, the party caucuses and the policy committees have never in any real sense functioned as policy-determining agencies. "Parties" within parties, such as the House Democratic Study Group, bear witness to the lack of party agreement on public policy.

Fourth, the very nature of the legislative process makes it difficult for the parties to function smoothly. For the party to maintain firm control, it must create majorities at a number of stages in the legislative process: first in the standing committee, then on the floor, and last in the conference committee. In the House of Representatives a majority will also be needed in the Rules Committee. Failure to achieve a majority at any stage is likely to mean the loss of legislation. Even those bills that pass through the "obstacle course" may be so sharply changed as to be scarcely recognizable by their sponsors. In contrast, the opponents of legislation have only one requirement: to splice together a majority at one stage in the decision-making process. Breaking the party leadership at some point in the chain requires neither great resources nor imagination. For these reasons, the adoption of a new public policy is immeasurably more difficult than the preservation of an old one. All the advantages, it seems, rest with those legislators bent on preserving existing arrangements.

Finally, the congressional party functions as it does because, by and large, it is a microcosm of the party in the electorate, beset by the same internal conflicts. The American political party is an extraordinary collection of diverse, conflicting interests and individuals brought together for the specific purpose of winning office. The coalition carefully put together in order to make a bid for power comes under heavy stress once the election is over and candidates have become officeholders. Differences ignored or minimized during the campaign soon come to the surface. Party claims become only one input among many the congressman considers in shaping his positions on policy questions. Not surprisingly, for reasons already noted, national party objectives may be disregarded as the congressman sorts out his own priorities and takes account of those interests, including his local party organization, whose support he deems essential to his election the next time around.

The astonishing fact about the congressional parties is that they perform as well as they do. One reason for this is the phenomenon of party loyalty —the typical member is more comfortable when he votes in league with his party colleagues than when he opposes them. Another reason is that most members within each party represent constituencies that are broadly comparable in makeup; in "voting their district" they are likely to be in harmony with the general thrust of their party.[34] A third reason is found in the informal powers of the elected leaders. Members who respond to their leadership may be given assistance in advancing their "pet" legislation, awarded with an appointment to a prestigious committee, or armed with important information. There are advantages to "getting along" with the leadership. Lastly, there is a great deal of evidence that presidential leadership serves as a unifying force for his congressional party. Members may not go along with the president gladly, but many of them do go along, and even those who do not give his requests more than a second thought.

NOTES

1. *Congressional Quarterly Weekly Report*, April 15, 1978, pp. 875–876.

2. For instructive studies of the congressional leadership, including patterns of leadership change, see Robert L. Peabody, *Leadership in Congress* (Boston: Little Brown, 1976); and Garrison Nelson, "Partisan Patterns of House Leadership Change, 1789–1977," *American Political Science Review*, LXXI (September 1977), pp. 918-939.

3. *The New York Times*, April 5, 1977. In discussing President Carter's many difficulties with Congress, Speaker O'Neill observed, "Maybe the President ought to go the route I go. I just come into a congressman's office and get down on bended knees." *U.S. News & World Report*, June 11, 1979, p. 17.

4. The Speaker's formal counterpart in the Senate is the vice-president. His role is simply that of presiding officer, since he is not a member of the body, cannot enter debate, and is permitted to vote only in the case of a tie. His influence on the legislative process is ordinarily insignificant.

5. Randall B. Ripley, *Party Leaders in the House of Representatives* (Washington, D.C.: The Brookings Institution, 1967), pp. 23–24.

6. "Leadership: An Interview with Senate Leader Lyndon Johnson," *U.S. News & World Report*, June 27, 1960, p. 88. Reprinted from *U.S. News & World Report*, copyright 1960 by U.S. News & World Report. See also Ralph K. Huitt, "Democratic Party Leadership in the Senate," *American Political Science Review*, LV (June 1961), pp. 333–344.

7. *Congressional Quarterly Weekly Report*, December 11, 1976, p. 3293.

8. "Leadership: An Interview with Senate Leader Lyndon Johnson," p. 90.

9. *The New York Times*, July 17, 1961, p. 11.

10. Changes in committee–subcommittee relations in the 1970s, including the adoption of a Subcommittee Bill of Rights, have had a major impact on decision-making in the House.

Subcommittees now have relatively clear-cut policy jurisdictions and, of more importance, substantial control over their own budgets, staffs, and agendas. Subcommittee chairmen commonly manage legislation on the floor. For analysis of the new role of subcommittees, see Norman J. Ornstein, *Congress in Change: Evolution & Reform* (New York: Praeger, 1975), pp. 88–114; and David W. Rohde, "Committee Reform in the House of Representatives and the Subcommittee Bill of Rights," *The Annals*, CDXI (January 1974), pp. 39–47.

11. *Pittsburgh Press*, September 23, 1978.

12. Concerning the middleman role of the floor leader, see these studies: David B. Truman, *The Congressional Party* (New York: Wiley, 1959), pp. 106–116 and 205–208; Barbara Hinckley, "Congressional Leadership Selection and Support: A Comparative Analysis," *Journal of Politics*, XXXII (May 1970), pp. 268–287; and William E. Sullivan, "Criteria for Selecting Party Leadership in Congress," *American Politics Quarterly*, III (January 1975), pp. 25–44.

13. *Congressional Quarterly Weekly Report*, May 27, 1978, p. 1304.

14. See a study by Randall B. Ripley, "The Party Whip Organizations in the United States House of Representatives," *American Political Science Review*, LVIII (September 1964), pp. 561–576.

15. For a detailed study of this committee, see Charles O. Jones, *Party and Policy-Making: The House Republican Policy Committee* (New Brunswick, N.J.: Rutgers University Press, 1964).

16. Hugh A. Bone, "An Introduction to the Senate Policy Committees," *American Political Science Review*, L (June 1956), p. 352. Also see Peabody, *Leadership in Congress*, pp. 337–338.

17. For analysis of the role and functions of informal party groups in Congress, see Kenneth Kofmehl, "The Institutionalization of a Voting Bloc," *Western Political Quarterly*, XVII (June 1964), pp. 256–272; and Sven Groennings, "The Wednesday Group in the House of Representatives: A Structural-Functional Analysis," a paper delivered at the annual meeting of the Midwest Political Science Association, Chicago, 1970. For a recent study of the behavior and effectiveness of the Democratic Study Group, see Arthur G. Stevens, Jr., Arthur H. Miller, and Thomas E. Mann, "Mobilization of Liberal Strength in the House, 1955–1970: The Democratic Study Group," *American Political Science Review*, XLVIII (June 1974), pp. 667–681. This study finds that, over the years, the DSG has become more cohesive than either Republicans or southern Democrats. With its heightened unity and an impressive rate of membership turnout on roll-call votes, the DSG has become a formidable liberal bloc in the House.

18. See Lewis Froman and Randall Ripley, "Conditions for Party Leadership: The Case of the House Democrats," *American Political Science Review*, LIX (March 1965), pp. 52–63.

19. See Edward V. Schneier's revised version of a classic study by Julius Turner, *Party and Constituency: Pressures on Congress* (Baltimore: Johns Hopkins Press, 1970), especially Chapters 2 and 3, from which the data of this paragraph were drawn. For another study of the differences between Democrats and Republicans in the period from 1947 to 1962, see David R. Mayhew, *Party Loyalty Among Congressmen* (Cambridge, Mass.: Harvard University Press, 1966). His analysis of the parties' performances during this period is instructive:

It can be said that the Democratic party in these years was transcendently a party of "inclusive" compromise. . . . Some congressmen wanted dams, others wanted mineral subsidies, others wanted area redevelopment funds, others wanted housing projects, still others wanted farm subsidies. As a result, the House Democratic leadership could serve as an instrument for mobilizing support among all Democrats for the programs of Democrats with particular interests. "Indifferent" Democratic congressmen frequently backed such programs "even against the debatable best interests of the people of their own communities." Republicans who characterized the Democratic party as a "gravy train" were quite right. . . . The essential point is that the program of the Democratic party in the House—of party leaders and of party majorities—was arrived at by adding together the programs of different elements of the party.... *Whenever possible*, most Republican congressmen opposed federal spending programs and championed policies favored by business. Thus, whereas "interested" minorities in the Democratic party typically supported each other's programs, each "interested" minority in the Republican party stood alone. The Republican leadership responded to the legislative demands of each minority by mobilizing the rest of the party to oppose them. City Republicans joined colleagues from the traditional "heartland" in voting against farm bills; Farm Belt members joined members from the "heartland" in opposing housing bills; almost everyone answered the party call in voting on labor or public power questions.

Reprinted by permission of the publishers from David R. Mayhew's *Party Loyalty Among Congressmen* (Cambridge, Mass.: Harvard University Press, 1966), pp. 150–153.

20. Barbara Deckard, "Political Upheaval and Congressional Voting: The Effects of the 1960s on Voting Patterns in the House of Representatives," a paper delivered at the Annual Meeting of the Midwest Political Science Association, Chicago, May 1–3, 1975.

21. *Congressional Quarterly Weekly Report*, April 15, 1978, pp. 917–929.

22. The key issues for the ADA and ACA in the Ninety-fifth Congress (first session) differ in some respects from those of the AFL–CIO. A senator voting a pro-ADA position in this session would have supported, among other things, efforts to: 1) halt the importation of Rhodesian chrome; 2) provide for public service job programs; 3) eliminate requirements that recipients pay for a portion of their food stamps; 4) promote federally assisted housing for low- and moderate-income persons; 5) implement the president's amnesty program for Selective Service violators; 6) provide federal funds for busing students and for abortions; and 7) prohibit production of the neutron bomb.

On the other hand, a senator voting in accordance with ACA positions would have opposed bills to: 1) promote the president's economic stimulus package (for instance, public service jobs); 2) provide increased funds for low-income housing; 3) terminate the development of the B-1 bomber; 4) provide any form of indirect U.S. assistance to certain countries such as Laos or Vietnam; 5) prohibit the acquisition of coal and uranium resources by major oil and natural gas producers; and 6) raise the temporary debt limit. In addition, a member would have favored proposals to: 1) repeal the pay raise for members of Congress and other high-level officials; 2) require recipients to pay for a portion of their food stamps; 3) prohibit HEW from using funds to enforce race or sex-related goals or quotas in hiring and admission policies; and 4) prohibit the use of federal funds for busing. For a complete listing of the ADA and ACA positions, see the *Congressional Quarterly Weekly Report*, April 15, 1978, pp. 917–923. For additional evidence of party voting along ideological lines, see William R. Shaffer, "Party and Ideology in the U.S. House of Representatives," a paper delivered at the Annual Meeting of the Southern Political Science Association, Atlanta, Georgia, November 9–11, 1978.

23. For more comprehensive evidence concerning the liberal "bias" of the Senate, see Sam Kernell, "Is the Senate More Liberal Than the House?" *Journal of Politics*, XXXV (May 1973), pp. 332–363.

24. Richard E. Neustadt, *Presidential Power: The Politics of Leadership* (New York: Wiley, 1960), p. 33.

25. James Sundquist, *Politics and Policy: The Eisenhower, Kennedy, and Johnson Years* (Washington, D.C.: The Brookings Institution, 1968), pp. 478–479.

26. There is additional evidence that a congressman's support for the president's policy proposals is influenced by how well the president ran in his district. In essence, the stronger the president runs in the member's district, the more policy support he will receive from that member. Presidential elections thus do more than select winners; they help to shape support patterns in Congress for presidential initiatives. See George C. Edwards III, "Presidential Electoral Performance as a Source of Presidential Power," *American Journal of Political Science*, XXII (February 1978), pp. 152–168.

27. From Randall B. Ripley, *Majority Party Leadership in Congress*, p. 175. Copyright © 1969, Little, Brown and Company, Inc. Reprinted by permission.

28. See Truman, *The Congressional Party*, especially pp. 279–319.

29. Charles O. Jones, *The Minority Party in Congress* (Boston: Little, Brown, 1970), especially pp. 9–24.

30. This study identifies eight strategies open to the minority party in the overall task of building majorities in Congress: support of the majority party by contributing votes and possibly leadership, inconsequential opposition, withdrawal, cooperation, innovation, consequential partisan opposition, consequential constructive opposition, and participation (the last strategy representing a situation in which the minority party controls the White House and thus is required to participate in constructing majorities). Strategies may vary within a single session of Congress and from one stage of the legislative process to the next. Jones, *The Minority Party in Congress*, pp. 19–24 and Chapters 4–8.

31. Charles L. Clapp, *The Congressman: His Work as He Sees It* (Washington, D.C.: The Brookings Institution, 1963), pp. 30-31.

32. For an analysis of the "credit claiming" activities of congressmen, see David R. Mayhew, *Congress: The Electoral Connection* (New Haven, Conn.: Yale University Press, 1974), pp. 52–61. The basic assumption of this remarkable little book is that reelection to Congress is the singular goal of members, and the relentless pursuit of it steadily influences not only their behavior but also the structure and functioning of the institution itself.

33. *The Washington Post*, June 17, 1975, p. 12. The statements are those of Congressman James O'Hara (D., Mich.) and the current Speaker of the House, Thomas P. ("Tip") O'Neill.

34. The typical northern Democrat is elected from a district with these characteristics: higher proportion of nonwhite population, lower owner-occupancy of dwellings, higher population density, and higher percentage of urban population. The typical northern Republican represents a district whose characteristics are just the opposite. Constituency characteristics undoubtedly have an important impact on congressional voting. See Lewis A. Froman, Jr., "Inter-Party Constituency Differences and Congressional Voting Behavior," *American Political Science Review*, LVII (March 1963), pp. 57–61.

Chapter 6

THE AMERICAN PARTY SYSTEM: PROBLEMS AND PERSPECTIVES

Extolling the virtues of the American party system is something of an anomaly in popular thought and scholarship. A few scholars, to be sure, have found substantial merit in the party system, particularly in its contributions to unifying the nation, augmenting political stability, reconciling social conflict, and institutionalizing popular control of government. But the broad thrust of commentary about this basic political institution has been heavily critical. American parties, a variety of indictments contend, are too much alike in their programs to afford voters a meaningful choice, are dominated by oligarchs or by organized special interests; are unable to deal imaginatively with national problems; are beset by a confusion of purposes; are ineffective because of their internal divisions; are short on discipline and cohesion; are insufficiently responsive to popular claims; and are deficient as instruments for assuming and achieving responsibility in government.

THE DOCTRINE OF RESPONSIBLE PARTIES

The major ground for popular distress over the parties may be simply that most people are in some measure suspicious of politicians and their organizations ("machines"). The criticism of scholars, on the other hand, has focused mainly on the lack of party responsibility in government. The most comprehensive statement on behalf of the doctrine of party responsibility is found in a report of the Committee on Political Parties of the American Political Science Association, *Toward a More Responsible Two-*

Party System, published in 1950. The report argues that what is required is a party system that is "democratic, responsible, and effective." In the words of the Committee:

> Party responsibility means the responsibility of both parties to the general public, as enforced in elections. Party responsibility to the public, enforced in elections, implies that there be more than one party, for the public can hold a party responsible only if it has a choice.... When the parties lack the capacity to define their actions in terms of policies, they turn irresponsible because the electoral choice between the parties becomes devoid of meaning.... An effective party system requires, first, that the parties are able to bring forth programs to which they commit themselves and, second, that the parties possess sufficient internal cohesion to carry out these programs.[1]

Two major presumptions underlie the doctrine of responsible parties. The first is that the essence of democracy is to be found in popular control over government rather than in popular participation in the immediate tasks of government. A nation such as the United States is far too large and its government much too complex for the general run of citizens to become steadily involved in its decision-making processes. But this fact does not rule out popular control over government. The direction of government can be controlled by the people so long as they are consulted on public matters and possess the power to replace one set of rulers with another set, the "opposition." The party, in this view, becomes the instrument through which the public—or more precisely, a majority of the public—can decide who will run the government and for what purposes. Government by responsible parties is thus an expression of majority rule.

The second tenet in this theory holds that popular control over government requires that the public be given a choice between competing, unified parties capable of assuming collective responsibility to the public for the actions of government. The contributions of a responsible party system would be three in number. One, it "would enable the people to choose effectively a general program, a general direction for government to take, as embodied in a set of leaders committed to that program." Two, it would help to "energize and activate" public opinion. Three, it would increase the prospects for popular control by substituting the collective responsibility of an organized group, the party, for the individual responsibility assumed, more or less inadequately, by individual officeholders.[2]

The responsible parties model proposed by the Committee on Political Parties is worth examination because it presents a sharp contrast to the contemporary party system. Disciplined and programmatic parties, offering clearer choices to voters, would replace the loose and inchoate institutions to which we are accustomed. The Committee's report deals with national party organization, party platforms, congressional party organization, intraparty democracy, and nominations and elections.

National Party Organization

The national party organizations envisaged by the Committee would be much different from those that exist today. The national convention, for example, would be composed of not more than 500 to 600 members, over half of whom would be elected by party voters. Ex officio members drawn from the ranks of the national committee, state party chairmen, and congressional leaders, along with certain prominent party leaders outside the party organizations, would make up the balance of the convention membership. Instead of meeting every four years, the convention would assemble regularly at least once every two years and perhaps in special meetings. Reduced in size, more representative of the actual strength of the party in individual states, and meeting more frequently and for longer periods, the "new" convention would gain effectiveness as a deliberative body for the development of party policy and as a more representative assembly for reconciling the interests of various elements within the party.

The most far-reaching proposal for restructuring national party organization involves the creation of a party council of perhaps 50 members, composed of representatives from such units as the national committee, the congressional parties, the state committees, and the party's governors. Meeting regularly and often, the party council would examine problems of party management, prepare a preliminary draft of the party platform for submission to the national convention, interpret the platform adopted by the convention, screen and recommend candidates for congressional offices, consider possible presidential candidates, and advise such appropriate party organs as the national convention or national committee "with respect to conspicuous departures from general party decisions by state or local party organizations." Empowered in this fashion, the party council would represent a firm break with familiar and conventional arrangements that contribute to the dispersion of party authority and the elusiveness of party policy. The essence of the council's task would be to blend the interests of national, congressional, and state organizations in such a way as to foster the development of an authentic national party, one capable of fashioning and implementing coherent strategies and policies.

Party Platforms

Party platforms, the report holds, are deficient on a number of counts. At times the platform "may be intentionally written in an ambiguous manner so as to attract voters of any persuasion and to offend as few voters as possible." State party platforms frequently espouse principles and policies in conflict with those of the national party. Congressional candidates and members of Congress may feel little obligation to support platform planks. No agency exists to interpret and apply the platform in the years between conventions. There is substantial confusion and difference of opinion over the binding quality of a platform—that is, whether party candidates are bound to observe the commitments presumably made in the adoption of the platform. Such are the principal shortcomings of this instrumentality.

To put new life back into the party platform, the report recommends that it should be written at least every two years in order to take account of developing issues and to link it to congressional campaigns in off-year elections; that it should "emphasize general party principles and national issues" which "should be regarded as binding commitments on all candidates and officeholders of the party, national, state and local"; that state and local platforms "should be expected to conform to the national platform on matters of general party principle or on national policies"; and that the party council should take an active role in the platform-making process, both in preparing tentative drafts of the document in advance of the convention and in interpreting and applying the platform between conventions. In sum, the report argues that party platforms and the processes through which they are presently formulated and implemented are inimical to the development of strong and responsible parties.

Congressional Party Organization

One of the most vexing problems in the effort to develop more responsible parties has been the performance of the congressional parties. The proliferation of leadership committees in Congress, the weakness of the caucus (or conference), the independence of congressional committees, and the seniority system have combined to limit possibilities for the parties to develop consistent and coherent legislative records. To tighten up congressional party organization would require a number of changes. First, each party in both the Senate and the House should consolidate its various leadership groups (for example, policy committees, committees on committees, House Rules Committee) into a single leadership group; its functions would be to manage legislative party affairs, submit policy proposals to the membership, draw up slates of committee assignments, and assume responsibility for scheduling legislation.

Second, there should be more frequent meetings of the party caucuses, their decisions to be binding on legislation involving the party's principles and programs. Moreover, members of Congress who ignore a caucus decision "should not expect to receive the same consideration in the assignment of committee posts or in the apportionment of patronage as those who have been loyal to party principles."

Third, the seniority system should be made to work in harmony with the party's responsibility for a legislative program. The report states:

The problem is not one of abolishing seniority and then finding an alternative. It is one of mobilizing the power through which the party leadership can successfully use the seniority principle rather than have the seniority principle dominate Congress. . . . Advancement within a committee on the basis of seniority makes sense, other things being equal. But it is not playing the game fairly for party members who oppose the commitments in their party's platform to rely on seniority to carry them into committee chairmanships. Party leaders have compelling reason to prevent such a member from becoming chairman—and they are entirely free so to exert their influence.

Fourth, the assignment of members of Congress to committees should be a responsibility of the party leadership committees. "Personal competence and party loyalty should be valued more highly than seniority in assigning members to such major committees as those dealing with fiscal policy and foreign affairs." At the same time, committee assignments should be reviewed at least every two years by the party caucus. A greater measure of party control over committee assignments is essential, if the party is to assume responsibility for a legislative program.

Finally, party leaders should take over the function of scheduling legislation for floor consideration. In particular, the power held by the House Rules Committee over legislative scheduling should be vested in the party leadership committee. If the party cannot control the flow of legislation to the floor and shape the agenda, there is little chance that it can control legislative output, which is the essence of responsible party performance in Congress.

Intraparty Democracy

The achievement of a system of responsible parties demands more than the good intentions of the public and of party leaders. It requires widespread and meaningful political participation by grass-roots members of the party, democratic party processes, and an accountable leadership. According to the report:

> Capacity for internal agreement, democratically arrived at, is a critical test for a party. It is a critical test because when there is no such capacity, there is no capacity for positive action, and hence the party becomes a hollow pretense. It is a test which can be met only if the party machinery affords the membership an opportunity to set the course of the party and to control those who speak for it. This test can be met fully only where the membership accepts responsibility for creative participation in shaping the party's program.

There is, of course, nothing easy about the task of developing an active party membership capable of creative participation in the affairs of the party. Organizational changes at both the summit and the base of the party hierarchy are required. "A national convention, broadly and directly representative of the rank and file of the party and meeting at least biennially, is essential to promote a sense of identity with the party throughout the membership as well as to settle internal differences fairly, harmoniously, and democratically." Similarly, at the grass-roots level, there is need for the development of local party groups that will meet frequently to generate and discuss ideas concerning national issues and the national party program. The emergence and development of local, issue-oriented party groups can be facilitated by national party agencies engaged in education and publicity and willing to undertake the function of disseminating information and research findings.

A new concept of party membership is required—one that emphasizes "allegiance to a common program" rather than mere support of party candidates in elections. Its development might take this form:

> The existence of a national program, drafted at frequent intervals by a party convention both broadly representative and enjoying prestige, should make a great difference. It would prompt those who identify themselves as Republicans and Democrats to think in terms of support of that program, rather than in terms of personalities, patronage, and local matters. . . . Once machinery is established which gives the party member and his representative a share in framing the party's objectives, once there are safeguards against internal dictation by a few in positions of influence, members and representatives will feel readier to assume an obligation to support the program. Membership defined in these terms does not ask for mindless discipline enforced from above. It generates the self-discipline which stems from free identification with aims one helps to define.

Nominations and Elections

The report's recommendations for changing nomination and election procedures fit comfortably within its overall political formula for strengthening the American party system. It endorses the direct primary—"a useful weapon in the arsenal of intraparty democracy"—while expressing preference for the *closed* rather than the open version. The open primary is incompatible with the idea of a responsible party system, since by permitting voters to shift from one party to the other between primaries, it subverts the concept of membership as the foundation of party organization. Preprimary meetings of party committees should be held for the purpose of proposing and endorsing candidates in primary elections. Selection of delegates to the national conventions should be made by the direct vote of party members rather than by state conventions. Local party groups should meet prior to the convention in order to discuss potential candidates and platform planks.

Three major changes should be made in the election system. The electoral college should be changed in order to give "all sections of the country a real voice in electing the president and the vice-president" and to help develop a two-party system in areas now dominated by one party. And second, the term of members of the House of Representatives should be extended from two to four years, with coinciding election of House members and the president. Were this constitutional change to be made, prospects would be improved for harmonizing executive and legislative power through the agency of party. Finally, the report recommends a variety of changes in the regulation of campaign finance, the most important of which calls for a measure of public financing of election campaigns.

The Promise of Responsible Parties

In the broadest sense, the publication of the report, *Toward a More Responsible Two-Party System,* was an outgrowth of the growing uneasiness among many political scientists over the performance of the nation's party system and the vitality of American government. Specifically, the report sought to come to terms with a problem that is central to the overall political system: the weakness of political parties as instruments for governing in a democratic and responsible fashion. The report is not a study in political feasibility. It does not offer a blueprint depicting where the best opportunities lie for making changes in the party system. What it does offer is a set of wide-ranging prescriptions consonant with a particular model of political organization. If the model sketched by the Committee were to come into existence, the American party system would bear only modest resemblance to that which has survived for well over a century. The key characteristics of the new parties would be the national quality of their organization, a much greater degree of centralization of party power, a tendency for party claims to assume primacy over individual constituency claims in public policy formation, a heightened visibility for the congressional parties and their leadership and for the president's role as party leader, and a greater concern over party unity and discipline.

To its credit, the report was not accompanied by the usual somnolence that settles over prescriptive efforts of this kind. Nor, on the other hand, did queues of reformers form in the streets, in the universities, or elsewhere to push for its implementation. What happened rather is that the report gave substantial impetus to the study of American political parties and helped to foster a concern for reform that, in one respect or another, continues to the present.

The goal of advocates of party responsibility is to place the parties at the creative center of policy-making in the United States. That is what party responsibility is all about. Voters would choose between two disciplined and cohesive parties, each distinguished by relatively clear and consistent programs and policy orientations. Responsibility would be enforced through elections. Parties would be retained in power or removed from power in terms of their performance and the attractiveness of their programs. Collective responsibility for the conduct of government would displace the individual responsibility of officeholders. Such are the key characteristics of the model party system discussed in these pages.

How well responsible parties would mesh with the American political system is another matter.[3] Critics have contended that disciplined parties might contribute to an erosion of consensus, to heightened conflict between social classes, to the formation of "splinter" parties (and perhaps to a full-blown multiple-party system), and to the breakdown of federalism. Moreover, the voting behavior and attitudes of the American people would have to change markedly in order to accommodate to the model of centralized parties, since many voters are more oriented to candidates than they are to parties or issues. The indifference of the public to the idea of programmatic parties would appear to be a major obstacle to rationalizing the party system along the lines of the responsible parties model.

RESPONSIBLE PARTIES AND PARTY REFORM

The reform wave of the last few years has produced a number of organizational and procedural changes in the American party system and in Congress. Perhaps as much by accident as by design, a surprising number of these changes are largely or fully compatible with the recommendations of the report, *Toward a More Responsible Two-Party System.*

Intraparty Democracy

Consider the steps that have been taken to foster intraparty democracy. No feature of the reform movement of the Democratic party—beginning with the guidelines of the Commission on Party Structure and Delegate Selection (the McGovern–Fraser Commission) in 1969 and extending through the report of the Winograd Commission in 1978—stands out more sharply than the commitment to make the party internally democratic and more responsive to its grass-roots elements.

Commenting on the overall process by which delegates were selected to the 1968 convention, the McGovern–Fraser Commission[4] observed that "meaningful participation of Democratic voters in the choice of their presidential nominee was often difficult or costly, sometimes completely illusory, and, in not a few instances, impossible." For example, the Commission found that: 1) in nearly half the states, rules governing the selection process were either nonexistent or inadequate, "leaving the entire process to the discretion of a handful of party leaders"; 2) over one-third of the convention delegates had, in effect, been chosen prior to 1968—well before all the possible presidential candidates were known and before President Johnson had withdrawn from the race; 3) "the imposition of the unit rule from the first to the final stage of the nominating process, the enforcement of binding instructions on delegates, and favorite-son candidacies were all devices used to force Democrats to vote against their stated presidential preferences"; 4) in primary, convention, and committee delegate selection systems, "majorities used their numerical superiority to deny delegate representation to the supporters of minority presidential candidates"; 5) procedural irregularities, such as secret caucuses, closed-slate making, and proxy voting, were common in party conventions from the precinct to the state level; 6) the costs of participating in the delegate selection process, such as filing fees for entering primaries, were often excessive; and 7) certain population groups—in particular blacks, women, and youth—were substantially underrepresented among the delegates.

To eliminate these practices and conditions, the Commission adopted a series of guidelines to regulate the selection of delegates for future conventions. Designed to permit all Democratic voters a "full, meaningful, and timely" opportunity to take part in the presidential nominating process, the guidelines set forth an extensive array of reforms to be implemented by state parties.

The initial step required of state Democratic parties was the adoption of a comprehensive set of rules governing the delegate selection process to which all rank-and-file Democrats would have access. Not only were these rules to make clear how all party members can participate in the process but they were also to be designed to facilitate their "maximum participation." In addition, certain procedural safeguards were specified. Proxy voting and the use of the unit rule were outlawed. Party committee meetings held for the purpose of selecting convention delegates were required to establish a quorum of not less than 40 percent of the members. Mandatory assessments of convention delegates was prohibited. Adequate public notice of all party meetings called to consider delegate selection was required, as were rules to provide for uniform times and dates of meetings.

The Commission enjoined state parties to seek a broad base of support. Standards eliminating all forms of discrimination against the participation of minority group members in the delegate selection process were required. To overcome the effects of past discrimination, moreover, each state was expected to include in its delegation blacks, women, and young people in numbers roughly proportionate to their presence in the state population.[5]

A number of specific requirements for delegate selection were adopted by the Commission. For example, provisions must be made for the selection of delegates in a "timely manner" (within the calendar year in which the convention is held), for selection of alternates in the same manner as delegates, for apportionment of delegates within the state on the basis of a formula that gives equal weight to population and to Democratic strength, and for the selection of at least 75 percent of the delegates at the congressional district level or lower (in states using the convention system). The number of delegates to be selected by a party state committee was limited to 10 percent of the total delegation.

One of the most remarkable aspects of this unprecedented action by the national party was the response of the state parties. To make a long story short, they accepted the guidelines, altered or abandoned a variety of age-old practices and state laws, and selected their delegations through procedures more open than anyone thought possible. And with "maximum participation" in mind, they produced a convention whose composition—with its emphasis on demographic representation—was vastly different from any previous one.[6] Whether for good or ill, the Democratic party had by 1972 accepted the main tenets of intraparty democracy.[7]

Strengthening the Congressional Parties

Reform, like conflict, is contagious. Essentially the same forces that produced major changes in the electoral structure of the Democratic party have produced major changes in the Democratic congressional party, particularly in the House of Representatives. The thrust of these changes is clearly in line with the theory of responsible parties. Advocates of this theory have sought not so much to promote the formation of a new party structure in Congress as to breathe new life into existing party structures and procedures. The changes have been impressive. Long dormant, the Democratic caucus is now a more influential force in the affairs of the House, particularly in terms of controlling committee assignments and in shaping rules and procedures. At the opening of the Ninety-fourth Congress (1975), the caucus removed three committee chairmen from their positions, increased party control over the committee assignment process, brought the Rules Committee more firmly under the leadership of the Speaker, and established a requirement that the chairmen of the appropriations subcommittees be ratified by the caucus. These were not stylized or marginal alterations. They should be seen for what they were: as systematically conceived efforts to reshape the power structure of Congress by diminishing the influence of the seniority leaders (who have often been out of step with a majority of the party) and augmenting the power of the party caucus and the leadership.

Organization/Platforms/Nominations and Elections

A potpourri of other recent party reforms was anticipated by the APSA report on responsible parties. Among them are the reassertion of the national convention's authority over the national committee, the selection of convention delegates by direct vote of the rank-and-file, the allocation of national committee members on the basis of the actual strength of the party within the areas they represent, the use of closed primaries for the selection of convention delegates, the public financing of presidential elections, and the provision for holding a national party conference between national conventions.[8]

In sum, many of the reforms that have been introduced in the party structure and in Congress are compatible with the model of responsible party government. They touch far more than the outer edges of the party and congressional systems. Nevertheless, there are no good reasons for supposing that party government is around the corner—that the raft of current reforms will result in the institutionalization of a durable, highly centralized, and disciplined party system. Traditional moorings throughout the political environment make change of this magnitude all but impossible. And the current trends in American politics, to which we now turn, have in fact done more to disable the parties than to strengthen them.

TRENDS IN AMERICAN POLITICS

Officeholding in the United States is dominated by the two major parties. The vast majority of aspirants for public office carry on their campaigns under the banner of one or the other of the two major parties. The most important fact to be known about the candidates in a great many electoral jurisdictions throughout the country is the party to which they belong, so decisive is party affiliation for election outcomes. Virtually everywhere, save in nonpartisan environments, the trappings of party—symbols, sponsorship, slogans, buttons, and literature—are in evidence. The parties and their candidates collect money, spend money, and incur campaign deficits on a scale that dwarfs their budgets of a generation ago. Party bureaucracies are larger than in the past. More than two out of three citizens continue to see themselves as Democrats or Republicans, however imperfectly they may comprehend their party's program or the performance of their party's representatives. Party-based voting decisions are common in numerous jurisdictions and especially in congressional elections. These are the signs of party vitality. Unfortunately, they are misleading. Indeed, the dominant trends in contemporary politics are largely "antiparty" in thrust:

1. *The loss of power by electoral party organizations.* At virtually every point associated with the recruitment and election of public officials, the party organizations have suffered an erosion of power. The reasons for this are many and varied. At the top of the list, perhaps, is the direct primary. "He who can make the nominations is the owner of the party," E. E. Schattschneider wrote some years ago, and there is no reason to doubt his observation.[9] In view of the fact that nonendorsed candidates may defeat party nominees in primaries, one may wonder whether, in some elections and in some jurisdictions, any one except the candidates really owns the parties. The party label has lost significance as candidates of all political colorations, with all variety of relationships to the organization, earn the right to wear it by capturing primary elections. Most important, a party that cannot control its nominations finds it difficult to achieve unity once it has won office and is faced with the implementation of its platform.

Candidates who defeat the organization may see little reason to subscribe to party tenets, defend party interests, or follow party leaders. Not only does the primary contribute to the fragmentation of party unity in office but it also divides the party at large:

> Primaries often pit party leaders against party leaders, party voters against party voters, often opening deep and unhealing party wounds. They also dissipate party financial and personal resources. Party leadership usually finds that it has no choice but to take sides in a primary battle, the alternative being the possible triumph of the weaker candidate.[10]

The weakening of the parties is nowhere more apparent than in the domain of presidential campaign politics. The spread of presidential primaries and the opening up of caucuses have curtailed the role of party leaders and organizations in the presidential nominating process. And of comparable importance, the introduction of public financing for presidential campaigns has drastically reduced the fund-raising role of party committees. Candidates for the presidency have less need of the party than perhaps at any time in party history. And it scarcely stretches the facts to argue that the national convention is a party convention in name only. The rapidity with which these changes have come about leaves most observers baffled and incredulous.

Still other reasons may be adduced for the atrophy of the party's role in the electoral process. The great urban machines of a generation ago have all but disappeared in many places. Employing an intricate system of rewards and incentives, the machines dominated the political process —controlling access to power, political careers, and, most important, votes. Their decline, due to a number of reasons, has contributed to a growth of independence both within the electorate and among politicians. "Antiparty" appeals are sometimes as effective as working within the party to gain office. Defeated in the Republican primary in 1969, John V. Lindsay ran on the ticket of the Liberal party, formed an Independent party to secure another line on the ballot, and won the New York mayor's office in a convincing victory over his Democratic and Republican rivals. In 1974, Maine voters rejected the candidates of both major parties and elected an independent as governor. In 1978, Wisconsin elected a governor who did not belong to any party before he sought the Republican nomination—"My mother," he observed, "always told me it was polite to join a party before you take it over." And Alabama elected to the governor's office a "born-again Democrat," a wealthy industrialist who had left the party in 1972 and then served four years as a member of the Republican state executive committee.[11] Party careers and party endorsements, it is evident, are less important in the new American politics. In addition, the decline in the volume of patronage due to extension of the merit system, the decline in the attractiveness of patronage jobs in times of affluence, the steady growth of a better-educated electorate, the mobility of voters, the awesome costs of campaigns, the requirement for technical skills in the use of the mass media and in other innovative forms of campaigning, the emergence of the celebrity candidate, and the inability of the parties to capture the imagination and esteem of the voters—all contribute to an easing of the party grip on the processes by which individuals are recruited and elected to office.

2. *The decline of partisanship.* Although evidence for the argument must be assembled in bits and pieces (and also treated warily), there are several reasons to believe that a marked decline in partisanship has taken place in the American electorate. In the first place, there has been a notable growth in the proportion of voters who describe themselves as independents rather than as partisans. Table 23 shows the political affiliation of a cross section of the general population and of the South in 1960 and 1978. According to the latter survey, 25 percent of southern citizens are classified as independents. Especially interesting is the finding that the proportion of southerners regarding themselves as independents was significantly larger in 1978 than in 1960—25 percent as opposed to 19 percent. Among voters in the 18–24 age group, according to a recent survey, 41 percent describe themselves as independents.[12] College students are even more likely to be independents than the general run of younger voters. To be sure, not all the voters who perceive themselves as independents actually behave as independents; many doubtless are undercover partisans who stay with the same party election after election. Nonetheless, as the proportion of self-styled independents rises, problems mount for the maintenance of a vigorous party system. Voter independence is to party vitality what coalition legislative voting is to party responsibility— a relationship of conspicuous incompatibility.

Another thread of evidence that party linkage between voters and government has diminished may be found in the contrast between presiden-

TABLE 23.   Political Affiliation in the Nation and in the South, 1960 and 1978*

	Democrat	Republican	Independent
National			
1960	47%	30%	23%
1978	48	24	28
South			
1960	59	22	19
1978	56	19	25

Source: The 1960 data were taken from the *Gallup Opinion Index*, Report No. 62, August 1970, p. 3; the 1978 data were furnished by the Gallup Poll (American Institute of Public Opinion, Princeton, New Jersey).

*The question asked was: "In politics, as of today, do you consider yourself a Republican, Democrat, or Independent?"

tial votes in the nineteenth and twentieth centuries. In the 16 presidential elections from 1836 to 1896, only the election of 1872 was of landslide dimensions—that is, an election in which the winning candidate received at least 55 percent of the two-party vote. By contrast, 9 of 20 presidential elections from 1900 through 1976 were decided by landslide margins. Movement across party lines from election to election has become increasingly common. Moreover, partisan swings have become substantially wider. To an important extent, the party-oriented voter of the nineteenth century has been displaced by the volatile voter of the twentieth century, resulting in a condition under which contemporary party organizations are "at best only indifferently successful at mobilizing a stable, predictable mass base of support."[13]

The growth in the incidence of ticket-splitting also suggests a deterioration in party ability to mobilize voters to cast a party vote—that is, to support the entire ticket. The magnitude of ticket-splitting today is undoubtedly much greater than it was a generation ago, though its precise dimensions in different kinds of elections are unknown. An important clue to this development may be found in an examination of the vote for presidential and congressional candidates within congressional districts. Table 24, the work of Milton Cummings, Jr., shows the number and percentage of congressional districts with split election results—districts won by the presidential candidate of one party and by the congressional candidate of another party—from 1920 to 1976.[14] It depicts a more or less steady increase in the number of split elections for these offices. A high point was reached in 1972 when 44 percent of all House districts split their results, doubtless due in great part to the voters' rejection of George McGovern. It is interesting to note that there were more split election outcomes in the five elections between 1960 and 1976 than in the ten elections between 1920 and 1956.

A phenomenon closely related to ticket-splitting is "party switching"—for example, voting for the presidential candidate of one party in one election and voting for the presidential candidate of another party the next election. Ordinarily, under two percent of the electorate will change its party identification in the period of a single year. Moreover, the net gain or loss to either major party is usually under one percent in a single year.[15] Such impressive stability can be misleading, for it is clear that, at times, citizens in far greater numbers abandon their parties at the polling place. Democrats by the millions deserted their party's presidential nominee in 1952, Adlai Stevenson, to vote for the Republican candidate, Dwight Eisenhower. Similarly, Republicans in droves cast their ballots for Lyndon Johnson in 1964 rather than for Barry Goldwater, thus contributing substantially to the landslide Democratic vote. Even more massive switches took place in 1968 and 1972. In the latter election, one-third of all Democrats voted for the Republican presidential candidate. Even in 1976, a presidential election in which party affiliation regained importance,

TABLE 24.   Congressional Districts with Split Election Results: Districts Carried by a Presidential Nominee of One Party and by a House Nominee of Another Party, 1920–1976

Year and Party of the Winning Presidential Candidate	Number of Districts	Number of Districts With Split Results	Percent
1920 R	344	11	3.2
1924 R	356	42	11.8
1928 R	359	68	18.9
1932 D	355	50	14.1
1936 D	361	51	14.1
1940 D	362	53	14.6
1944 D	367	41	11.2
1948 D	422	90	21.3
1952 R	435	84	19.3
1956 R	435	130	29.9
1960 D	437	114	26.1
1964 D	435	145	33.3
1968 R	435	141	32.4
1972 R	435	193	44.4
1976 D	435	124	28.5
Total	5973	1337	22.4

Source: Milton C. Cummings, Jr., *Congressmen and the Electorate* (New York: Free Press, 1966), p. 32, as updated. Presidential returns for some congressional districts were not available between 1920 and 1948.

nearly one out of five Democratic identifiers voted for the Republican presidential candidate.

Finally, an ebbing of partisanship among the American people can be detected in a miscellany of public opinion surveys. It is common to find many voters, for example, who believe that it will not make much difference which party wins an election or that there is not much difference in the capacity of the parties to solve certain public problems. Doubtlessly, some cleavages that divided society in the past have lost their political and emotional significance. As an element in the "cognitive map" of many voters, partisanship is of slight importance.

3. *The escalation of interest group activity.* The growth in the number and influence of interest groups—particularly those organized around narrow, special causes—is one of the key developments in American politics in recent years. Members of Congress have become acutely sensitive to the power of lobbies. To quote Senator Abraham Ribicoff (D., Conn.): "Lobbying has reached a new dimension and is more effective than ever in history. It has become a big computerized operation in which the Congress and the public are being bombarded by single-issue groups."[16]

The increasing influence of interest groups undoubtedly has contributed to the weakening of the parties. Parties and interest groups compete for the same political space. When legislators are more concerned with satisfying interest group claims than with supporting party positions and leaders, the vitality of legislative party organizations is sapped. When party lines collapse, collective responsibility for decisions is diminished. Increasingly, individual members are on their own, crowded and pressured by groups intent on getting their way. Congressman David Obey (D., Wis.) has put it this way: "It's a lot more difficult to say no to anybody because so many people have well-oiled mimeograph machines."[17] Or, in the grimly blunt words of Senator Edward M. Kennedy (D., Mass.): "We have the best Congress money can buy. Congress is awash in contributions from special interests that expect something in return."[18]

Single-issue groups in particular present serious problems for the legislator. Their issue is *the* issue; their position is the one on which legislators are to be judged. The compromises that occur naturally to practical politicians seldom carry much weight with the leaders of single-issue groups: members are either for or against the Panama Canal treaties, gun control, abortion, tax reductions, equal rights, nuclear power, environmental safeguards, prayer in the public schools, or any of a number of other issues including certain foreign policies for which there are active domestic constituencies. There are, of course, insistent groups on each side of each of these troublesome questions. And legislators do not find it easy to hide from them, especially since decision-making processes have become increasingly open as a result of the reform wave of the 1970s.

The broad point is that weakened parties provide slim protection for the harassed legislator in a free-for-all system. Middle-of-the-road politicians find themselves in trouble. Public service itself becomes increasingly frustrating in a politics of tiptoe and tightrope. Shortly before he was defeated for reelection in 1978, a northern Democratic senator observed:

> The single-interest constituencies have just about destroyed politics as I knew it. They've made it miserable to be in office—or to run for office—and left me feeling it's hardly worth the struggle to survive.[19]

The "special cause" quality to much of contemporary politics is also reflected in these comments by a leading official in Minnesota's Democratic–Farmer–Labor party:

> Frankly, there are very few of us in the party leadership now whose primary goal is the election of candidates committed to a broad liberal agenda. Most of the people in control are there to advance their own special causes. From the time we spend on it, you would think the most important problem in the world is whether there should be speedboats on six lakes in northern Minnesota.[20]

The arrival of narrow "issue" politics has changed the American political landscape. Pragmatic politics has been diminished and compromise has declined as a way of doing business. In forming their positions on certain inflammatory, "high principle" issues, members believe that there is a reduced margin for error. A "wrong" vote can cost them electoral support and produce new challenges to their reelection. And not in a few cases members believe they are faced with a "no win" vote—where a vote on either side of a controversial, high-visibility issue appears likely to damage their electoral security.

4. *The public's declining confidence in political institutions.* A sharp decline in the American mass public's confidence in its social and political institutions is among the most conspicuous trends of the last decade. So wide-ranging is the evidence of declining trust in government and growing cynicism toward political institutions that we shall have to be content with describing only certain dimensions of the problem. Figure 19, the work of Arthur H. Miller, shows a profile of the public's growing discontent over leaders, parties, and elections. The figure indicates clearly that

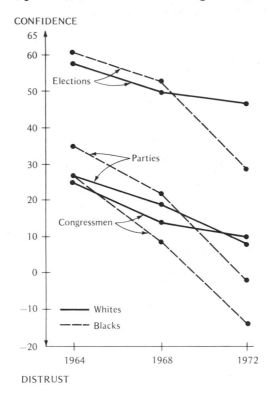

Figure 19.
CONFIDENCE IN LEADERS, PARTIES, AND ELECTIONS, 1964–1972
Source: Arthur H. Miller, "Rejoinder to 'Comment' by Jack Citrin: Political Discontent or Ritualism?" *American Political Science Review,* LXVIII (September 1974), p. 990.

the public evaluates its leadership and institutions differentially. Confidence in elections (to make government responsive) has not declined as sharply as has confidence in political leaders and parties. The decline in each case, moreover, has been more severe among blacks than whites. The trend line for blacks suggests that the first signs of discontent are reflected in attitudes toward leaders and parties, followed by a decline in confidence in elections.[21]

Overall, it is important to stress that the erosion of public confidence in elites and parties is closely associated with popular evaluation of the broader political system. Those people who express a high degree of general trust in government, for example, are significantly more likely to be supportive of the party system and elections than those who are cynical toward the system at large.[22]

It is also worth emphasizing that popular disillusionment concerning politics and political institutions did not emerge with the revelations and dislocations of Watergate. This trend, Figure 19 makes plain, began much earlier. The disclosures of criminal activities by leading officials of the White House, including the president, in this infamous affair merely accentuated it. (See Table 25.)

There is no simple explanation for the decline of trust in government. A variety of factors have been at work, probably the most important of which center in acute public dissatisfaction with policy outcomes—involving urban unrest and riots, the Vietnam war, and a range of social and economic problems (for example, inflation, race relations, poverty, campus disturbances, crime). It is probable that the public's negative evaluation of the performance of a series of incumbent presidents also contributed to the erosion of the political system's claims to legitimacy.[23]

Whatever the explanation, it is obvious that a sense of alienation and powerlessness is prevalent in the American public. Figure 20 shows certain dimensions of the phenomenon. Sixty percent of the public believes, for example, that "People running the country don't really care what happens to you" and that "What you think doesn't count much anymore." It is a startling fact that these propositions were accepted by about twice as many people in 1977 as in 1966.

The generalized lack of trust in government undoubtedly has affected the party system. Though the evidence is elusive, it seems likely that the loosening of ties to party (as manifested in the growing number of independents and the increase in ticket-splitting), the influx and successes of "celebrity" candidates, the increase in candidate-centered campaigns, the sapping of the organizational vitality of parties, the fascination with "new politics" solutions to current stresses, and the successes of party reform efforts all bear a relationship to the depletion of popular goodwill toward government.

Nothing about these trends, however, is immutable. Changes in political leadership, reorientations in governmental policies leading to the amelio-

TABLE 25. Popular Trust in Government, 1964–1976

How much of the time do you think you can trust the government in Washington to do what is right—just about always, most of the time, or only some of the time?

Response	1964 All Respondents (N = 4658)	1970 All Respondents (N = 1514)	1972 Whites (N = 1963)	1972 Blacks (N = 207)	1974 Whites (N = 2293)	1974 Blacks (N = 224)	1976 Whites (N = 2416)	1976 Blacks (N = 272)
Always	14.0%	6.4%	6%	3%	3%	2%	4%	4%
Most of the time	62.0	47.1	51	30	36	17	32	20
Some or none of the time	22.0	44.2	43	67	61	81	64	76
Don't know	2.0	2.3						
	100.0%	100.0%	100%	100%	100%	100%	100%	100%

Source: Data drawn from the election studies of the Center for Political Studies of the University of Michigan, as reported in Arthur H. Miller, "Political Issues and Trust in Government: 1964–1970," American Political Science Review, LXVIII (September 1974), p. 953; and Arthur H. Miller, Jeffrey Brudney, and Peter Joftis, "Presidential Crises and Political Support: The Impact of Watergate on Attitudes Toward Institutions," a paper delivered at the Annual Meeting of the Midwest Political Science Association, Chicago, May 1–3, 1975, p. 9. Data for 1976 from Center for Political Studies.

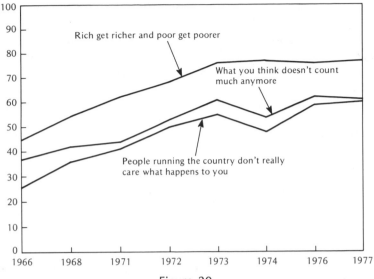

Figure 20.
EVIDENCE OF THE GROWING ALIENATION OF THE PUBLIC
Source: Adapted from Louis Harris survey data as found in *Public Opinion* (May/June 1978),
p. 23. The question asked was: "I want to read you some things that people have felt from time
to time. Do you tend to feel or not that (read list)?"

ration or resolution of nagging problems, successful new ventures by government, and the more complete fulfillment of popular expectations about government could well lead to a revival of trust in the political system. No one ought to lie awake nights, however, awaiting the arrival of this era of domestic good feeling.

5. *The growing importance of professional campaign management firms and the media in politics.* American party organizations no longer dominate the process of winning political support for the candidates who run under their labels. This is one of the principal facts to be known about the party system today. The role of party organizations in campaigns has declined as professional management firms, pollsters, and media specialists—stirred by the prospects of new accounts and greater profits—have arrived on the political scene. Indeed, so important have they become in political campaigns, especially for major offices, that it often appears as if the party has been reduced to the role of spectator. To be sure, the parties continue to raise and spend money, to staff their headquarters with salaried personnel and volunteers, and to mobilize their precinct officials to turn out the vote on election day. What they do matters, of course, but much less so than in the past.

The center of major political campaigns now lies in the decisions and activities of individual candidates and in their use of consultants, campaign management firms, and the mass media—not in the party organizations or in the decisions of party leaders. Modern political campaigning calls for resources and skills, which for the most part the party organization cannot furnish. Public opinion surveys are needed to pinpoint important issues, to locate sources of support and opposition, and to learn how voters appraise the qualities of the candidate. Electronic data processing is useful in the analysis of voting behavior and for the simulation of campaign decisions. For a fee, the candidate with sufficient financial resources can avail himself of specialists of all kinds: public relations, advertising, fundraising, communications, and financial counseling. He can hire experts in film-making, speech-writing, speech-coaching, voter registration, direct-mail letter campaigns, computer information services, time-buying (for radio and television), voter analysis, get-out-the-vote drives, and campaign strategy. Fewer and fewer things are left to chance or to the vicissitudes of party administration. What a candidate hears, says, does, wears, and possibly even thinks bears the heavy imprint of the specialist in campaign management.

Campaign consulting is a growth industry. Consultants whose candidates win upset or overwhelming victories are celebrated by politicians and the media alike. They are "hot" commodities, and candidates vie to purchase their services. Folklore develops that the "right" consultant is the key to victory. Reportedly, both candidates for the Democratic nomination to the U.S. Senate in New Jersey in 1978 sought to hire the same consultant, one who had gained fame for "his" victories in the mayoralty race in New York City and the governor's race in New Jersey.[24]

There is, it seems, no end to the variety of services made available to candidates by management firms. The Campaign Communications Institute of America, Inc., has an arrangement under which a candidate low on cash can charge services on his American Express Card. A glimpse of the other services CCI provides may be gained from this account:

> Under a middleman arrangement with some 35 manufacturing and service firms, [CCI] has produced a swollen bag of personalized vote-getting tricks. There are the routine items—bumper stickers, buttons, litter bags, matchbooks, posters, and flags. But there is also a $19.95 tape-playing machine that enables the candidate to carry his inspirational messages into the homes of voters over the telephone. There are Hertz rental cars equipped with bullhorn sound systems. And there is a $39.95 portable projector that flashes slogans, pictures, and platforms on anything from a living-room wall to the side of an office building. "Our job," the board chairman of CCI has said, "is to enable the low-budget candidate to get the most votes for his bucks."

> For well-heeled candidates, CCI will also arrange mass telephone campaigns at a cent and a half a call, state-wide voter polls (sample prices: $4,000 for Vermont, $9,000 for New York) and direct campaigns through Western Union Services or New York's big Reuben H. Donnelly Corporation.... "Whenever and wherever people elect people, we'll be there," says the CCI board chairman. "That's our market."[25]

How much American politics and parties will be affected by the coming of age of the mass media, technocracy, and the techniques of mass persuasion is hard to say, though their impact is already sizable. It is a good guess, say a variety of students of the media and politics, that the party organizations of the future will be stripped of most of their electoral functions, at least in major national campaigns. In their place will be a new politics dominated by image-makers and technical experts of all kinds—men who know what the public wants in its candidates and how to give it to them. Consider these facts and prognoses for an issueless, pseudopolitics:

It is not surprising . . . that politicians and advertising men should have discovered one another. And, once they recognized that the citizen did not so much vote for a candidate as make a psychological purchase of him, not surprising that they began to work together. . . . Advertising agencies have tried openly to sell Presidents since 1952. When Dwight Eisenhower ran for reelection in 1956, the agency of Batton, Barton, Durstine and Osborn, which had been on a retainer throughout his first four years, accepted his campaign as a regular account. Leonard Hall, national Republican chairman, said: "You sell your candidates and your programs the way a business sells its products."[26]

Day-by-day campaign reports spin on through regular newscasts and special reports. The candidates make their progress through engineered crowds, taking part in manufactured pseudo events, thrusting and parrying charges, projecting as much as they can, with the help of makeup and technology, the qualities of youth, experience, sincerity, popularity, alertness, wisdom, and vigor. And television follows them, hungry for material that is new and sensational. The new campaign strategists also generate films that are like syrupy documentaries: special profiles of candidates, homey, bathed in soft light, resonant with stirring music, creating personality images such as few mortals could emulate.[27]

In all countries the party system has folded like the organization chart. Policies and issues are useless for election purposes, since they are too specialized and hot. The shaping of a candidate's integral image has taken the place of discussing conflicting points of view.[28]

[Party] organizations find themselves increasingly dependent on management and consultant personnel, pollsters, and image-makers. The professional campaigners, instead of being the handmaidens of our major political parties, are independent factors in American elections. Parties turn to professional technicians for advice on how to restructure their organizations, for information about their clienteles, for fund-raising, and for recruiting new members. Candidates, winning nominations in primaries with the aid of professional campaigners rather than that of political parties, are increasingly independent of partisan controls. The old politics does not rest well beside the new technology.[29]

No matter what happens, the national political parties of the future will no longer be the same as in the past. Television had made the voter's home the campaign amphitheater, and opinion surveys have made it his polling booth. From this perspective, he has little regard for or need of a political party, at least as we have known it, to show him how to release the lever on Election Day.[30]

6. *The increasing nationalization of politics.* So unobtrusively has the change taken place that a great many American citizens are doubtless unaware of the extent to which sectional political alignments have been replaced by a national political alignment. The Republican vote in the South in the 1952 presidential election was, it turns out, more than a straw in the wind. General Dwight Eisenhower carried four southern states, narrowly lost several others, made the Republican party respectable for many southern voters, and, most important, laid the foundation for the development of a viable Republican party throughout the South.

From the latter part of the nineteenth century until recently, the principal obstacle to the emergence of a national politics was the hold of the Democratic party on the South. Presidential, congressional, state, and local offices were won, as a matter of course, by the Democratic party. Today, the Democratic grip on the southern states is no longer firm. Taken as a whole, since 1952, southern states have been almost as likely to vote Republican as to vote Democratic in presidential elections. Probably of greater significance has been the growth of "congressional Republicanism" in the South. Table 26 attests to the striking gains made by the Republican party in congressional elections from the early 1950s to the late 1970s. Democratic candidates for Congress in Arkansas, Florida, North Carolina, Tennessee, and Virginia can no longer take elections for granted. Even in the Deep South—Alabama, Georgia, Louisiana, Mississippi, and South Carolina—Republican congressional candidacies have assumed new life. Fewer and fewer southern Democratic candidates for Congress can expect to win election by default, no Republican opponent having been nominated to oppose them. And when a Democratic incumbent retires, the chances are about four out of ten that a Republican candidate will win that seat.[31] There is a strong new breeze of Republicanism coursing through southern electorates. The insulation of southern politics from national political trends has not broken down completely, to be sure, but it has become remarkably porous.[32]

The movement from parochial to national politics has not been limited to the South. No matter what its history of party allegiance and voting, no state is wholly secure from incursions by the minority party. The vote in presidential elections now tends to be distributed more or less evenly throughout the country; fewer and fewer states register overwhelming victories for one or the other of the major parties. One-party political systems dwindle. "It is probably safe to say that in national and state-wide politics we are in the time of the most intense, evenly-spaced, two-party competitiveness of the last 100 years."[33]

TABLE 26.   Republican Percentage of the Statewide Major Party Vote for the U.S. House of Representatives, Selected Years, Southern States

State	Republican Statewide Percentage				
	1950	1952	1968	1974	1978
Alabama	0.7	5.4	30.8	50.2	42.9
Arkansas	0.0	14.3	53.0	37.6	66.1
Florida	9.6	25.9	42.8	54.5	41.7
Georgia	0.0	0.0	20.5	33.7	32.6
Louisiana	0.0	8.7	18.8	36.9	50.0
Mississippi	0.0	2.5	7.5	54.9	36.9
North Carolina	30.0	32.2	45.4	41.8	35.9
South Carolina	0.0	2.0	32.8	41.5	37.6
Tennessee	30.3	29.8	51.1	57.4	47.3
Texas	9.5	1.3	28.1	39.8	40.6
Virginia	24.9	31.0	46.4	47.7	50.2

Source of data: *The 1968 Elections* (Washington, D.C.: Republican National Committee, 1969), pp. 115–116; and *Congressional Quarterly Weekly Report*, issues of November 9, 1974, pp. 3084–3091, and November 11, 1978, pp. 3283–3291. The strength of the Republican party in congressional elections is less impressive than shown in this table because southern states typically do not report the vote of the winner if he or she is unopposed by a major party candidate. In the 1978 general election, for example, there were 33 congressional candidates who had no major party opposition; 26 were Democrats while 7 were Republicans.

The sources for the growing nationalization of American politics are both numerous and varied. Social changes, rather than conscious party efforts to extend their spheres of influence, have provided the principal thrust for the new shape given to American party politics. Among the most important of these has been the emergence and extraordinary development of the mass media in political communications. Through the electronic media, national political figures can be created virtually overnight, national issues can be carried to the most remote and inaccessible community, and new styles and trends can become a matter of common knowledge in a matter of days or weeks. Insulation, old loyalties, and established patterns are difficult to maintain intact in the face of contemporary political communications. Consider these observations by Harvey Wheeler:

Eisenhower was himself a newcomer to party politics. . . . He was heavily financed. He employed expensive and sophisticated mass media experts. "Madison Avenue" techniques were devised to project a predesigned "image." A new kind of electoral coalition was formed, composed largely of urban, white-collar people dissociated from the grass roots traditions of the agrarian past. His campaign cut across traditional party lines to orient itself about the personality of the candidate rather than the machine or the party. The new coalition of voter groups was socially and geographically mobile. The new politics required image manipulators rather than ballot box stuffers. The new organizations were ad hoc affairs created overnight by national cadres of advance men. The presidential primary overshadowed the party convention. This was to be the wave of the future. Television truly nationalized campaign communications and undermined the federal structure of the old machines. Party politics gave way to personality politics.[34]

For all their importance to the changes under way, the electronic media have not by themselves transformed the face of American politics. Changes in technology, the diversification of the economic bases of the states, the growth of an affluent society, the higher educational attainments of voters, the mobility of the population, the migration of black citizens to the North, the illumination of massive nationwide problems, the growth of vast urban conglomerations, and the assimilation of immigrant groups have all contributed to the erosion of internal barriers and parochialism and, consequently, to the strengthening of national political patterns. Whatever the complete explanation for this phenomenon, one thing is clear: the forces for the nationalization of politics are far more powerful today than the forces for localism and sectionalism. A changing party system is the inevitable result.

7. *A continuation of party competition based on meaningful policy differences between the parties.* The American parties are often criticized for being "Tweedle-dum and Tweedle-dee"—for being so similar that even an attentive voter can miss the alternatives they present. This indictment is not persuasive. The attitudes of Democratic and Republican elites toward certain major policy questions are, in fact, substantially different. Interesting new evidence on this score is found in a *Washington Post* survey of the policy attitudes of each party's 1976 national convention delegates, conducted about a year before the 1980 conventions. Figure 21 shows the results. The largest difference appears on the question of a national health care program. Sixty-three percent of the Democratic delegates favor such a program, as contrasted with a mere 5 percent of the Republican delegates. The other contrasts, similarly consistent along liberal and conservative lines, are almost as stark. Republican delegates attach much more importance to tax cuts and to a balanced budget than their Democratic counterparts. A much smaller defense budget wins the approval of a majority of Democrats but only 11 percent of Republicans. Four times as many Democrats as Republicans believe racial integration is not going fast enough. And three times as many Republican as Democratic delegates believe the United States should try to maintain military superiority over Russia—as opposed to seeking an arms limitation agreement that would leave the two countries as equal as possible in military strength.

The important point to recognize is that the parties' loss of vitality in recent years—particularly apparent in their electoral organizations—has not clouded the ideological differences between their leaders. Meaningful differences separate the parties in Congress. Even larger differences di-

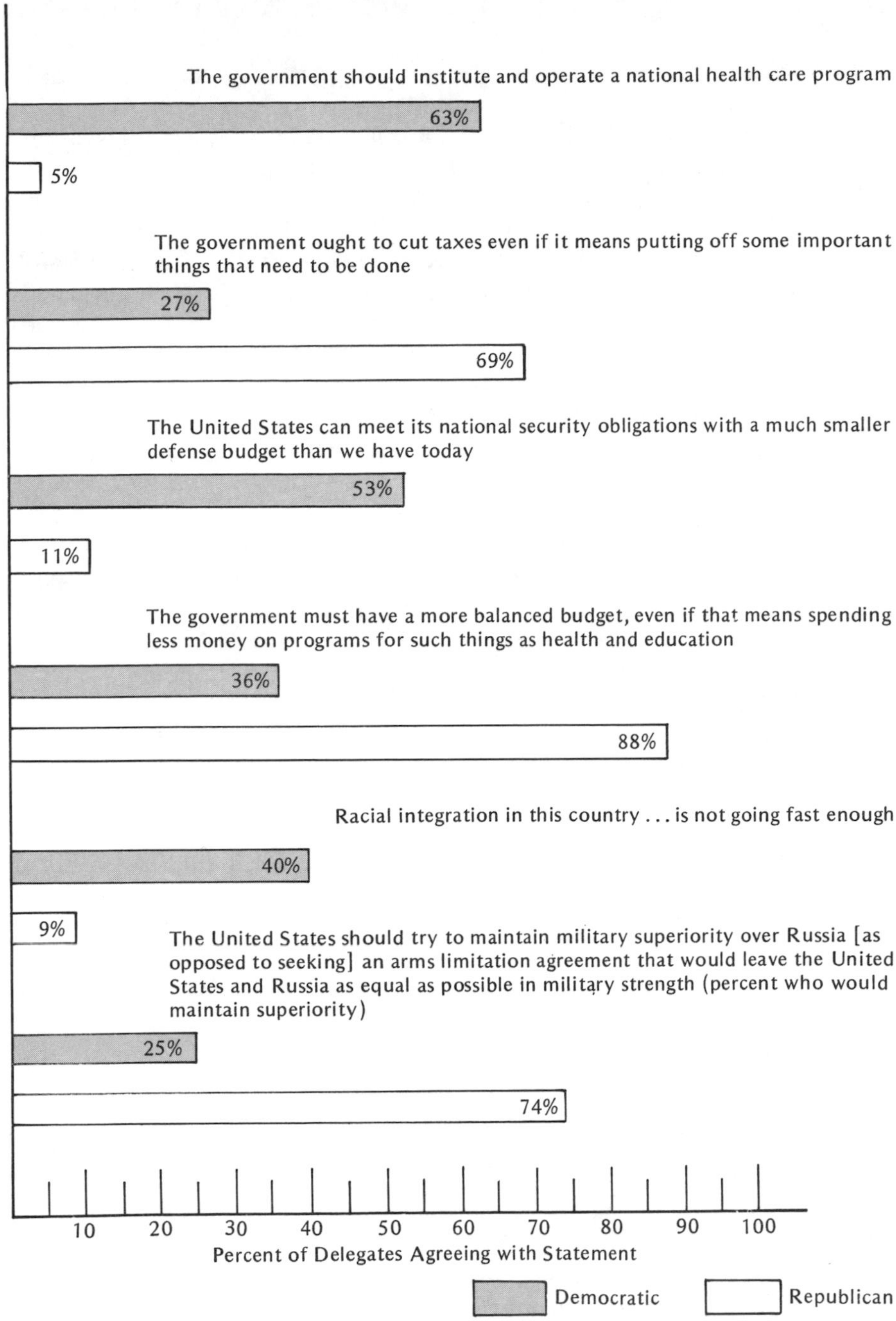

The government should institute and operate a national health care program

63%

5%

The government ought to cut taxes even if it means putting off some important things that need to be done

27%

69%

The United States can meet its national security obligations with a much smaller defense budget than we have today

53%

11%

The government must have a more balanced budget, even if that means spending less money on programs for such things as health and education

36%

88%

Racial integration in this country ... is not going fast enough

40%

9%

The United States should try to maintain military superiority over Russia [as opposed to seeking] an arms limitation agreement that would leave the United States and Russia as equal as possible in military strength (percent who would maintain superiority)

25%

74%

10   20   30   40   50   60   70   80   90   100

Percent of Delegates Agreeing with Statement

Democratic   Republican

Figure 21.

THE ATTITUDES OF DEMOCRATIC AND REPUBLICAN NATIONAL CONVENTION DELEGATES TOWARD MAJOR POLICY ISSUES

Source: Data derived from "Leadership Survey," *The Washington Post,* July 20, 1979. The survey included 1600 Democratic and 1310 Republican delegates.

vide the national convention delegates of the parties. Quite plainly, these party elites do not evaluate the problems of the nation in the same light. Nor are they attracted to the same solutions. The parties, in sum, stand for much more than most people give them credit.

8. *A turn toward party and governmental reform.* It is a fundamental rule for those in power (perhaps especially for those who hold political power) that no problem should ever be attacked directly if it can possibly be absorbed, put off, finessed, or avoided—at least, so it often appears to outsiders. The rule is not difficult to follow under ordinary circumstances. One result of this is that changes in American politics do not come easily. The large-scale reforms that have found their way into the party structure, into Congress, and into public policies that shape and regulate the political process did not arrive during a period of "politics as usual." Quite the contrary, they began to take shape and were adopted during a time in which the political system was in substantial disarray. In the midst of an unpopular war, challenged on nearly all sides, President Johnson withdrew from the presidential election of 1968. Senator Robert F. Kennedy was assassinated. The Democratic convention, meeting in Chicago, was an ordeal of rancor, tumult, and rioting. And then came Watergate. Public alienation toward the political system, which had been building for years, reached a high point. The stage was set for reform. More than anything else, the success of those who brought it about was due to their capacity to seize upon these unusual and transitory circumstances to develop sharply new ways of carrying on political business.

From almost any perspective, the changes appear notable. More reforms, in fact, were adopted between 1968 and 1974 than at any time since the early nineteenth century.[35] The power of the national party agencies to establish standards for state party participation in national nominating conventions was established—and the Supreme Court added its imprimatur to this development. The first national party charter was adopted. At the state level, a number of presidential primary laws were adopted. Nor was Congress immune to change. Though not toppled, the seniority system was weakened. The filibuster rule was revised, making it easier for a Senate majority to assert itself. The party caucus took on new roles and new vigor. A campaign finance law that provides for the use of public funds to finance presidential campaigns was adopted. In sum, a whole new range of choices and opportunities was opened up, for the politician as well as for the public.

The overall effects of these changes are not yet well understood. But certain observations appear appropriate. A more open political process does not necessarily contribute to the increased participation of the general public, to a heightening of political trust, or to the revitalization of the parties. A demographically more representative convention does not necessarily lead to the selection of candidates who can best represent the party, who can unify it, or who can be elected. A strengthened congressional party does not necessarily make different choices or produce different policy outcomes. A national party charter does not necessarily diminish the prevailing federalism of American politics or reduce the autonomy of state and local parties on most matters that count.[36]

Indeed, the "reform" of the party system must be taken with a grain of salt—for a reason that is obvious to anyone who has read this far. American parties are to an important extent the "dependent variable" in the scheme of politics, more the products of their environment than the architects of it. The only governmental system the parties have known is Madisonian, marked by division of power and made to order for weak parties. Federalism, the separation of powers, and all manner of structural arrangements and election laws (for example, direct primary, candidate-oriented campaign regulations, nonconcurrent terms for executive and legislature, nonpartisan elections, and staggered elections) militate against the development of strong parties. By diminishing party control over the presidential nominating process, the reforms have undermined an institution already feeble.[37] The massive use of television for political campaigns, the increasing power of special-interest groups, and the arrival of public relations, media, survey, computer, and fund-raising experts have also contributed heavily to our current candidate-centered system that stresses personality over party and, frequently, style over substance. And for an American public that has never had much enthusiasm for parties, their current desuetude is not likely to be cause for concern.

THE PROSPECTS

The American party system has been shaped more by custom and environment than by intent. Indeed, in broad contour, the parties of today resemble closely those of previous generations. For as long as any of us can remember, the major parties have been loose and disorderly coalitions, heavily decentralized, lacking in unity and discipline, preoccupied with winning office, and no more than erratically "responsible" for the conduct of government and the formation of public policy. There is, of course, another side to them. They have performed at least as well as the parties of other democratic nations—and perhaps far better. Democratic politics requires the maintenance of a predictable legal system; institutionalized arrangements for popular control of government and the mobilization of majorities; methods and arenas for the illumination, crystallization, and reconciliation of conflict; and means for endowing both leaders and policies with legitimacy. To each of these requirements the parties have contributed steadily and often in major ways.[38]

It is a truism of American politics that it is invariably difficult to cut free from familiar institutions. Old practices die hard. Conventional arrangements hang on and on. Change arrives incrementally and unnoticed. Not only are most Americans habituated to weak parties but the parties themselves are accustomed to the environment in which they function. It would seem that prospects for the development of a system of responsible parties are thin at best. But the matter deserves a closer look.

It seems clear that on most counts the parties have lost ground in recent years. The electoral party organizations undoubtedly have been weakened. Their control over the nominating process, once a virtual monopoly, has gradually slipped away. Primary battles for major offices appear to occur more and more frequently. So-called independent candidates seem to be both more numerous and more successful than in the past. Indeed, many candidates use the party label "in the same spirit that ships sail under Liberian registry—a flag of convenience, and no more."[39] A gradual loosening of the electorate's ties to the parties is also evident. There are more people who regard themselves as independents today than ever before—more, in fact, than those who describe themselves as Republicans. The power of local party bosses probably never has been less formidable than it is today. The media, public relations consultants, and campaign management firms are now as much a part of political campaigns as the party organizations themselves—at least, when important offices are at stake. In sum, in the recruitment–campaign–election stages of the political process, American parties gradually have lost power. They compete within the political process but do not dominate it. A great deal of contemporary politics, in fact, lies outside the parties and beyond their control.

The current deterioration of the parties makes the prospects for the development of a full-blown, responsible party system, along the lines described at the outset of this chapter, anything but bright. Too many obstacles—constitutional, political, and otherwise—stand in the way. But this is not to say that responsible party performance in government is unattainable. The way in which parties govern is far from dependent upon the strength and vitality of the electoral party organizations or upon the way in which men and women are elected to office. The party-in-the-government, it is worth remembering, is both different from the party-in-the-electorate and largely independent of it.

The essence of a responsible party system is not to be found in party councils, closed primaries, demographically representative national conventions, off-year party conventions, government financing of elections, or in intraparty democracy. Rather, the key idea is represented in party responsibility for a program of public policy. Such responsibility requires, in the first place, a strong measure of internal cohesion within the party-in-the-government in order to adopt its program and, in the second place, an electorate sufficiently sensitive to party accomplishments and failures that it can hold the parties accountable for their records, particularly in the case of the party in power. At times, neither requirement can be met to any degree. When the executive and legislative branches are controlled by different parties, for example, party responsibility goes by the boards. Nevertheless, there are occasions when American political institutions function in a manner largely consonant with the party responsibility model.

A responsible party system at the national level demands a particular kind of Congress—one in which power is centralized rather than dispersed. Over long stretches of time, Congress has not been organized in such a way as to permit the parties, *qua* parties, to govern. The seniority system, the independence of committees and their chairmen, the filibuster, the weaknesses present in elected party positions and agencies, and the unrepresentativeness of Congress itself have made it difficult for party majorities to assert themselves and to act in the name of the party. Nevertheless, as we have seen, these barriers to party majority-building have been notably diminished in recent years.

Every so often the congressional party comes fully alive. Consider the first session of the Eighty-ninth Congress (1965)—"the most dramatic illustration in a generation of the capacity of the president and the Congress to work together on important issues of public policy":

In part a mopping up operation on an agenda fashioned at least in spirit by the New Deal, the work of the 89th Congress cut new paths through the frontier of qualitative issues: a beautification bill, a bill to create federal support for the arts and humanities, vast increases in federal aid to education. . . . [The] policy leadership and the legislative skill of President Johnson found a ready and supportive response from a strengthened partisan leadership and a substantial, presidentially oriented Democratic majority in both houses. A decade of incremental structural changes in the locus of power in both houses eased the President's task of consent-building and of legislative implementation.

Yet Congress was far from being just a rubber stamp. On some issues the President met resounding defeat. On many issues, presidential recommendations were modified by excisions or additions—reflecting the power of particular committee chairmen, group interests, and bureaucratic pressures at odds with presidential perspectives.

[The lessons of the Eighty-ninth Congress] proved that vigorous presidential leadership and sizable partisan majorities in both houses of the same partisan persuasion as the President, could act in reasonable consonance, and with dispatch, in fashioning creative answers to major problems. The nation's voters could pin responsibility upon a national party for the legislative output. If that partisan majority erred in judgment, it could at least be held accountable in ensuing congressional and presidential elections.[40]

The chances are that there will be future Congresses like "the fabulous Eighty-ninth"—the label bestowed on it by President Johnson. No one, of course, should expect them to be strung together, one following another. The conditions must be right: a large partisan majority, more or less ideologically unified, and a vigorous president are essential. A long policy agenda may also be required. In any case, the point not to be missed is that, under the right circumstances, the deadlocks in American politics can be broken and the political system can function vigorously and with a high degree of cooperation between the branches of government. "Party responsibility" can thrive even if unrecognized and unlabeled. The evidence of the Eighty-ninth Congress suggests that the first requirement for government by responsible parties—a fairly high degree of internal party agreement on policy—can, at least occasionally, be met.

The second requirement—an electorate attuned to party performance in government—is a much different matter. The total system of responsible parties breaks down at precisely this point:

> What the public knows about the legislative records of the parties and of individual congressional candidates is a principal reason for the departure of American practice from an idealized conception of party government.... The electorate sees very little altogether of what goes on in the national legislature. Few judgments of legislative performance are associated with the parties, and much of the public is unaware even of which party has control of Congress.... Many of those who have commented on the lack of party discipline in Congress have assumed that the Congressman votes against his party because he is forced to by the demands of one of several hundred constituencies of a superlatively heterogeneous nation. In some cases, the Representative may subvert the proposals of his party because his constituency demands it. But a more reasonable interpretation over a broader range of issues is that the Congressman fails to see these proposals as part of a program on which the party—and he himself—will be judged at the polls, because he knows the constituency isn't looking.[41]

Experiments with forms of party responsibility, like fashion, will perhaps always possess a probationary quality—tried, neglected, forgotten, and rediscovered. The tone and mood of such a system will doubtless appear on occasion, but without the public's either anticipating it or recognizing it when it arrives. More generally, however, the party system is likely to resemble, at least in broad lines, the model to which we are adjusted and inured: the parties situated precariously atop the political process, threatened and thwarted by a variety of competitors, uncomfortably coalitional, active in fits and starts and often in hiding, beset by factional rifts, frustrated by the growing independence of voters, and moderately irresponsible. From the vantage point of both outsiders and insiders, the party system ordinarily will appear, to the extent that it registers at all, in disarray. And indeed it is in disarray—more so than at any time in the last century—but not to a point that either promises or insures its enfeeblement and disintegration.

NOTES

1. All of the proposals for reforming the party system cited in this section, along with quoted material, are drawn from the Committee on Political Parties of the American Political Science Association's report, *Toward a More Responsible Two-Party System* (New York: Holt, Rinehart and Winston, 1950). The longer quotations appear on these pages of the report: definition of party responsibility (pp. 1, 2, 22); seniority (pp. 61–62); intraparty democracy (p. 66); and party membership (pp. 69–70).

2. For a comprehensive development of the themes of this and the previous paragraph, see Austin Ranney, *The Doctrine of Responsible Party Government* (Urbana, Ill.: University of Illinois Press, 1954), pp. 10–16.

3. There are a number of excellent analyses of party responsibility. See Austin Ranney, "Toward a More Responsible Two-Party System: A Commentary," *American Political Science Review*, XLV (June 1951), pp. 488–499; T. William Goodman, "How Much Political Party Centralization Do We Want?" *Journal of Politics*, XIII (November 1951), pp. 536–561; Evron M. Kirkpatrick, "Toward a More Responsible Two-Party System: Political Science, Policy Science, or Pseudo-Science?" *American Political Science Review*, LXV (December 1971), pp. 965–990; Gerald M. Pomper, "From Confusion to Clarity: Issues and American Voters, 1956–1968," *American Political Science Review*, LXVI (June 1972), pp. 415–428; Michael Margolis, "From Confusion To Confusion: Issues and the American Voter (1956–1972)," *American Political Science Review*, LXXI (March 1977), pp. 31–43; and David S. Broder, "The Case for Responsible Party Government," in Jeff Fishel (ed.), *Parties and Elections in an Anti-Party Age* (Bloomington, Ind.: Indiana University Press, 1978), pp. 22–32.

4. The recommendations of the Commission are found in *Mandate for Reform* (Washington, D.C.: Commission on Party Structure and Delegate Selection, Democratic National Committee, 1970).

5. Most of the McGovern–Fraser guidelines were incorporated in new party rules and in the party charter. But a few important changes were made. The quota system was dropped in favor of an "affirmative action" provision. Going beyond the guidelines, winner-take-all primaries were banned and state parties are required to "take all feasible steps to restrict participation in the delegate selection process to Democratic voters only"—the effect of which is to require closed primaries.

6. The price of these reforms was high. Delegates of the new-enthusiast variety were far more numerous than party professionals. Also, the ideological cast of the delegates was markedly different—that is, much more "liberal"—from that of the general run of Democrats. And fewer delegates belonging to labor unions were present than is ordinarily the case. In some respects the new rules produced a most unrepresentative convention. The candidate it nominated, George McGovern, was overwhelmingly defeated in the election—undoubtedly due in part to the defection of party moderates and conservatives. Ironically, though it was expected that the quota system for blacks, women, and youth would increase support among these groups in the election, nothing of the sort happened. Blacks and youths supported the 1972 Democratic presidential candidate in about the same proportion as they did the 1968 candidate. Support among women voters declined notably. See Austin Ranney, *Curing the Mischiefs of Faction: Party Reform in America* (Berkeley, Calif.: University of California Press, 1975), pp. 153–156, 206–208.

7. To achieve a system of responsible parties, according to the *Toward a More Responsible Two-Party System* report, "The internal processes of the parties must be democratic, the party members must have an opportunity to participate in intraparty business, and the

leaders must be accountable to the party." Committee on Political Parties of the American Political Science Association, *Toward a More Responsible Two-Party System*, p. 23.

8. In addition, though tangential to this account, certain major recommendations of the report have been met through action by the federal government. A number of barriers to voting have been eliminated as a result of the passage of the Voting Rights Act of 1965 and the adoption of the Twenty-sixth Amendment to the Constitution in 1971.

9. E. E. Schattschneider, *Party Government* (New York: Holt, Rinehart and Winston, 1942), p. 64.

10. Frank J. Sorauf, *Political Parties in the American System*, p. 102. Copyright © 1964 Little, Brown and Company, Inc. Reprinted by permission.

11. See an account of "party crashers" in the *Congressional Quarterly Weekly Report*, October 28, 1978, pp. 3107–3109.

12. *Gallup Opinion Index*, December 1977, p. 30.

13. For further analysis of this theme, see Walter Dean Burnham, "The Changing Shape of the American Political Universe," *American Political Science Review*, LIX (March 1965), pp. 7–28. For the period 1872–1892, the mean national partisan swing in presidential elections was 2.3 percent; for 1896–1916, 5 percent; for 1920–1932, 10.3 percent; and for 1936–1964, 5.4 percent. These data and the quotation are drawn from pp. 22–23. See another article by Walter Dean Burnham, "The End of American Party Politics," *Trans-Action*, VII (December 1969), pp. 12–22.

14. Milton Cummings, Jr., *Congressmen and the Electorate* (New York: Free Press, 1966); the extent and consequences of ticket-splitting are considered on pp. 28–55. The data of Table 24 provide only a partial view of the dimensions of ticket-splitting in contests for these offices. For example, substantial ticket-splitting nevertheless could be present even though the presidential candidate and the congressional candidate of the same party received total votes of the same size. The totals would be the same if, say, those voters who voted for the Republican presidential candidate and the House Democratic candidate were balanced by an equal number of voters who voted for the Democratic presidential candidate and the House Republican candidate.

15. William H. Flanigan, *Political Behavior of the American Electorate* (Boston: Allyn and Bacon, 1968), p. 44.

16. *Time*, August 7, 1978, p. 15.

17. *Time*, January 29, 1979, p. 12.

18. *U.S. News and World Report*, January 29, 1979, p. 24.

19. *The Washington Post*, September 13, 1978. The comment was made by Senator Wendell R. Anderson (D., Minn.) to columnist David S. Broder.

20. *The Washington Post*, September 13, 1978.

21. Arthur H. Miller, "Rejoinder to 'Comment' by Jack Citrin: Political Discontent or Ritualism?" *American Political Science Review*, LXVIII (September 1974), pp. 990–991. Also, consult a study by Benjamin Ginsberg and Robert Weissberg which finds that elections help to generate citizen support for leaders and the regime itself. Many citizens who view the responsiveness of government with skepticism prior to the election change their minds after they have voted. "Elections and the Mobilization of Popular Support," *American Journal of Political Science*, XXII (February 1978), pp. 31–55.

22. See Miller, "Rejoinder to 'Comment' by Jack Citrin: Political Discontent or Ritualism?" p. 991; and Jack Dennis, "Trends in Public Support for the American Political Party System," a paper delivered at the Annual Meeting of the American Political Science Association, Chicago, August 29–September 2, 1974, p. 22.

23. See Arthur H. Miller, "Political Issues and Trust in Government: 1964–1970," *American Political Science Review*, LXVIII (September 1974), pp. 951–972; Arthur H. Miller, Jeffrey Brudney, and Peter Joftis, "Presidential Crises and Political Support: The Impact of Watergate on Attitudes Toward Institutions," a paper delivered at the Annual Meeting of the Midwest Political Science Association, Chicago, May 1–3, 1975; and for a different per-

spective, Jack Citrin, "Comment: The Political Relevance of Trust in Government," *American Political Science Review,* LXVIII (September 1974), pp. 973–988.

24. See an account in the *Congressional Quarterly Weekly Report,* July 22, 1978, pp. 1857–1860. The consultant was David Garth. He chose to work for Richard Leone, former New Jersey State Treasurer. Bill Bradley, known for moving without the ball better than anyone on the Knicks and probably better at this than anyone in the NBA except John Havlicek, then hired Michael Kaye. Bradley overwhelmed Leone, and a new star was born: Michael Kaye.

25. *Newsweek,* April 29, 1968, p. 76. For a comprehensive study of the public relations man in politics, see Stanley Kelley, Jr., *Professional Public Relations and Political Power* (Baltimore: Johns Hopkins Press, 1956).

26. Joe McGinniss, *The Selling of the President, 1968,* p. 27. © 1969 by Joemac, Incorporated. Reprinted by permission of Trident Press/Division of Simon & Schuster, Inc.

27. Robert MacNeil, *The People Machine: The Influence of Television on American Politics* (New York: Harper & Row, 1968), p. xvii.

28. Marshall McLuhan, as quoted by McGinniss, *The Selling of the President, 1968,* p. 28. © 1969 by Joemac, Incorporated. Reprinted by permission of Trident Press/Division of Simon & Schuster, Inc.

29. Dan Nimmo, *The Political Persuaders: The Techniques of Modern Election Campaigns* (Englewood Cliffs, N.J.: Prentice-Hall, 1970), p. 197.

30. Harold Mendelsohn and Irving Crespi, *Polls, Television, and the New Politics* (Scranton, Pa.: Chandler, 1970), pp. 310–311.

31. See Richard G. Hutcheson III, "The Inertial Effect of Incumbency and Two-Party Politics: Elections to the House of Representatives from the South, 1952–1974," *American Political Science Review,* LXIX (December 1975), pp. 1399–1401.

32. The best evidence that the "Solid South" has expired as a political entity will appear when Republicans contest vigorously with Democrats over state and local offices. During the 1960s and 1970s, Republican gubernatorial candidates were elected in Arkansas, Florida, North Carolina, South Carolina, Tennessee, Texas, and Virginia. As of 1980, only three southern states—Tennessee, Texas, and Virginia—had Republican governors. Republican gains at the state legislative level have been greatest in Florida and Tennessee. Local offices continue to be dominated overwhelmingly by Democrats throughout the South.

33. From Frank J. Sorauf, *Party Politics in America,* p. 48. Copyright © 1968 Little, Brown, and Company, Inc. Reprinted by permission.

34. Harvey Wheeler, "The End of the Two Party System," *Saturday Review,* November 2, 1968, p. 20. Copyright 1968, Saturday Review, Inc.

35. Ranney, *Curing the Mischiefs of Faction,* p. 3.

36. Apart from its provisions concerning intraparty democracy, there is little that is new in the Democratic party charter. The mid-term party convention that adopted the charter in 1974 rejected numerous provisions designed to centralize the party and to alter its federal character, including a dues-paying membership, a mandatory national party conference every other year, an independent national chairman elected for a four-year term (to reduce the presidential nominee's influence over the chairman), an elaborate regional party organization, and a strong national party executive committee. Few changes were made in the major organs of the party: the national convention, national committee, and the office of the national chairman. The vast majority of the compromises reached both prior to and during the convention were struck on the side of those who wanted to preserve a party system notable for its decentralization. See an interesting account of the convention's issues involving centralization versus decentralization by David S. Broder, *The Washington Post,* December 1, 1974.

37. See a provocative essay by Jeane Jordan Kirkpatrick, which argues that the most important cause for the decline of the parties has been the reforms of the 1970s. She recognizes, of course, that social, cultural, and technological factors have also contributed to

their weakening. *Dismantling the Parties: Reflections on Party Reform and Party Decomposition* (Washington, D.C.: American Enterprise Institute for Public Policy Research, 1978).

38. To explore the literature that defends the American party system, see in particular Herbert Agar, *The Price of Union* (Boston: Houghton Mifflin, 1950); Pendleton Herring, *The Politics of Democracy* (New York: Norton, 1940); Arthur N. Holcombe, *Our More Perfect Union* (Cambridge, Mass.: Harvard University Press, 1950); and Edward C. Banfield, "In Defense of the American Party System," in Robert A. Goldwin (ed.), *Political Parties, U.S.A.* (Chicago: Rand McNally, 1964), pp. 21–39.

39. *Time*, November 20, 1978, p. 42.

40. Stephen K. Bailey, *Congress in the Seventies* (New York: St. Martin's, 1970), pp. 102–103. Among the other major accomplishments of the first session of the Eighty-ninth Congress were the passage of bills to provide for medical care for the aged under Social Security, aid to depressed areas, the protection of voting rights, federal scholarships, the Teacher Corps, immigration reform, and a variety of programs to launch the war on poverty.

41. Donald E. Stokes and Warren E. Miller, "Party Government and the Saliency of Congress," in Angus Campbell et al. (eds.), *Elections and the Political Order* (New York: Wiley, 1966), pp. 209–211.

Index